The Way We Lived

The Way We Lived

CALIFORNIA INDIAN STORIES, SONGS & REMINISCENCES

Edited with Commentary by Malcolm Margolin

Foreword by Michael Connolly Miskwish

Heyday, Berkeley, California
California Historical Society

CALIFORNIA HISTORICAL SOCIETY since 1871

Library of Congress Cataloging-in-Publication Data
Names: Margolin, Malcolm, editor. | California Historical Society.
Title: The way we lived : California Indian stories, songs & reminiscences /
    edited with commentary by Malcolm Margolin ; foreword by Michael Connolly
    Miskwish.
Description: 35th anniversary edition. | Berkeley, California : Heyday, 2017.
    | "Copublished by Heyday and the California Historical Society."
Identifiers: LCCN 2017005938 | ISBN 9781597143936 (pbk. : alk. paper)
Subjects: LCSH: Indians of North America--California--Folklore. | Indians of
    North America--California.
Classification: LCC E78.C15 W39 2017 | DDC 398.2089/97--dc23
LC record available at https://lccn.loc.gov/2017005938

Editing, typesetting, interior design, indexing, and production: Wendy Low
Interior design, indexing, and coordination: Jeannine Gendar
Cover design: Ashley Ingram
Cover photo: Hunge Ka Pu, Chaw'se, 1995, by Dugan Aguilar

Printed in Peoria, Illinois, by Versa Press, Inc.

Copublished by Heyday and the California Historical Society.

Published by Heyday
P. O. Box 9145, Berkeley, California 94709
(510) 549-3564
heydaybooks.com

10 9 8 7 6 5

Acknowledgements

I am, as always, immeasurably grateful to the partnership of Rina Margolin whose ideas and standards suffuse this book.

Those who graciously provided a variety of advice, insight, criticism, technical expertise, or other help in putting together the first edition of this book include: Dave Chamberlin, Larry Di Stasi, Donna Dumont, Joan Feldman, Vera Mae Frederickson, Robin Freeman, Dennis Gallagher, Amy Godine, Georgianna Greenwood, Francine Hartman, Jose Hatier, Rob Hurwitt, Bruce Kaiper, Christina Kessler, Rebecca Kurland, Frank Lobo, Red McClintock, Randy Milliken, Frank Norick, Peter Palmquist, Gene Prince, Celia Ramsay, Elitha Rea, Sara Satterlee, Erich Schimps, David Sheidlower, Mrs. Thomas (of the National Anthropological Archives), Linda Tontini, Paul Velde, and Christopher Weills.

The second edition of this book has grown to include over a hundred selections and nearly as many photographs, and my indebtedness and gratitude have increased proportionately. This book and its editor have been the recipient of so much generosity over so long a period that to even begin to name all those who taught, corrected, and who gave gifts of photographs, text, wisdom, and effort would be too daunting.

To mention only a few, I would like to thank:

—Wendy Low, who pulled together the manuscript and the photos, tracked down references, copyedited, did the typesetting and much of the page-by-page design, and produced the index, all with the greatest imaginable skill and kindliness;

—Jeannine Gendar, who oversaw the project, provided editing suggestions, designed the interior, and who has been an invaluable co-worker, friend and ally for several years now;

—the contributing editors and writers of *News from Native California* who have taught me so much, and its support group, Friends of *News from Native California*, for having kept it all afloat;

—Sharon Smith, who kindly offered advice and consultation on cover design; and

—Lee Swenson and Lexi Rome, whose generosity and wonderful friendship have meant so much.

I would finally like to acknowledge the extraordinary involvement of Canterbury Press, Berkeley, and its owner, Ian Faircloth, in the production of this book and in everything else we have done for many years now. His marvelous skill and gentle, noble spirit have enabled us to do not just good work but occasionally truly beautiful work. Deepest gratitude.

Grateful acknowledgment is made to the following for permission to reprint material copyrighted or controlled by them:

THE BANCROFT LIBRARY REGIONAL ORAL HISTORY OFFICE and HELENE H. OPPENHEIMER for "The Judge's Visit" by Geneva Mattz from "Salmon War on the Klamath, 1978—Remembered by a Yurok Family Project."

BEAR STATE BOOKS and FRANK F. LATTA for "I Am the Last" from *Handbook of Yokuts Indians* by Frank F. Latta. Copyright 1949 by Frank F. Latta; revised and enlarged edition copyright 1977 by Bear State Books.

WILLIAM BRIGHT for "Coyote's Journey" excerpted from *American Indian Cultural and Research Journal*, 4, 1980.

CALIFORNIA HISTORICAL SOCIETY for "My Grandpa, Before White People Came" from "Out of the Past" edited by Edith V.A. Murphey, *California Historical Society Quarterly*, December 1941, "The Death of Father Quintana" from "The Assassination of Padre Andrés Quintana by the Indians of Mission Santa Cruz, 1812" edited by Edward D. Castillo, *California History*, 68, No.3, Fall 1989, and "The Stone and Kelsey Massacre" by William Ralganal Benson, *California Historical Society Quarterly*, 11, September 1932.

DUKE UNIVERSITY PRESS and WILLIAM J. WALLACE for "The Men I Knew" excerpted from "Personality Variation in a Primitive Society'" by William Wallace in *Journal of Personality*, 15, No. 4. Copyright 1947 Duke University Press (Durham, NC).

MALKI MUSEUM PRESS and WENDY ROSE for "For the White Poets" from *Lost Copper* by Wendy Rose. Copyright 1980.

NATUREGRAPH PUBLISHERS, INC. for "Childhood Games" from *Northern Maidu* by Marie Potts. Copyright 1977.

REDDING MUSEUM AND ART CENTER for "Becoming a Man" from *Samson Grant, Atsuge Shaman* by Susan Park. Copyright 1986.

FLORENCE CONNOLLY SHIPEK for "We Had to Move Again" from *Delfina Cuero*, Ballena Press. Copyright 1991.

STEIN AND DAY for "A Man Without Family" from *Deep Valley* by B.W. and E.G. Aginsky. Copyright 1967 and 1971.

UNIVERSITY OF WASHINGTON PRESS for "When I Was a Child," "A Great and Wise Shaman," and "I No Longer Believe" from *Primitive Pragmatists* by Verne F. Ray. Copyright 1963.

UNIVERSITY OF WISCONSIN PRESS and ELIZABETH COLSON for "My Grandfather" and "Crying" excerpted from *Autobiographies of Three Pomo Women* by Elizabeth Colson. Published by The Archaeological Research Facility, Department of Anthropology, University of California at Berkeley, 1974.

Contents

III: An Ordered World

IV: Old Age and Death

V: The Aliveness of Things

VI: Getting Power

VII: Dream Time

VIII: Mythic Time

List of Photographs

Foreword

Michael Connolly Miskwish (Kumeyaay)

As a boy growing up in California in the sixties, I was exposed to the same California story as most people who attended the public schools. Indians were the Apache, Cherokee, or Sioux. Indians were the warriors of the Plains or the Eastern Woodland. They greeted the Pilgrims and taught them to farm. As I grew older I learned of other tribes, like Pueblo Indians, Navajo, and Apache. I was taught that I was an Indian too, but we seemed so different. Our houses weren't teepees, we didn't hunt buffalo, and turquoise was a color, not a stone. When I spent time on the Reservation, my Uncles would tell stories from their lives—World War II, fighting with the BIA, working on local ranches. But little of Kumeyaay history was mentioned, other than references to our land being stolen and our people killed. It seemed that the Mission narrative, taught by teachers and historians, must indeed be true.

It was only as I approached adulthood that I learned there was more to the story of my people. I gained snippets of information from newspaper articles, magazines, or talks with elders. But still, the colonial narrative dominated my perspective, particularly regarding other California Indians. At one point, I believed that whatever other California Indian cultures were left from the Missions had been swallowed up by the powwow culture brought in from other states.

In the days before Google and Amazon, written research started in the libraries. I started to seek out more information on my own people, the Kumeyaay. As a by-product, I came across histories and accounts regarding other California Indians. It was readily apparent to me, by this time, that history had been whitewashed and sanitized for the most part. Some of the accounts and opinions regarding California Indians were so racist and dehumanizing, they approached the absurd. Yet these were the scholarly sources of the day. During one of these searches I stumbled upon a copy of *The Way We Lived* in a public library. It was a discordant element among the status quo of historical references. Here was a publication that was unafraid to step outside the politically correct California narrative and show the California Indian people for all their breadth and diversity as vibrant, intelligent, loving, jocular human beings. I had never read a book on California Indians that gave me such a kaleidoscope of mental images across time, or that covered so many California tribes from periods of routine normality to the horrors of genocide. It was one of a few writings that inspired me to learn more about my own history and culture. Surely, we too had corresponding tales of the hunt, creation, survival, and our common humanity.

Years later, I reread *The Way We Lived*. After researching, learning, and writing about my own people's history and culture, I went back to turn more experienced eyes on the text. I read with a critic's perspective, wanting to poke holes in the narration, as I felt it was my cynical duty to question all historical sources. Yet, as I read, I found myself once again caught up in the stories. Rather than critiquing, I found myself rediscovering the book through the commonalities between my own culture and so many other California Native cultures.

Of course, California is an artificial construct. That is very apparent to the Kumeyaay, as the California–Mexican border bisects our traditional territory. Still, for its geographical size, this constructed political boundary encompasses a richness of language families and cultures that is unmatched in North America and perhaps the world. These diverse perspectives on relationships with each other, the world around us, and the spiritual realm are valuable to our ability to adapt to the rapid changes around us. The commonalities of these stories underlie our shared humanity, something that invaders worked so diligently to destroy. This balance of diversity and commonality is exceptional in books about California Indians.

I confess, I had not thought about the book for many years until asked to write this foreword to the new edition. Now, with the insights that age can bring to a more mature scholar, I willingly allowed myself to be carried on the current of the narration. Passing from one story to the next, I began to realize that many of these stories have become part of larger works over recent decades. Researchers and writers have taken these moments in time and magnified them into theses, dissertations, and documentaries. Were these authors inspired as I was so long ago? Maybe, but we can never really know. So much historical research and writing has developed over the last thirty years that a great synergy is coming forth, spilling over into other media forms. California Indians are rediscovering much of their heritage. In the age of YouTube, regional documentaries, and Native authors, a new narrative is forming. In this context, is a collection such as this book still important? Reading it for the third time, I found myself jotting down notes about more that I need to research and learn. Perhaps, for me personally, the book has morphed from inspiration to muse. I hope it serves you the same.

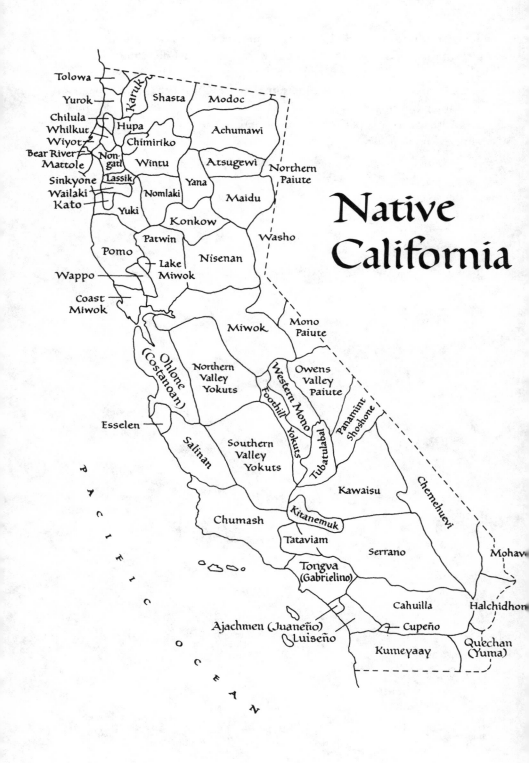

Tolowa
Yurok
Chilula
Whilkut
Wiyot
Bear River
Mattole
Sinkyone
Wailaki
Kato

Karuk
Hupa
Chimiriko
Non-gatl
Lassik
Yuki

Shasta
Wintu
Nomlaki
Konkow
Patwin

Modoc
Achumawi
Atsugewi
Yana
Maidu

Northern
Paiute

Pomo
Wappo
Coast
Miwok

Lake
Miwok
Nisenan

Washo

Esselen

Ohlone
(Costanoan)

Northern
Valley
Yokuts

Salinan

Southern
Valley
Yokuts

Miwok

Western Mono

Foothill Yokuts

Tubatulabal

Mono
Paiute

Owens
Valley
Paiute

Panamint
Shoshone

Kawaisu

Chemehuevi

Chumash

Kitanemuk

Tataviam

Serrano

Mohav

Ajachmen (Juaneño)
Luiseño

Tongva
(Gabrielino)

Cahuilla

Cupeño

Kumeyaay

Halchidhom

Quechan
(Yuma)

PACIFIC OCEAN

Native
California

Introduction

The following collection of reminiscences, stories, and songs reflects the diversity of the people native to California. The magnitude of that diversity is obvious in any gathering of California Indians, with great differences quickly apparent not only between those from northern and those from southern California, but often between groups of people living only a few miles apart.

In the days before the coming of whites those differences were even greater. Picture, for example, a typical spring afternoon in California two hundred years ago. On the prairies of the northeastern part of the state a man, hiding behind a clump of sagebrush, waves a scrap of deerskin in the air, trying to rouse the curiosity of a herd of grazing antelope and draw them within range of his bow and arrow. Along the Klamath River a boy crawls through the circular doorway of a large plank house and walks downstream to watch his father and uncles fish for salmon beneath the redwoods. In the Central Valley a group of women, strings of wildflowers in their hair, wade out into the deep sea of rippling grass to gather roots. As they push forward herds of elk scatter before them. In San Francisco Bay two men paddle a rush boat through the quiet channels of a saltwater marsh. East of the Sierra, families—eager for change and weighed down with burden baskets—leave their winter homes in the desert and trek through pine forests toward thawing mountain lakes and the promise of good fishing. At the edge of the Mohave Desert men and women plant corn, bean, and pumpkin seeds in the warm, fertile mud of the Colorado River.

People first started appearing in California more than twelve thousand years ago. Perhaps they were placed here by the Creator, as many traditional people still insist, each group rooted in its own territory by divine ordinance. Or perhaps, as archaeologists tell the story, they were bands of bold explorers or maybe desperate refugees who had been ousted from homelands elsewhere, who came into California from many places and over the course of many thousands of years.

Their languages are many and varied. Some California groups speak languages of the Algonkin family of eastern North America. Others speak

1

an Athapascan language related to languages of Canada. There are also speakers of languages from the Uto-Aztecan or Shoshonean language family; speakers of the Hokan languages more commonly found in the southwest; speakers of Penutian languages whose linguistic relatives may include the Tsimshian of British Columbia and perhaps even the Mayans of Central America; and at least two groups of Yukian speakers whose language can be linked convincingly to no other surviving languages in the world.

As group after group appeared in California, they gradually dispersed along the ocean beaches, settled into secluded mountain valleys, moved out into the open desert, and established villages in the oak savannahs of the Sierra Foothills. They built wooden houses in the redwood and pine forests, underground earthen houses in the grasslands of the Central Valley, rush and willow houses along the fringes of marshlands. Centuries, sometimes thousands of years passed, and people of the same language family lost contact with each other. Some became almost totally isolated within their narrow valleys, some merged with neighboring groups of different linguistic stock. As a result, when white explorers first set foot in California, they found as many as 100 languages being spoken, seventy percent of them as mutually unintelligible as English and Chinese. Stephen Powers, a nineteenth century ethnologist, complained of traveling for "months in regions where a new language has to be looked to every ten miles sometimes."

The great variety of languages was matched by a great variety of customs, technologies, beliefs, and physical characteristics. The Yuman people of southernmost California and the Modoc of the northern border were among the most warlike people in North America, while residents of the central part of the state were among the most peaceful. The Mohave who lived along the Colorado River were the tallest of all Native Americans, the Yuki of Mendocino County the shortest. Dances, religious practices, foods eaten and shunned—indeed, almost every aspect of culture varied widely throughout the state.

As one example of California's extraordinary diversity, consider the matter of boats. The Yurok at the mouth of the Klamath River made dugout canoes out of redwood logs—crafts of "wonderful symmetry and elegance," according to an early visitor, "the sides as smooth as if they had been sandpapered." These Yurok boats were blunt and sturdy, made to withstand the battering of rocks and the scraping of river bottoms. The Modoc, by comparison, made extremely delicate dugouts hollowed out to an amazingly thin shell—boats well suited to the calm waters of Tule and Lower Klamath Lakes.

The Chumash of the Santa Barbara Channel had a totally different concept of boatbuilding. They fashioned boats, sometimes over thirty feet long, out of thin planks. Lacking nails they drilled holes in the planks and sewed them together with thongs of deer sinew. Then they caulked the seams with asphaltum, painted the sides red with hematite, and decorated the bows with white sea shells. These were ocean-going vessels in which the maritime

Chumash voyaged to the Channel Islands, Santa Catalina, and even to remote San Nicolas Island sixty-five miles from shore.

The Choinumni, a Yokuts group of the San Joaquin Valley, bound tule (bulrush) together with willow withes to make barges fifty feet long. They outfitted these immense barges with bedding, baskets of acorns and dried meat, even clay-lined fireplaces. Firewood was taken aboard, and one or more families embarked onto the sloughs, waterways, and lakes of the Central Valley, for a combined fishing expedition and vacation that often lasted weeks.

Even this does not come close to exhausting the types of boats used in California. Dugouts were made in a variety of designs out of locally available wood: redwood, fir, cottonwood, juniper, and pine. Tule craft ranged from tiny floating platforms from which Tubatulabal fishermen hurled harpoons to thirty-foot boats that once plied Clear Lake carrying several persons or over a ton of freight. Some groups lashed logs together to make rafts. Others used large baskets or even clay pots—towed by strong swimmers—to ferry children and goods across a river.

The variety of watercraft in California suggests the remarkable variety of people and culture. The people we call "Native Californians" actually belonged to over five hundred independent tribal groups. Such diversity boggles the modern mind, overtaxing our systems of categorization and nomenclature. Consequently we moderns have tended toward generalization. We refer, for example, to the "Pomo" as if there had once been a Pomo tribe or a Pomo culture. Before the coming of whites, however, the Pomo were several dozen independent tribal groups—small nations, as it were— each with its own territory and chief. Pomo groups who lived in the interior valleys differed widely in customs, beliefs, and languages from those who lived along the coast. The major justification for grouping such diverse people under a single name is that the languages they spoke—seven different, mutually incomprehensible languages—are linguistically related and of common origin.

Pomo, in short—like Miwok, Maidu, Yokuts, etc.—is largely a concept of our own invention. Nevertheless for over a hundred years stories and songs, accounts of daily life, baskets and other artifacts have been collected from people described simply as "Pomo." Also, as generations have passed, the unique identities, characteristics, territories, and sometimes even the names of the many independent tribal groups have become obscured. Thus this book has no choice but to follow the conventional nomenclature and refer to people as Pomo, Maidu, or Miwok, however misleading. In fact this book does something much worse. In the following pages mention is often made of "Native Californians," "California Indians," or of a "California" way of thinking or acting. California, of course, is our own way of defining the world; the area it describes holds together as a unit only in the modern mind. In terms of native culture, "California" is utterly meaningless. So be forewarned. References to California, even more than references to Pomo,

3

Watercraft

LEFT: A Pomo tule canoe or "balsa" on Clear Lake. Harry Holmes at the stern. *Archival photo courtesy of Phoebe Apperson Hearst Museum of Anthropology.*

BELOW: A Chumash plank canoe, constructed and launched by native builders in 1976 under the direction of the Santa Barbara Museum of Natural History. *Photo by Rick Terry, courtesy of Santa Barbara Museum of Natural History.*

RIGHT: Karuk dugout canoe, possibly with Jim Pepper. *Archival photo courtesy of California Department of Parks and Recreation.*

BELOW: Mohave raft loaded with melons and squash. *Photo by Edward S. Curtis, 1907. Courtesy of Smithsonian Institution.*

are concessions to modern perspective and definition, rather than adequate descriptions of the incalculable human richness and multiformity that existed here two hundred years ago.

California is thought to have had the densest pre-Columbian population anywhere north of Mexico. In 1769, when the first Spanish colonists arrived, an estimated 310,000 native people were living within the borders of the present state. Then came the missions and the *ranchos;* the goldminers, loggers, and farmers; the silting of streams, clearing of forests, draining of marshes, fencing of grasslands, and elimination of game; the diseases, the hatred, and the violence; the unspeakable tragedy. By the beginning of the twentieth century fewer than 20,000 native people were left in the state.

After 1900 California's Indian population began to increase, but many of the survivors were children of mixed marriages and broken traditions. Those who spoke native languages and who remembered and valued native culture continued to decline. The twentieth century saw a steady, inexorable shrinking of witness to the old ways of life. Anthropologists and other scholars scurried among the survivors, trying to salvage what they could from those who still remembered. Carobeth Laird, wife of the linguist-anthropologist John P. Harrington, described the mood: "The vessel of the old culture had broken, and its precious contents were spilling out and evaporating before our very eyes. Harrington, like a man dying of thirst, lapped at every random trickle."

Harrington was not alone. Although it is dreadful how much has been lost—whole tribal groups have disappeared with scarcely a word recorded—it is nevertheless astounding how many Native Californian songs, stories, speeches, and reminiscences have been preserved: literally thousands of dictaphone cylinders, disks, records, and tapes; folders, boxes, and filing cabinets filled with field notes; and thousands upon thousands of pages of material published as monographs, books, or in scholarly journals; and (amazingly) innumerable songs, stories and reminiscences still part of the ongoing cultures of California Indians.

It has been several years since I took my first plunge into this vast sea of linguistic and ethnographic material. I originally had, if I remember correctly, a rather lofty ambition. I planned a comprehensive survey of Native California literature—one which would be, if not complete, at least representative. As time went on the impossibility of the task gradually dawned on me. Not only was I overwhelmed by the mass and variety of material available, but much of that material was in itself simply bewildering.

How could I deal, for example, with the large number of "autobiographies" which gave no details about birth, marriage, or occupation, but instead consisted of meticulous recountings of dreams and contacts with the spirit world? Such autobiographies made perfect sense in a cultural context. Native Californians traditionally lived in small tribal groups in which the external details of each person's life were intimately known. It would never occur to a woman, for instance, to talk about how she made baskets, how she pound acorns, or who her children were, for such things were known by everyone. To mention them would have been too obvious—like mentioning the fact that she had two legs and a nose. The subject of autobiographies is what other people do not know—in this case the world of one's dreams and the nature of one's spirit-world contacts, which for most Californians were the most important and most individual aspects of their lives. Yet while I recognized that such dream and spirit autobiographies were typical and thoroughly indicative of the native thought process, I found the bulk of them so foreign to the modern experience as to be inaccessible to all but the most dedicated student. Thus in preparing this collection I tended to pass over most of such material in favor of those autobiographies that were less typical but were structured more in line with our own conventions.

Similarly many Indian stories and myths seem rambling and plotless by modern standards. Originally there was no real need for plot. After all, the entire audience—except for the very young children—had heard each story and myth many times. Since everyone knew the plot, the storyteller was free to concentrate instead on voice, cadence, and performance. Especially performance! Imagine, for example, a rainy winter night. People have crowded into the assembly house or large dwelling. A fire is lit—it crackles and smokes from the moisture in the wood—and the storyteller launches forth, voice rising and falling; now talking, now singing; adopting the tone of one character, then another; shouting, whispering, grunting, wheedling, laughing—and all in a language molded to the story by centuries of previous performances; all in an energized setting in which family and friends are crowded together.

Anthropologists, linguists, and folklorists have painstakingly recorded and transcribed many stories. Yet when such stories are stripped of the richness of human voice and the presence of living audience, cut off from cultural knowledge and tradition, translated into a distant language and set into type, they are often so diminished that many of them seem formless, empty, and incomprehensible to us.

Songs in particular suffer in translation. The tune, the rhythm, the nonsense syllables, the very life is often pressed out of a song as it passes into written English. How can one even begin to translate a Maidu shaman's recital, described by a listener as a "tangle of breathing and blowing sounds, bilabial trilling, nonsense syllables, and esoteric utterances?" How can one capture songs in Lower Lake Pomo, a language full of hissing sounds and sharp clicks such as one finds in certain African languages? Indeed, how can one convey any song except to sing it? Once again a huge body of very typical material had to be passed over in my final selection.

Thus my plan to present a comprehensive, or at least representative survey of Native Californian literature quickly ran into trouble. In fact as time went on I strayed further and further from the goal, so that the reminiscences and stories, songs and speeches that follow—while thoroughly authentic and (as nearly as possible) true to tone—are basically a personal selection. Here, then, is what seemed to jump out of the mass of collected material, suddenly illuminating some aspect of native life, or presenting me with something that I found beautiful, tragic, terribly interesting, or simply funny. Here are the selections that transported me, for a few minutes at least, into another world—that made me feel what it must have been like to have been a shaman dancing for power, a young boy awaiting initiation, an old man gazing at a pine tree he could no longer climb, a young girl hearing for the first time the mourning cries of her mother, a member of an audience listening to Coyote tales in an atmosphere of shared laughter. Here are the selections that have filled me with wonderment and have given me a deeper understanding not only of Native Californians, but of all humanity.

Why a Second Edition?

I finished compiling material and writing commmentary for the first edition of *The Way We Lived* in 1981; I did not, however, finish learning. In the years that followed, my understanding of California Indians has grown and changed, as has my increasing personal involvement with contemporary native communities and individuals.

The vehicle for much of this personal growth has been *News from Native California*, a quarterly devoted to the history and ongoing cultural concerns of California Indians, which I co-founded in 1987 and continue to publish through Heyday Books. *News* has attracted many native writers and scholars and has become a means by which they have been able to tell their own stories and define their own realities. As publisher and co-editor I surely learn more from each issue than any of our readers.

News has further provided me with an introduction to hundreds of people I would never otherwise have met. Not of Indian descent myself, I seem to have been generally accepted into various communities as some kind of odd, well-meaning, benign, and occasionally useful "friend of the family," a role which I have eagerly embraced. In this role I have sat in many kitchens drinking coffee; been present at the sidelines of many traditional ceremonies; and attended numerous baby namings, weddings, shamans' healings, tribal council meetings, conferences, art shows, picnics, all-night stick game tournaments, and a variety of other events, some traditional, some modern; some public, some private. I have developed a wide network of acquaintances, and within this network even a few dear and true friends. I have also engaged in what must now amount to thousands of hours of conversations, and in the course of these conversations I could feel old certainties dissolve and new understandings grow. Some of what I thought I knew needed to be modified or expanded, while things that I had never conceived of before now needed to be said.

Most of these new understandings were, of course, quite specific—a certain phrase or "fact" about some particular aspect of Indian life was faulty and had to be changed. More importantly, though, I came to recognize the inadequacy of a way of thinking that I had never clearly articulated but was at the root of how I had structured the first edition of *The Way We Lived*. I had originally conceived of California Indian culture as having been complete at the time of contact with Europeans. From that point on, I had envisioned it as decaying inexorably, sometimes dramatically, as each generation of Indians forgot more and more of the old ways and assimilated into the dominant culture. Although there is something to be said for this viewpoint—it should not be dismissed too lightly—I came to feel that it was incomplete. Why should we hold Indian culture to standards and demands that we do not apply to ourselves? Do we envision the culture of the dominant society as having reached its fullness at a particular moment of history, say, 1776, from which point it has degenerated? Do we demand that a person wear a powdered wig, speak in the cadences of Benjamin Franklin, and plow the fields with a horse in order to be called an "American?"

Living cultures change and adapt—they have no choice if they are to remain living. So it has been with California Indian cultures. When George Blake (Hupa/Yurok) uses a chainsaw to carve out a traditional dugout canoe, or Margaret Baty (Mono) uses a blender to process acorns, they are not turning their backs on their cultural traditions. They are doing what Indian boatbuilders and cooks have been doing for thousands of years—using the best available tools at their disposal for the job at hand. Seen this way, shaping a canoe with a chainsaw or processing acorns in a blender are, paradoxically, traditional, a continuation rather than a denial of cultural values.

What I have come to appreciate then, is the vitality, ingenuity, dignity, and strength of contemporary Indian culture, even as it is changing before my very eyes. I had not quite achieved this appreciation when I wrote the first edition of *The Way We Lived*, and consequently I ended it with a feeling of great sadness at the loss of languages, of cultural knowledge, of traditions. In the edition before us the sadness is still present—there is indeed much to be sad about—but it is now balanced by what I have been feeling more and more with each passing year, namely a genuine and thorough admiration not only for the past but also for the ongoing cultural life of these most remarkable people.

1. Growing Up

Lively, lively, we are lots of people.

from the "Duck Dance Song"
Amanda Wilson, Maidu

The Cradle

A Native Californian child was born into a tightly-woven family, into a small tribal group, into a people whose lives were influenced by traditions many hundreds of years old. The men hunted the way their fathers, grandfathers, and great-grandfathers had hunted—indeed, they hunted in the very same meadows and woodlands, and the deer they stalked were the direct descendants of the very deer their forefathers had stalked. The women gathered basketry roots from the same sedge beds and in the same ways their mothers, grandmothers, and great-grandmothers had done before them. It was an ancient, intimately-known world into which an infant was born. A child in its lifetime would never be expected to improve or alter things—change was seen as disruptive—but rather to fit in with the old ways, to adapt to its customs. This was a world in which innovation and independence were discouraged, and in which the prime virtues were obedience, moderation, and restraint.

Soon after a baby was born, it was swaddled tightly into a basketry cradle. There were practical reasons for restraining a child: California had grizzly bears, rattlesnakes, scorpions, poisonous plants, rushing water, and numerous other dangers. Also, a swaddled baby seldom cried or fussed. Yet surely those early months packed into a basketry cradle must have greatly influenced personality. The severe restriction of movement curbed independence and a sense of experimentation. A child watched the world rather than acted upon it. Perhaps in the process the child developed an attitude of acceptance toward the world—an attitude that throughout a person's life would be amplified by other cultural experiences, until in the end acceptance of the world would become the very center of a complex system of belief and value.

They have an extra basket for a child when it is born; an aunt might have given an old one, or a grandmother might have made one especially. They roll the inside bark of red or white willow (rich people use maple bark) into soft balls that they use as diapers. Layers of it are put in the baby's basket, and the baby is laid on it. The diaper material is changed; it might be washed once or twice but, if possible, clean material is used. They are always very particular to keep these things nice and clean. When the baby is first put into the basket, they have a peculiarly shaped rock as a pillow for the head. They keep it there for about a week and then take it away. The baby stays in the basket until he is old enough to crawl, and sometimes he crawls with the basket still on.

JEFF JONES, NOMLAKI*

The rock pillow helped flatten the back of the baby's head, for in much of California a flattened head was considered a mark of beauty. Thus a child was from its first moments literally molded by cultural values. Indeed, the image of the baby crawling turtle-like with its cradle on its back describes not only the circumstances of California Indians, but the fate of all humanity. We may have

*For information about sources, see notes beginning on page 232.

been born free, but by the time we are ready to crawl we already bear the weight of our culture upon our backs—a culture which is at once our burden and our refuge.

Baby in cradleboard (Washo). *Photo courtesy of California Department of Parks and Recreation.*

When I Was a Child

Most native people remembered their childhood with fondness, even yearning. Childhood in California tended to be a time of relative freedom, of games and competitions, of the first tentative explorations into the adult world.

The Modoc lived in the high plateau country of northeastern California. They were among the most warlike of the California peoples, and their relatively arid environment—bitterly cold in the winter, hot in the summer—was hardly the most luxurious. Yet in recalling his childhood, Peter Sconchin remembers neither the terrors of warfare nor the threat of famine, but rather a world of peace and plenty.

When I was a child the first thing I did in the morning was to go out and play. I played around Tule Lake where the tules and grass grow thick on the north shore. Many of us boys played there together. We used to go out in the high tules, about six of us. There three of us sat down and closed our eyes while the other three went off to hide.... After we played this game for a while we went swimming in the lake. We had races to see who could swim farthest under water, or stay under longest. I played this game often when I was young.

Every boy had bows and arrows that his father had made for him. The bows were made of young juniper. We used to go out in the tall grass of the lake and look for chub fish. When the chubs moved around, the grass waved. Then we knew where to go; we pushed the grass aside and shot at the chubs with our arrows.

I killed frogs too, with small arrows that my father made for me. I also killed lots of watersnakes. I was afraid of them, but shot at them just the same...

When I came back to lie down before going to sleep, I used to hear my father's mother tell stories of the mythological times.

PETER SCONCHIN, MODOC

North Fork Mono girls swimming, before 1910. *Photo by Nellie MacGraw. Courtesy of Phoebe Apperson Hearst Museum of Anthropology.*

A bark slab house of the
Sierra foothills, Mono.
*Photo courtesy of the
Field Museum, Chicago.*

Childhood Games

In early childhood, girls and boys played together, spontaneously and with
little adult supervision. As children grew older, however, they moved—for the
most part naturally and easily—into sexually determined roles. The boys
learned hunting, fishing, regalia-making, and other manly arts from male
relatives; the girls, on the other hand, spent more and more time learning
basketry, plant lore, and an array of womanly arts from female relatives.

O ur young people of all ages, both boys and girls, had many contests
and races. Swimming was popular, including diving. One contest was
to take a rock, mark it by wrapping it in string, and throw it into the river
to see who could retrieve it first. There were foot races, sometimes in relays,
passing a rock or stick. There was competition in the broad jump and the
high jump, and often ball games in which the object was to kick a wrapped-
up ball of skins through goal posts. When the girls played they were
permitted to throw the ball. Many times, the girls were the winners.

In one race, rocks were placed in succession along parallel lines, with one
line of rocks for each player. Each contestant had to run to the first rock
on his line and return it to his goal, then return with the next rock to the
goal, and so on. The game was won by the first player to bring all his rocks
to his goal.

Another contest was one in which rocks were thrown, starting with small
ones, and working up in size to big ones, until the rocks were too heavy to lift.

Our children also had fun with supple young trees (saplings), pulling one
down and riding it like a horse or swinging on it. Sometimes someone would
take hold of the end and switch it from side to side, to see if he could buck
the rider off.

When I was a small girl, I went on root digging trips with my mother and helped her to collect plenty of roots to dry for winter use. These would be gathered in baskets. Some were cooked whole, or sometimes we pounded them up and cooked them like mush....

I also remember as a child living in the cedar bark house with my grandparents. How wonderful it was lying awake at night sometimes, to hear the coyotes bark, and the hoot owls uttering their calls among the trees. Sometimes there would be the running clatter of squirrels on the bark slabs above us; and in spring and summer, just as it grew light before the sun rose, there came the enchantment of the bird chorus, the orchestra of the Great Spirit all around us. That clean pine smell on the morning wind—where can we find it now?

MARIE POTTS, MAIDU

My Grandfather

As a child grew older family members—often aunts, uncles, or grandparents—took more interest in its education. The child received practical instructions in a variety of skills, as well as repeated lectures on being virtuous. On a deeper level the child absorbed (without quite realizing it) attitudes, manners, and values from the people around it. There was a right and wrong way of doing everything—of singing, of talking, of eating.

A Pomo woman, speaking broken English, gives an affectionate remembrance of her grandfather, a man who did things in the old manner—fastidiously and correctly.

Grandfathers don't teach much. Only "Don't run around with another man or married man. Be good to people. Be kind to people. Don't run around in the night time." That's what my grandfather said to me. Not to go to different houses; not to visit people. That's what my grandfather said, my mother's father. They don't teach much. But they tell you lots of stories, lots of old kinds of stories. How things happen, and how a person do long time ago. Sing some kind of song.

He was a great hunter, that old fellow. One time I saw him, he made traps for birds—all kinds of birds, for larks and quails and cottontails. He used to make old time traps. He used to put lots of them out in the evening. He used

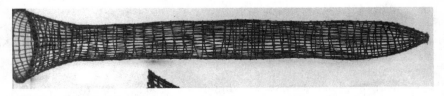

Pomo bird trap. *Photo courtesy of Phoebe Apperson Hearst Museum of Anthropology.*

to have baskets and used to fill them up with the game: rabbits, cottontails, birds. He used to have all of them in the basket [traps], and next morning early he would go out to get them. And when he bring them home in the morning, he used to build a fire, and he take all the feathers off. He cleaned all the birds, and he cooked it. He was the only one got to cook it. None of us helped with that. And when we ate the bird, we never bite it or break the bone. We just pull the meat off with the fingernails. It would have made him have bad luck if we bite it and break the bones. That's the way we did things. He used to cook it on the coals. He had acorn mush and acorn bread too. Tastes good with acorn mush—cold acorn mush cooked last night and left to set overnight....

My grandfather said he put the deer head on [as a disguise] when he want to go out hunting. He used to go out among the deer. The deer wanted to smell his behind. He always just turn around and sit down. It used to make me laugh when he tell that story.

POMO

Learning to Hunt

The name Kumeyaay has come to denote the people who have long occupied the desert area of extreme Southern California and the northern portions of Baja California. They are also sometimes known as the Diegueño—so called after Mission San Diego into which many of them were drawn over two centuries ago—or as the *Tipai* and *Ipai*, words meaning "person" in the two major dialects of the Kumeyaay language. The variety of names reflects, in part, the fact that while the Kumeyaay share a language and many other cultural characteristics, they are not a "tribe" in any political sense. Historically, they have consisted of some thirty independent, semi-nomadic clans. Some clans were traditional allies, others were enemies. Each clan generally wintered in its own sheltered valley, and as spring unfolded it followed the ripening plants higher and higher into the mountains, migrating back into the valley floors each fall.

While men and boys hunted as a matter of course, carelessness toward the animal world was severely disapproved of everywhere in California, especially among the Kumeyaay. Big game was relatively scarce in their arid environment, and a boy underwent a long and detailed training as a hunter. If he displayed proficiency and luck at hunting rodents, lizards, and other small game he would be taught to hunt rabbits. If successful at that he might eventually be trained to stalk deer and perhaps even mountain sheep. The hunting of big game animals fell under the close supervision of the clan's huntmaster, and was invested with considerable ritual and honor.

When I was a boy I always hunted with my father's younger brother. I remember when he first took me hunting. I had a small bow and arrows, little better than toys. My uncle told me to poke into a pack rat's nest with a long stick. I asked him instead to let me shoot when the rat sat outside,

17

but he said, "No, you can't wound him." I insisted and shot, but the arrow failed to penetrate for lack of power. I cried and shuffled my feet in chagrin. My uncle told me that it was no use for me to try, anyway, because he would not let me eat it. "If you eat the rat, or anything you kill, you will have worms in your stomach." Up to the time I married I never ate what I killed. Others can eat the game, but a boy cannot eat his kill until he is adult. One who refrains is always lucky. When I was a grown boy, whenever I went to hunt, I killed several rabbits almost immediately.

JIM MCCARTHY, KUMEYAAY

From his first fumbling efforts as a child to the time he became an accomplished hunter, the Kumeyaay youth was guided closely by tradition. For him—as for all California Indians—hunting was not a direct, primal confrontation between hunter and quarry. Rather the hunter throughout his life moved in a world complexly defined by ritual and custom.

The unmarried Kumeyaay hunter was warned against eating the game he killed lest he get worms and bring bad luck upon himself. But the taboo had broad and important social consequences as well. It meant that as the youth grew in skillfulness he would not become independent; instead he would continue to provide food for his family, while his own meat would be supplied by his father, uncles, and older brothers. In this way family ties were maintained and even strengthened during adolescence. Even after marriage, when the hunter was free to eat what he had killed, he would continue to share his game with family, repaying those who had fed him during his apprenticeship and providing meat for younger brothers and nephews who were themselves just learning to hunt.

When a man was in his prime he probably gave more than he received, but when he reached old age, unable to get about easily, his membership in the clan would provide him with the fruits of a nephew's or grandson's first hunting. It was membership in clan and family—rather than individual skills—that provided one with identity and security.

A Man Without Family

Before the coming of whites the Sonoma and Mendocino County area held a diversity of people. Among them were those who spoke seven different but related languages and who have come to be known collectively as the "Pomo." Arts were highly developed, and indeed Pomo basketmakers have been considered among the most accomplished and sophisticated visual artists the world has ever seen. Ceremonial life, too, was immeasurably rich: secret societies, initiation rites, cult performances, shamans, festivals, and elaborate dances were a major part of life, suffusing everyday affairs with a strong sense of the sacred. The complexities of Pomo social, religious, and artistic life are many. But underlying the complexities and elaborations was the institution of family, the solid foundation upon which Pomo life rested.

What is man? A man is nothing. Without family he is of less importance than that bug crossing the trail, of less importance than spit or dung. At least *they* can be used to help poison a man.

A man must be with his family to amount to anything with us. If he had nobody else to help him, the first trouble he got into he would be killed by his enemies because there would be no relatives to help him fight the poison of the other group. No woman would marry him because her family would not let her marry a man with no family. He would be poorer than a newborn child; he would be poorer than a worm, and the family would not consider him worth anything. He would not bring renown or glory with him. He would not bring support of other relatives either. The family is important. If a man has a large family and a profession and upbringing by a family that is known to produce good children, then he is somebody, and every family is willing to have him marry a woman of their group. It is the family that is important....

The family was everything, and no man ever forgot that. Each person was nothing; but as a group, joined by blood, the individual knew that he would get the support of all his relatives if anything happened. He also knew that if he was a bad person the head man of his family would pay another tribe to kill him so that there would be no trouble afterward and so that he would not get the family into trouble all of the time. That is why we were good people.

POMO

The importance of family. Jim Pepper (Karuk) with wives and neighbors.
Photo courtesy of California Department of Parks and Recreation.

19

So deep did the sense of family go that the Pomo, in common with other Native Californians, tended not to view the individual as a complete, self-sufficient entity. *Family* was seen as the basic unit of humanity, individuals as mere components. A person isolated from family was grotesque, frightening, pitiful, and ultimately unable to survive—like a finger severed from a hand. Individuals were incomplete, transitory beings; only family persisted, only family had meaning and authority, only family could bestow complete personhood.

Becoming a Man

Children were relatively well respected in California and were generally treated with kindliness and even indulgence. They were, of course, instructed and lectured at. But more importantly they were expected to learn, and learning, it was felt, came from within. Thus, for example, when an Indian child asked an especially important question of an elder, the elder often did not answer directly, but might instead tell a seemingly irrelevant story. Other stories might follow in days to come, or maybe the elder might set up an experience. Eventually, the child would put together the various stories and experiences and come to recognize that he or she could now provide the answer to the original question. This is how the elders taught; had they answered such questions directly, they felt that they would have robbed the child of the experience of learning.

It was further understood that knowledge was not just a body of facts, a code of beliefs, or a series of rules that the elders could impart. True knowledge (as well as power) resided in the world, and the youth would have to go out into the world—not to "get" knowledge—but rather to receive it. Perhaps if one were virtuous or fortunate, if one acted properly and followed instructions, the beings of the spirit world would come with gifts of knowledge and power.

W hen I was a boy, I wanted to learn. I wanted to know. I wanted to know about history. I went to the old people, and I got to learn all about this whole history. So I used to go to the old people every evening. I had to go because I had to learn. I had to go, so I fixed my bed there where the old man was. This old man was the oldest Indian. The old man who was going to tell all about history was there.

He told all about history. He began with old Flint (*sat ta che huey*). This old man knew how they lived. He knew how to live now. He knew what to do. He told me what to do. He told me this, "First thing in the morning you get up and you go out to the spring. You take a bath every morning. You have to do this."

So I had to do this. I had to take a bath every morning. I kept on doing this every morning, and I kept on running every night until my voice changed.

My voice changed, and my father was watching for this. He said, "Now, my son, your voice is changing, and I want you to go up in the mountain to the big lake." He named the lake.

20

He took me outside the house, and he took a bow string and he doubled it. He made me bend over and put my hands on the ground. My father licked me with the bow string. He gave me five licks and then I stood up. My father said to me, "Now, my son, you listen to me. Your voice changed, and I want you to go to the mountain to the big lake.

"You take five loads of wood to the mountain. Don't pick up sticks that are lying on the ground. Pull dead branches off trees. If you pick up a stick that is lying on the ground, you will have rheumatism.

"On the top of the mountain build a fire so that I can see it. Then go to the lake; [again] he named the lake. A hundred yards from the lake pull off your shoes and start to run. Before you get to the lake, pull your clothes off and throw them down. Don't stop running. Make a big jump into the lake and dive right down. When you get to the bottom, take a mouthful of water; wash your mouth out. Spit this water out and take another mouthful and swallow it before you come to the top of the water...."

Then he said, "You make a big fire on the top of the mountain. You do this five times tonight and I will watch you.

"After you fix the fires, fix your bed. Don't fix a good bed. Just sit up and don't sleep.

"Get some rocks and pile them up. Pick up a rock and throw it toward the east; then pick up another rock and throw it toward the west; then pick up another rock and throw it toward the south.

Old style sweat-house (Atsugewi). *Photo courtesy of Phoebe Apperson Hearst Museum of Anthropology.*

21

"When you have done this, take another rock and make a pillow out of it. Then you will dream something. Maybe you will dream of gambling or of a hunter killing a deer or about doctoring. If you dream one of these things, you must remember it. Don't go back in the water again; don't throw those dreams away. Come right back. When you come to the house, come to that tree. I'll watch for you.

"If you don't come back, I'll know that you didn't dream of those things, so then I will think you dreamed something bad, like fighting or killing a man or stealing. If you dream something bad, you must go into the water and swim again and throw the bad dreams away."

That is what he told me.

When I came back, I was a man, no longer a boy.

SAMSON GRANT, ATSUGEWI

Puberty Dance Song

For girls, childhood ended with the first menstruation. In these tightly-knit family and tribal groups, the event was hardly a secret, but rather an occasion for public acknowledgement and elaborate ritual. Throughout most of California the girl's family—and in some cases the entire tribal group—might hold a coming-of-age feast and, in many places, a dance.

> Thou art a girl no more,
> Thou art a girl no more;
> The chief, the chief,
> The chief, the chief,
>   Honors thee
> In the dance, in the dance,
> In the long and double line
> Of the dance,
>   Dance, dance,
>   Dance, dance.

WINTU

Rolling Head

Throughout California menstruation was regarded as an important event. A menstruating woman was generally seen as unclean, defiled, injured. At the same time menstruation gave her extraordinary magical powers, able to inflict illness or bad luck upon her enemies. Rituals were needed to restore the woman's "health" lest she come to harm and to neutralize her power lest she inadvertently bring harm to others.

Thus during menstruation a Wintu woman had to undergo a variety of restrictions: she lived alone for several days in a separate dwelling; abstained

22

from meat, fish, and salt; refrained from sexual activity; and ate from special baskets and utensils. The first menstruation—the onset of puberty—demanded even more severe restrictions. For a full month the pubescent girl lived alone in a brush shelter several yards from the family dwelling. She struggled to remain awake for the first five days to prevent dangerous dreams. She ate nothing but acorn soup; she could not comb her hair or even touch her own body. She had to keep out of sight, and whenever she left the shelter to relieve herself she covered her head with a basket or deerskin lest a glimpse of her face bring bad luck to others.

The fears and rituals that surrounded menstruation—common everywhere in California—seem puzzling to us. We view menstruation as a relatively minor and decidedly personal occurrence. But in a society in which everyone was organically connected nothing was *personal*. The perceived dangers of menstruation affected not only the "moon-sick" woman, but other people to whom she was linked. A husband, for example, would not go hunting during his wife's menstrual period because her condition would affect his prowess and luck: after all, they were of the same family and thus connected as a unit. And a woman who was careless about her menstrual obligations, especially at puberty, would bring ruin not only upon herself, but upon her entire family— one of the underlying themes of the following Wintu "horror" story.

L
ong ago people came into being and lived at a village; it was filled with people. People lived both on the flat on the west side of the river, and on the flat on the east side of the river too. There was a chief at the head of the people who had two daughters. The younger one reached puberty, but she did not tell her mother. However, her parents knew it. So they were to call a puberty dance, and they met and discussed it. In the evening the father spoke. "Early in the morning go strip bark for a maple bark apron," he said. "But don't take the girl who has reached puberty with you. Go secretly," he said.

The rest of the women got up early in the morning. They all went secretly, quite a little way north they went, and even some went north uphill and crossed the ridge to the north. Then later she woke up, the one who had reached puberty. And she went, though she was forbidden to go she went, going behind the others. She kept going until she reached them. Some were stripping bark and others already had much. She went right up to them and cut off maple bark.

All at once, she stuck her little finger with a splinter. It bled. Her older sister came up to her and wiped it with dead leaves. Then they said, "When will it leave off? The blood cannot stop flowing." And the rest of them all left, they knew already and were afraid so they left. She and her older sister were left behind alone. Some who had already gone reached the house and told the father. "She got stuck with a splinter while stripping bark," they said. And the old man said, "She does not listen to me."

She who had reached puberty, who was downhill to the north, now sucked blood and spat it out. Then more blood came and though she sucked the blood she could not stop its flow. Meanwhile the sun began to set. Until early evening she sucked, she kept on sucking, not being able to help herself. Then she got tired, not being able to stop it in any way. Suddenly she happened to swallow blood and smelled the fat. It tasted sweet. So now she ate her little finger, she ate it, and then ate her whole hand. Then she ate both her hands, devoured them. Then she ate her leg, ate both her legs. Then she ate up her whole body. Then her head alone was left and rolled about. She went rolling over the ground, her sister still beside her.

The old man in the house said, "From the north she'll come, she who went to strip maple bark. Put on your clothes, people. Get your weapons. We people are gone." And the people dressed themselves and got their weapons. And from the north they saw her come, she came rolling toward the house. She arrived in the early evening and lay there. After she had stayed there a while, she bounced up to the west across the river to the flat on the west, where she threw the people into her mouth. She did not linger, she turned the village upside down as she devoured them all. Then she fell to the east across the river and lay there, and the next morning she threw those of the east flat into her mouth, ate them, devoured them all. Only her eldest sister she left for a while. And she went about the world, and when she saw people she threw them into her mouth and ate them. Each evening she came home, each morning she went about the world looking for people. Always she went searching.

One day she climbed up to the northern edge of the sky and looked all over the world, but she saw no one. So in the evening she came home, and the next morning she got up and threw her elder sister into her mouth. Then she came on her way, until she reached the edge of a big creek. She did not know how to cross. And from the other side she called. A man was sitting there. He threw a bridge over from the other side. She was crossing, and when she had gone halfway he jerked it, and it went down at Talat. And she fell into the river, and as she fell into the water a riffle pike jumped and swallowed her. And it is finished. That is all.

SYKE MITCHELL, WINTU

Sand Painting Sermon

The Luiseño were a number of tribal groups who lived in Southern California. Their villages—each with thatched conical dwelling houses, shade houses, semi-subterranean sweat-houses, and a fenced ceremonial enclosure (*wamkis*)— dotted the land from Mount Palomar to the coast. The Luiseño spoke a Shoshonean language, itself one of the Uto-Aztecan languages that flourished throughout the American Southwest, and indeed Luiseño culture (as well as Southern California culture in general) bears certain similarities to the cultures of Arizona and the Southwest.

The Luiseño boy's initiation ceremony was a long and especially dramatic affair. Tribal leaders had each initiate purify himself, drink the hallucinogenic drug *toloache* (Datura), and then dance until unconscious. This often produced a colorful, mystical vision. In the weeks of heightened sensitivity that followed, elders imparted songs, dances, and sacred knowledge. A sand painting, representing the entire cosmos, was made on the ground. Here, laid before the initiate's eyes, was a symbolic universe that consisted of astronomical and spiritual phenomena interspersed with "avengers" such as bear-cougar and raven. As the youth studied the sand painting, an older man explained its meaning.

S ee these [sand painting figures], these are alive, this is bear-cougar; these are going to catch you if you are not good and do not respect your elder relatives and grown-up people. And if you do not believe, these are going to kill you; but if you do believe, everybody is going to see your goodness and you then will kill bear-cougar. And you will gain fame and be praised, and your name will be heard everywhere.

See this, this is the raven, who will shoot you with bow and arrow if you do not put out your winnowing basket. Harken, do not be a dissembler, do not be heedless, do not eat food of overnight [do not secretly eat food left after the last meal of the day]. Also you will not get angry when you eat, nor must you be angry with your elder relations.

The earth hears you, the sky and wood mountain see you. If you will believe this you will grow old. And you will see your sons and daughters, and you will counsel them in this manner, when you reach your old age. And if when hunting you should kill a hare or rabbit or deer, and an old man should ask you for it, you will hand it to him at once. Do not be angry when you give

Luiseño sand painting at girls' ceremony, 1906. *Photo courtesy of San Diego Museum of Man.*

25

it, and do not throw it to him. And when he goes home he will praise you, and you will kill many, and you will be able to shoot straight with the bow....

Heed this speech and you will grow old. And they will say of you: "He grew old because he heeded what he was told." And when you die you will be spoken of as those of the sky, like the stars. Those it is said were people, who went to the sky and escaped death. And like those will rise your soul.

LUISEÑO

Initiation into the Ghost Society

A major event in a boy's life was, in some places, his initiation into a secret society. Such societies flourished in north-central California, preserving sacred knowledge, ritual, songs, and dances, and passing them on to a younger generation. The Ghost Society, widespread among many different tribal groups, was apparently of ancient origin. Ghost Society members impersonated the spirits of the dead—a dangerous and fearful undertaking—and cured illnesses caused by ghosts. Their dance costumes consisted of long black poles, elaborate featherwork, and bodies painted with black, red, and white stripes. Such spectacular regalia combined life images with death images, thereby symbolizing the society's position as mediator between the world of the living and the world of the dead. By sponsoring initiation rites, the Ghost Society also mediated between the world of childhood and that of adulthood. A Yuki man, looking back upon his youth, recalls his initiation into the Ghost Society—although he is careful, of course, not to divulge any of the sacred knowledge that his grandfathers gave him at the time.

For the Ghost-Society Initiation everyone moved to the village of Ushichma'lha't, and the same day a dance house was put up. The logs were cut and everybody helped in their erection. That night the old men discussed among themselves how they could best catch me the next day.

In the morning they went out to cut the large center post and took me along. They found a good white oak in the canyon and cut its roots. They had no steel axes and worked with a large stone. When they were about to fell the tree itself they ordered me up into it. I was to sit on the crotch with my arms folded. They wanted to test me and see if I was a man and make me into someone who would be a chief. But they made the tree fall as lightly as they could so as not to hurt me. Then they chopped off the top above the fork in which I still sat. Now one of my uncles took off my boy's fawnskin and gave me a man's deerskin to wear. Then they took the log away. I lay flat on it. Thus they brought it into the dance house. They set it up in its hole and still I kept my place. Then my maternal grandfather reached up and took me off, laid me on his lap and cried over me. Then I could not help but cry too.

When the sun went down, they built a large fire and sweated themselves, but did not trouble me. For four days I was in the dance house with many other boys, all of us eating nothing. My maternal grandfather, and also my paternal grandfather, Lamsch'ala, talked to me about the Ghost Society.

This was late in the fall, when the river first began to rise. After four days I was allowed to eat and drink again, but all winter they kept me hidden away in the dance house. Whenever I went outdoors my face was covered. All through the winter at intervals they had the Ghost Society performance for four days at a time. They made it for themselves, not to teach me. But my grandfathers told me to watch them and to see everything that they did. Between times they kept me well covered up. Every evening they sweated. This they did until late spring when the grass seeds were ripe.

The second time I went through the Initiation was at Suk'a. I was a big boy now. This time the ceremonies lasted only four days. After the meal at the end I belonged to the dance house [as a full initiate] and went with the others to bring wood for sweating. Between the first ceremony and this one my grandfathers had taught me fully all the songs that I must know.

The third time I took part I was a grown and married man. Now I took part in the building of the dance house and all the other work. I danced and helped to give orders. I was practicing to be an important man.

YUKI

The first Ghost-Society Initiation lasted from the time "when the river first began to rise" until the time "when the grass seeds were ripe"—from early December until May or June, a six month period during which the youth kept to the dance house and devoted himself exclusively to religious instruction. No one considered this excessive. Throughout life a proper person would put large amounts of time aside for dancing, singing, praying, fasting, and other ritual observances. For Indian people everywhere in California, such activities were as fully necessary for human life as the hunting of game or the gathering of acorns.

27

II: The Conflict of Love

I am a fine-looking woman;
Still, I am running with my tears.

From a traditional song
Amanda Wilson, Maidu

How the Woman Got Even

When it came time to marry, the prospective groom approached his family to give or lend him the "bride-price"—gift baskets, money beads, skins, featherwork, and other treasure objects that he would have to pay to the bride's family. If his relatives were poor, he might (among some groups) be allowed to perform labor for the bride's family in lieu of material payment.

Bride-price was an honored custom almost everywhere in California, absent only at the fringes of the state—east of the Sierra and along the Colorado River. Among some groups, such as the Yokuts, it had become reduced to a gesture—a symbolic gift passed from the groom's family to the bride's family to legitimize the union. In northwestern California, however, bride-price was extraordinarily important. Among the Hupa, for instance, a woman's status was judged entirely by the bride-price she had fetched. So was her children's status. If a man's mother had gotten a huge bride-price he would be highly esteemed and assumed to be of noble character and unassailable integrity. Throughout his life people would treat him with honor and respect. A man whose mother had received only a small bride-price was considered ill-bred and was constantly suspected of lying and cheating. As for a man whose mother had received no bride-price at all, he was called *tintailtcwen*, "born-in-the woods." Such a man was a social outcast, generally a slave. He was never allowed to set foot in the sacred sweat-house. If he ever married it was only to someone of the same caste. If he was killed, no money could be exacted from his murderer. Throughout his life he would be addressed in terms generally used for dogs.

Along with the strong emphasis on bride-price, the northwestern California people tended to have austere attitudes toward sex. Men generally slept separately from women, and innumerable restrictions and taboos discouraged too frequent love-making. In fact among the Hupa the taboos were so prevalent that almost all sexual contact was said to have taken place in late summer and early fall when people left their villages (and ordinary lives) to camp in the hills. Almost all Hupa babies were born in the late spring.

A similar austerity prevailed among the Hupa's neighbors, the Karuk. For the Karuk, as for the Hupa, marriage was basically a financial transaction rather than a romantic fulfillment. The woman whom the Karuk held out as an ideal was the one who got—not the man she *loved*—but rather the highest possible bride-price.

A woman was walking upslope to Ipputtatc; she was going for wood, and she was packing along fire at the same time. Then all at once she saw somebody downriver coming in the upslope direction. He stopped; he looked. He was carrying his quiver, holding it high up. He said: "What are you packing fire for?" She answered: "I am cold." "What, the quail is already hollering, and nobody is carrying fire; nobody will feel cold," he said laughing. "I am going to Amekyaram. They are catching salmon already at Amekyaram." He was laughing, he was just laughing; he was making fun of her packing fire. Then he went on upriver. The woman too went on upslope. She was going to get wood. After walking a little way, she looked up in the air. "Behold it is going to rain. It is all clouded over." Then she thought: "Oh, I wish it would rain; oh, I wish it would snow." Then she prepared the wood, chipping off dry fir bark with a wedge. After a while it was snowing, dry snow; it was snowing a big fall of dry snow. The girl made a big fire there, where she was getting the wood ready. Then she thought: "Just a little later now and I will go downslope." All she could think about was that man. She was mad at him because, "Why did he laugh at me? That fellow said: 'I will be passing through here on my way back this evening, at sundown.'" She thought: "I guess he is about coming back." Then she put the load on her back. The snow was up to her ankles. She was walking along. She carried the fire back again as she went downslope; she was carrying it in her bowl basket, and she had the wood, too, on her back.

Then all at once there was a noise behind her. It was the man who hollered: "Stop, I want to talk with you." She stopped.

He said: "Do something good for me; make a fire for me. I am cold." The woman laughed. Then she said: "The quail is hollering; nobody ever feels cold. Nobody feels cold. You are not cold, I think you are telling a story." "Make a fire for me. I am carrying here in my hand a head-cut of salmon. Make me a fire for that. I am carrying here in my hand a head-cut of salmon." "No!" "I have here a pair of hair club bands with woodpecker scalps on them." Then she said: "No!" "Well then, I will give you my quiver, and all that is inside of it; all that I will give you." "No!" "I will give you my fishery, Ickecatcip." "No!" "I am carrying inside here a flint knife." "No!" "Well then, my armor; I will give you my armor." "No!" "Well then, let me marry you then; you can make a slave out of me." "Well then, I will make a fire." So she made a fire, a fire. The man warmed himself. Then he was all right; he warmed himself thoroughly.

Then they went home, to Xavnamnihitc, to the woman's house. She had him for her slave, and they were going to live at her house [not the man's house, the more usual marital arrangement]. She was happy, she was laughing all the time. That is what Xavnamnihitc-woman did.

PHOEBE MADDUX, KARUK

Thus Xavnamnihitc-woman got a fine bride-price—not only treasure, but ownership of the man himself. No wonder she was laughing! She was the idealized Karuk heroine: calculating, firmly insistent that her rights be respected, quick to take advantage of a situation, and *always* attentive to wealth and material possessions.

Although the Karuk and their neighbors emphasized bride-price far more than did other California Indians, their attitudes were not so much an exception as an extreme development of attitudes common throughout much of the state. Why was bride-price so important? Perhaps because (despite the story of Xavnamnihitc-woman) it generally gave family control over the marriage. The groom, scarcely more than a youngster, would not have acquired sufficient treasure to legitimize his marriage, and the penalties for marrying without

31

bride-price were too severe to be borne. Thus the groom would have to go to his family, which would thereby have power over whom the son would marry. Similarly, by accepting or rejecting the offer, the bride's family had control over their daughter. Indeed, throughout California marriages were generally arranged by the family. Love—the passionate desire of one individual for another—was not held to be a necessary foundation for a successful marriage. The honor and economic advantage of the family was the foremost concern, the passion of the individual (as always) was secondary.

Three noted fishing places on the Klamath River.

OPPOSITE: A Karuk fishing place named Shanamkarak.

RIGHT: A Yurok fishing place, name not recorded.

BELOW: A Yurok fishing place at Kenek, near Weitchpec, named Woweyek. *All photos courtesy of Phoebe Apperson Hearst Museum of Anthropology.*

Three Love Songs

Despite the austerity of people in northwestern California, despite the prevalence of arranged marriages everywhere, and despite the many restrictions on sex, love still raged beneath the surface—as poignant, pressing, and irreducibly tender as it is throughout the world.

I.

Before you go over the snow-mountain to the north,
Downhill toward the north,
Oh me, do look back at me.

You who dwell below the snow-mountain,
Do look back at me.

HARRY MARSH, WINTU

Hupa man hunting deer
with decoy mask.
*Photo courtesy of Field
Museum, Chicago.*

II.

When he walks about,
When he walks about,
Pushing the deer decoy back away from his face,
Right there in front of him
May I come gliding down and fall!

HARRY MARSH, WINTU

III.

The sleeping place
Which you and I hollowed out
Will remain always,
Will remain always,
Will remain always,
Will remain always.

FANNY BROWN, WINTU

The Handsome Man

Amidst the restrictions and family pressures, people gave themselves over to love—sometimes tragically, sometimes foolishly, sometimes comically, often hopelessly. And they gave themselves over to love stories, too—stories that explored love in all its pleasant and all its painful aspects. The Wintu called love stories "Nini," because they were ritually preceded and followed by the refrain, *hinini,* repeated again and again.

There was a couple who had one son. The little boy grew up and became handsome. No one ever saw him. The people talked among themselves. "They say he is a handsome man," they said. Women from all over heard about him. They came in numbers to where the man dwelt, and surely it was because they wanted to see him. The women who came lived in houses nearby. They watched, but they did not see him.

Now at daybreak that man used to go bathing in the creek, but no one saw him. So the women who had come watched three and many days for him, yet they did not see him. Other women came from the west and from the north. They continued to come, and new ones arrived, and they all talked among themselves. The man heard them. He disliked all the women, so he did not want to stay.

Now all the women went to bathe where the man was accustomed to bathe. They saw damp tracks on the ground, and in the water they found a long hair. When they found the hair they all rushed to get it. Once they had

35

seen the hair, they all wanted to see the man, saying, "It must have fallen from his head." So they thought, "Let's watch tomorrow."

The man, disliking them all, spoke to his father and mother, saying, "I am not going to stay here."

The next morning the women went to bathe, planning to catch a glimpse of the man; but the man had gone to bathe before them. So when the women went downhill to the creek there were already damp tracks returning. They were all very much annoyed.

In the evening the women lay talking to one another. "Let us watch this evening," they said. So early in the evening they went along the trail to the creek. Two went south and sat along the creek. A little further up, west of the trail, two more sat. But the man knew already that they were there to watch for him. Now the women sat watching all night. They sat, and sat, and sat, all of them. And the dawn came, and they slept sitting as they were. When they were asleep for a short while, the man went to the water, bathed, and after bathing came back to his house. Then the women woke up, went down to the water, and behold! there were wet tracks already returning. They were all annoyed, and talked together. They almost wept.

The man, after he got home, warmed himself by the fire and after warming himself he parted his hair and spread it out. After a time it dried and the old woman got the meal ready. When he had eaten, he spoke. "I will go away this morning," he said to his parents. So after he had finished eating and had combed his hair, he got some red rock powder and some tail fat and mixed them together. Then he painted himself and took his weapons and said, "Well, I'm going." And they said, "Yes," to their son. He then went outside and stood in front of his house, and the women now saw him.

Among the women were two sisters who had wanted terribly to see him, and they too saw him. So the man stood around, wishing that all should see him. Then he went off toward the west. The two sisters went into the house, got their carrying baskets, and followed after him, running. They went at a running pace over North Flat, wishing to see the man who had gone before them. The man was not to be seen, but there lay his tracks going forward. And they ran, they went at a running pace; they went rapidly. At South-Slope-Climb they looked northward, but did not see him. "We'll see him going uphill at Waitisawi," they thought to themselves. But they did not see him; he had already gone by.

The women went on running. They came to the ridge north of Dula and looked across the canyon, saying, "He'll be going that way." Still they did not see him. "*Hala*, he must be hurrying terribly much," they said.

So they ran, they went at a running pace across the canyon and up Nosono, and then they came to a stop. Looking down on the ground, behold! there were tracks going eastward. When they saw the tracks they ran toward the east until they came in sight of Rock-House-Lowland-Walk. There was a creek with running water. And when they looked, behold! that was where the man had stopped to drink, dipping water up in wild rhubarb leaves, and leaving the rhubarb leaves behind. Behold! there were damp tracks, he had just gone by that way. They pounced on the rhubarb leaves. Each girl pressed the rhubarb leaves against her heart, put them against her body here and there, because the man had held them in his hands.

Then they went on; they went running, running up the hill. When they reached the top they could look far ahead, but they could not see him. They kept on going at a rapid pace, and when they reached the top they looked to the north. They still did not see him. So they went on running; they kept on going at a rapid pace, and they arrived in sight of Digger-Pine-Broken-Off-In-Front. And behold! to the north they saw the man sitting, sitting with his face to the east. And they ran fast, keeping their eyes on him. One sat down on one side of him, the other sat down on his other side. Then they put their arms around him, and both said, "Why did you hurry so?" The man said, "I did not hurry." "We came at a rapid pace, so you must have run," they said. And he said, "No, I didn't." And they both sat there.

Then the man said, "I thirst for water. Do go and bring water, you two." "Where may the water be?" they asked. "Down the hill to the north, there is water in West Creek," he said. And they said, "You are finding an excuse because you want to go and leave us." "I won't," he said: "no, one of you two go and bring the water." However, they did not want to go and bring water. Then one said, "Younger sister, you had better go and bring water." Still they were unwilling to go, grudging each other the man. Then the man said to them, "I am thirsty. Hurry and get me water, you two, then we can start on our way." Still they did not want to go. Then he said, "Both of you go. I'll wait for you." Finally they said, "We'd better go. Don't leave us." And he said, "I won't."

They took out the drinking baskets that they had brought with them and went. They went running. They went running down the hill to the creek, and when they got there, they sipped water; they dipped up water and drank it. Then they dipped up another cupful and brought it running to where the man had sat. But when they reached the place, behold! the man was not there. Then they said to each other, "You were the one who wanted to go," they said. And the women threw themselves on the ground and wept, and after a while they saw smoke in the east. They waited, and soon they saw smoke even further toward the east. And they wept. "We won't go," they said. They lay there and lay there until afternoon. "We won't go," they said. Finally they sat up. Then they sang.

Ni, ni, ni, ni, ni, ni,
East and north from Skunk Mountain.
Lutustini's child,
Lutustini's child,
Goes east and north.
Along his going
Smoke rises.

It hangs over the south.
Lutustini's child
Goes east and north.
Ni, ni, ni, ni, ni.

Then they went home, they went home crying.

JENNY CURL, WINTU

Football Free-for-All

People throughout California certainly fell in love. Even in the northwestern part of the state, tender stories were told of poor young men who by magic and hard work accumulated enough of a bride-price to marry the women they loved. Also, most groups in varying degrees were tolerant of premarital sex, homosexuality, certain cases of infidelity, polygamy, divorce, and remarriage. People of all ages relished sexual jokes and delighted in the raunchiest of Coyote stories. Among many groups there were certain seasons and certain ceremonies during which sexual looseness was not only permitted but even encouraged.

S ometimes a football game was called, the women playing the men, putting up valuables and even money to bet with each other. The men kicked the ball with the foot while the women caught it with the hand and ran with it. The men hugged the woman who carried the ball. When they tickled her belly, she threw the ball to another woman.

If that woman missed, a man kicked the ball with the foot. Another woman caught it with the hands and ran with it towards their goal. Then a man hugged her again. When he threw her on the ground and rolled her around, she threw the ball. In that way another woman caught it and brought it towards their goal.

The men played with the foot, the women played with the hand: that was their playing together so that a man could hug the woman he loved. The women on their part took every opportunity to hug the men they loved; the game was like that so that this could be done.

WILLIAM JOSEPH, NISENAN

Tolowim Woman and Butterfly Man

Native Californians had paradoxical and complex attitudes toward sex. On one hand people fell in love and some had wide sexual experiences. On the other hand, sex was seen as threatening, dangerous, inimical to spiritual pursuits. People about to hunt, gamble, dance, seek power, collect medicine, or engage in any serious venture were warned to avoid love-making. Against the passion of the individual, the voice of society repeated its message: be prudent,

38

moderate, obedient, restrained. Yet how difficult it was to heed that message! A woman gathering food in a meadow might stop now and then to indulge in a fantasy. How wonderful it would be, she might daydream, if an irresistible lover were suddenly to appear.

A Tolowim-woman went out to gather food. She had her child with her; and while she gathered the food, she stuck the point of the cradle-board in the ground, and left the child thus alone. As she was busy, a large butterfly flew past. The woman said to the child, "You stay here while I go and catch the butterfly." She ran after it, and chased it for a long time. She would almost catch it, and then just miss it. She wore a deer-skin robe. She thought, "Perhaps the reason why I cannot catch the butterfly is because I have this on." So she threw it away. Still she could not catch the butterfly, and finally threw away her apron and hurried on. She had forgotten all about her child, and kept on chasing the butterfly till night came. Then she lay down under a tree and went to sleep.

When she awoke in the morning, she found a man lying beside her. He said, "You have followed me thus far, perhaps you would like to follow me always. If you would, you must pass through a lot of my people." All this time the child was where the woman had left it, and she had not thought of it at all. She got up, and followed the butterfly-man. By and by they came to a large valley, the southern side of which was full of butterflies. When the two travellers reached the edge of the valley, the man said, "No one has ever got through this valley. People die before they get through. Don't lose sight of me. Follow me closely."

They started and travelled for a long time. The butterfly-man said, "Keep tight hold of me, don't let go." When they had got halfway through, other butterflies came flying about in great numbers. They flew every way, about their heads, and in their faces. They were fine fellows, and wanted to get the Tolowim-woman for themselves. She saw them, watched them for a long time, and finally let go of her husband, and tried to seize one of these others. She missed him, and ran after him. There were thousands of others floating about; and she tried to seize, now one, now the other, but always failed, and so was lost in the valley.

She said, "When people speak of the olden times by and by, people will say that this woman lost her lover, and tried to get others but lost them, and went crazy and died." She went on then, and died before she got out of the valley. The butterfly-man she had lost went on, got through the valley, and came to his home.

MAIDU

To desert child and family and run with complete abandon after love and beauty—this is indeed at the heart of many a daydream. But as the fate of the Tolowim-woman poignantly suggests, destruction awaits those who seek freedom and unrestrained joy. The moral is clear: freedom leads to ruination and one had best follow the middle way—the way of moderation and restraint, the way of the family.

Women are Troublemakers

Perhaps because marriages were often arranged by family, and perhaps because of the sense that love-making was harmful to spiritual and other valued activities, the relationship between husband and wife tended to be somewhat aloof. The woman associated with other women throughout the day, making baskets, grinding acorns, collecting roots and berries. The man kept company with other men—in some tribal groups even living together in the sweat-house apart from the women and children. Marriage did not seem to be the most important relationship in one's life, and generally a person had closer ties to natal family than to a spouse.

W omen are troublemakers: an old woman said that to me when I was young. Out of my four women, only one got along with me nicely. Indian women are jealous. Children will get you into trouble. The older people teach us not to get in the habit of fussing with our wives, and if one starts complaining, to walk away if you can. A woman is more jealous than a man. A man isn't after a woman for nothing.

As a rule, a poor man has more children, but I guess he lies around and has more babies. A man of importance isn't around the house very much. Such a person hardly ever jokes with his wife. He may only be around in the evening. He may lie down alone for a while and then come to her to get warm. There are some men who like to be around their women all the time. They get to hating each other bitterly after a little while....

A couple can decide to separate by agreement. If a woman who is a basketmaker wants to leave a man, she will make him a real nice basket, mad and pouting all the time. This may take her from six months to a year. She will remain there and work for him and talk to him, but the two will simply not be getting along very well. When she finishes the basket she will hand it to him, saying that she is leaving. He gives it to his mother and tells her what has happened. Now the man's parents have to give her parents something. That is a friendly separation.

JEFF JONES, NOMLAKI

The marriage might break up, but as always the deep, organic relationship between children and parents survives.

House in Hoopa Valley, 1890. *Photo by Col. C.E. Woodruff. Courtesy of National Museum of the American Indian.*

LEFT: Doorway of a Yurok house. *Photo courtesy of California Department of Parks and Recreation.*

BELOW: "Calendar stones" at entrance to Hupa house. *Photo courtesy of Peabody Museum, Harvard University.*

ABOVE: Interior of Hupa house, with house "pit" in the foreground, storage baskets on the "shelf" in the background, 1890. *Photo by Col. C.E. Woodruff. Courtesy of National Museum of the American Indian.*

RIGHT: Interior of a Yurok house, with stairs leading toward entrance. *Photo courtesy of Phoebe Apperson Hearst Museum of Anthropology.*

III: An Ordered World

The young chief is going to do the same as his father used to do.
Now all of you men get ready.
Put those poles up for him.
All of you men get ready.
Have the ceremonial house ready just the same as for his father.
The young chief is going to do just the same as his father.
He is going the same way as his father did.
It is just the same, just the same.

Speech upon inaugurating a new chief,
Tom Williams, Miwok

Tarantula

A couple began their married life together in a world where custom determined much of one's behavior, custom as ancient as time itself. Among California people, there was a deep sense that when the world was created the Creator Beings instituted the rules by which everything—plants, animals, people, streams, mountains, etc.—should live. A deer, for example, was given particular foods to eat, particular places where it should bed, particular ways in which it should mate, raise its young, and grow old. How ridiculous if a deer were to attempt to hunt meat like a grizzly bear or climb trees like a squirrel!

For people, too, there was a correct way of doing everything—collecting shellfish, making baskets, building a house—and to deviate from the accepted and ordained was unthinkable. Knowledge of how to live a good life did not lie in the future, to be discovered by experimentation and change. Rather, such knowledge lay in the past, in the actions of the Creator Beings, and could be attained only by following ancient rules. Innovation was generally avoided and even mocked; the old ways were the right ways, the elders respected, traditional knowledge revered. Only a complete idiot would try to do things differently. Among the Coast Yuki a man named Tarantula was such an idiot.

There was a man named Tarantula. He had a wife. Tarantula did not know much. His wife had to tell him everything. They lived, lived together, all right.

Once Tarantula went to the beach at Mussel Rock [*Lilem*]. He was going to make himself a basket. He did not break up the hazel brush like anyone else; instead he bunched it as it stood growing. He made a basket, working around and around, until it was very big and high. When he finished with that, he collected mussels and filled the basket with them. Then he attached a pack strap, so he could carry it. He got under the basket and tried to lift, but could not, because it was fastened by the roots. He tramped around and strained and made a large hole where he was trying to get it up.

After a while his wife found him. She looked for him, because she did not know what had become of him.

She said: "My goodness, you crazy thing. You don't know anything. You ought to die!"

She transferred the mussels to another basket and took them and him home. They built a dwelling house. They got redwood bark for the sides. They kept at it until it was finished. She told him: "When you finish the house put earth around the bottom." He went out and threw up earth. He kept throwing up earth, until it was all covered like an assembly house. She went out to see what he was doing. There he was throwing up earth as fast as he could.

"You crazy thing, what is the matter with you?" she asked. "You ought to go off and die; you don't know anything." They finished the house. Everything was done.

46

After completing the house, Tarantula went after more mussels. She said: "Now, you get hazel twigs, break them off and make a basket. Don't make a basket growing." "Hech," Tarantula said. Then he went to Mussel Rock. He made a basket, kept working, working until he could no longer reach; then he quit. He broke off the twigs this time. He got mussels and started back. He did not return by the trail, but went under the ground like a gopher.

His wife was sitting on the ground in their house. She felt something moving the ground, like a gopher. She got up and looked and got ready with a pestle to strike the gopher when it came up. The ground kept moving, moving. She stood with pestle poised to strike.

Pretty soon Tarantula's head appeared. "You crazy thing, you ought to go off and die," she said. "You don't know anything, you crazy thing. People who go to get mussels should come by the trail." Then Tarantula went back into the ground. He went out of his tunnel at its starting point; then came up the trail.

When he returned by the trail, he did not put his basket down when he arrived, but stood with it on his back. She went out of the house and found him standing there with the basket on his back. He had not taken it off yet.

She said: "When people come up the trail with mussels or anything they should lay their basket down, then go inside and sit down." He went in and sat down; never moved, just sat there. He sat there.

"My goodness," she said, "when people come up the trail with mussels or anything and sit down, they should move around a little and eat." She fixed food and he ate. He kept eating, would not stop. She said: "Some time, when you get enough, stop for a while. Sometimes men and women play together." "Hech," he replied. He played with her, squeezed and hugged her; they played like two children. Pretty soon, she got tired. "Oh my goodness," she said, "sometimes they have to quit playing." "Hech," he said. He quit. The woman said: "Sometimes they sit down and talk." "Hech," he said. He sat there saying nothing; sat there as though he were dead, did not look around, did not say a word. "My goodness," she said, "sometimes people lie down."

He lay down; lay there, lay there, lay there. "Oh," she said, "sometimes people pack wood and make a fire."

He went out and got wood, packed wood, and packed wood, without stopping. Finally, she made him stop.

One day it was raining. The house was leaking. She said: "You'd better go out and find some redwood bark to stop this leak." He went on top of the house and lay his body over the leaky place, instead of getting bark. He lay there a long time and his wife did not know what had become of him. He almost died of the cold, as he lay there wet and shivering.

"I'd like to know what's the matter with you," she said. "You ought to go off and die. You don't know anything, you crazy thing."

COAST YUKI

47

The Osegen Slave at Espeu

Yurok villages dotted the downstream portions of the Klamath River and the coast nearby. In the Yurok vision of the world, they had been set down here at the very creation of the human race. Deeply rooted, they knew their land with profound intimacy. Large trees, clumps of bushes, even modest-size river rocks had proper names and stories. Villages like Osegen and Espeu—clusters of large, redwood-plank, pitched-roof houses—were viewed as ancient features; once established they were like rivers and mountains in their apparent permanence, and such villages had hundreds of stories and associations attached to them. Individual houses—or rather the house sites they were resting on—also had ancient names and histories. For a Yurok to say, "My father is from the house named *wogwu*, my mother from the house *sohtsu*," (as the narrator of the following account once described himself) was to communicate something rich in meaning and connotation, rich in history and myth. A person who was born on a prestigious house site, it was felt, had absorbed the power and history which the house site had collected from previous generations. The Yurok inhabited an old, well-established, deeply-experienced world in which the interactions between families had been regulated for centuries by a complex, sophisticated legal system of liabilities and penalties—a legal system serviced by professional mediators who were paid for their judicial roles.

A young man from Espeu had been visiting at Welkwau. On his way back they asked him at Osegen to stay overnight, for it was getting late. In the morning three brothers at Osegen went to hunt sea lions on a rock about three-fourths of a mile opposite Emets Beach. They did not invite the young man from Espeu, but he went along. From on top of the rock they saw a squall off Rekwoi. They started home at once, but the squall caught them and the Espeu young man was drowned on the beach. Espeu talked of destroying Osegen, so Osegen offered to settle. They claimed that they had not invited him, but a Turip woman there said they had asked him to stay overnight. Anyway, even if he had been all alone and had lost his life on their beach, Osegen would have been liable. Nevertheless, it was a close case, and Espeu knew they could not exact too much, so they insisted merely on getting a slave, and did get him. He was the youngest brother of the three who had taken the dead man out.

So the slave stayed a long time. He had gone as a young man and was elderly now. His master let him go overnight to his old home sometimes. Then he began to stay longer, and finally he did not come back.

Then his owner, with his two sisters, came after him to Osegen and found him on the beach, surf fishing, with his relatives the Osegen people. The Espeu man promptly claimed him. Then the slave's nephew said that he was not going back any more. The Espeu man said that he would take him right then and there. Thereupon the Osegen man shot him with three arrows. His sisters tried to protect him, but it was too late. One of them did break the bow that shot the third arrow.

Then the older sister stayed with the body, while the other one ran home and summoned help to bring the dead man back. Besides his two sisters, who were unmarried, the dead man had two brothers and a son. They did not try to fight until after the burial.

Meanwhile the Osegen people talked it over and said they must make a settlement as soon as possible. They asked a man from a Big Lagoon village to come at once and act as their go-between. So on the seventh day three men from Big Lagoon went to Espeu. They had a smoke and then reported to Espeu that Osegen wanted to settle. The next day they brought the pay that was proffered: a red obsidian, a woodpecker headband, four strings of large dentalium money, two otterskins, and a large deerskin blanket.

But Espeu had already said the day before that they would not take any property; they wanted the killer's sister. They were meeting halfway between Espeu and Osegen, so that the go-betweens would not have to walk so far. For a day they argued with Osegen, but the man who had done the killing did not want to let his sister go. His relatives kept urging him, and after two days he finally said, "I will give her if Espeu lets the slave go free." So the girl from Osegen was married to the son of the man who had been killed.

ROBERT SPOTT, YUROK

From a Yurok point of view, the story of the Osegen slave had a happy ending. The settlement was to the advantage of the murdered man's son, who acquired a wife without having to pay the steep bride-price that would ordinarily have preceded such a marriage. As for the woman, she would have been considered properly married and her children would have been considered legitimate—very important in the Yurok world. In fact she would have been very well thought of by everyone, since her bride-price had been established as more than "a red obsidian, a woodpecker headband, four strings of large dentalium money, two otterskins, and a large deerskin blanket," a rather significant amount of treasure. Everyone, in short, made out well, and the account of the Osegen slave—with its careful attention to the details of negotiation—would have been preserved as a legal "case" to be used as precedent for the resolution of similar conflicts in the future.

"Slavery," it might be pointed out, was not primarily an economic institution among the Yurok. A slave may have fetched firewood, hauled animal carcasses, and done other chores; but the family that "owned" a slave was not overly interested in exploiting the slave's labor. Rather it held the slave mostly to exalt its own status—and perhaps to socially humiliate the family of the slave. Indeed, the word *slave*—with all the connotations and images it invokes in the modern mind—should probably not be used to describe this relationship; but since we have no equivalent institution, the English language has no really suitable word.

Wealth—the great obsession of northwestern Californians—also had a rather different meaning. Almost never did a person use wealth to buy food, clothing, or other necessities. In fact acorns, salmon, and other basic needs were not for sale. Thus wealth was not really something to be spent, but rather to be conserved within a family, for it was wealth alone that conferred status. The more treasure one had, the greater one's social prestige. Wealth was also proof and measure of virtue. The phrases "a good person" and "a wealthy person" were completely synonymous and interchangeable in the Yurok mind. And for good reason. In this extremely litigious society anyone who was not virtuous—who transgressed in any manner upon others—would be sued and fined, and would ultimately lose wealth. Thus the accumulation of wealth—far from being socially destructive—was a sure sign that one was constantly and unfailingly devoted to socially approved behavior.

Elsie Frank (Yurok) of Requa in ceremonial dress, 1901. *Photo by Pliny Goddard. Courtesy of Phoebe Apperson Hearst Museum of Anthropology.*

Property

The Nomlaki lived along the Sacramento River and in the hills to the west, in what are now Glenn and Tehama Counties. The Hill Nomlaki differed culturally from the River Nomlaki, and they were further subdivided into a number of distinct dialect groups. Political units consisted of tiny, independent village-states, each with a population of no more than twenty-five to 200 people.

Like most Native Californians, the Nomlaki were so-called "hunter-gatherers." Each fall people heaved carrying nets and burden baskets onto their shoulders and left the major villages to gather acorns in the hills. They made similar treks for greens, roots, elk, salmon, and other commodities, often staying away from the major villages for weeks at a time as they ranged over their land.

The lack of large political units and the wandering style of life might lead one to think that the Nomlaki—who were fairly typical of Central California people—lived with a looseness of organization that bordered on anarchy. Yet the impression is false. The wanderings followed a distinct yearly pattern, and—as the following reminiscence indicates—the landscape over which people "wandered" was far from a trackless wilderness.

T he land does not [generally] belong to individuals. Dominic's grandfather [a chief], by being such a big and good man, was favored. He was left a big valley. He owned one big oak tree of a special kind. It was a singular tree called *nuis*. There was a village nearby, but old Dominic's grandfather owned that tree and got all the acorns from it. He also owned a valley of about 2,000 acres of open land. It was two or three miles away from his home. This valley was staked off—each different division [kin group] got a different part of the valley for themselves. They had poles to mark the different persons' territories....

Where there is a tree of small acorns, some family owns that tree. He [the family head] will lean a stick against the tree on the side toward which he lives. Thus the people know what family owns it. He may set up too many and will give away the others to his relatives. This person kind of owns the tree—like you would a fruit tree. In those days the families owned them. They own trees in the mountains, too. They maintain border lines, but if you are friendly with them they may give you a tree in time of need.

JEFF JONES, NOMLAKI

Very Strict Laws

Many different people lived along the Klamath River and its major tributaries, the Trinity and Salmon Rivers. Among the languages that were spoken along these waterways were Yurok, Karuk, Shasta, Hupa, Chimariko, and Wintu. Within these language groups were numerous independent and interdependent political entities.

However much people may have differed, everyone along the river system depended upon the annual run of salmon for their sustenance. They were rarely disappointed. Salmon crowded the rivers each season in runs so thick that at their height people found it difficult to ford the river.

People fished heavily, each village pulling thousands of salmon out of the water. Yet at the beginning of the next season, when the priests had sung the right songs and performed the right ceremonies, the teeming salmon returned, year after year, without diminishment. The health and magnitude of the annual run was not due to the sparseness of human population, or to the "low" level of technology by which people fished. The Indians of northwestern California were very competent at building fish dams that could have easily reduced or even wiped out the run of fish. Instead, a series of laws and regulations, respected and strictly enforced throughout the river system, ensured that only an appropriate number of salmon would be caught, that upstream people would receive their fair share, and (most importantly) that an optimal number of salmon would eventually reach their spawning grounds.

Fish weir across the Trinity River, Hupa, 1906. *Photo by Pliny Goddard. Courtesy of Phoebe Apperson Hearst Museum of Anthropology.*

W hen the fish dam is put in, they have very strict laws governing it. There are nine traps which can be used: one belongs to Lock* and his relatives, one to Lock-nee and his relatives, one to Nor-mer and her relatives, and so on down the line. These families come in the morning, and

---

*Lock was the person in charge of installing the fish dam; Lock-nee and Nor-mer, male and female respectively, were his ritual assistants.

each one takes from the trap that which belongs to them, as many salmon as they need, by dipping them out with a net that is made and used for this purpose; and they must not let a single one go to waste, but must care for all they take or suffer the penalty of the law, which was strictly enforced. After all these get their salmon, then comes the poor class, which take what they can use, some of which they use fresh and the rest they cut up, smoke them lightly, then they are dried. When they are dried, they are taken down and packed in large baskets, with pepperwood leaves between each layer so as to keep the moths out of them, and then they are put away for the winter. The Indians from up the river, as far as they are able to come, can get salmon, and down the river the same.

In these traps there gets to be a mass of salmon, so full that they make the whole structure of the fish dam quiver and tremble with their weight, by holding the water from passing through the lattice-work freely. After all have taken what they want of the salmon, which must be done in the early part of the day, Lock or Lock-nee opens the upper gates of the traps and lets the salmon pass on up the river, and at the same time great numbers are passing through the open gap left on the south side of the river. This is done so that the Hupas on up the Trinity River have a chance at the salmon catching. But they keep a close watch to see that there are enough left to effect the spawning, by which the supply is kept up for the following year.

LUCY THOMPSON, YUROK

Tree Care

California was a land of unbelievable fecundity. Great flocks of waterfowl darkened the skies in their autumn migrations; herds of deer, elk, and prong-horn antelope spread out over the prairies; fish crowded the streams and rivers. Each spring meadows brought forth luxuriant stands of plants that offered edible seeds, greens, and roots for eating and for basketry; mudflats and offshore rocks offered a seemingly inexhaustible supply of shellfish; trees provided nuts, firewood, and medicines.

The people who lived here for so many thousands of years did not take this abundance for granted. Rather, throughout California people adopted conservation practices and laws that maintained and even increased the richness of their land.

The Indians were preservers of the sugarpine timber which grew on the high ranges of mountains on the north side of the river, and there was a very heavy fine and also death to the Indian that willfully destroyed any of this timber. The sugar from these trees was also used by them as a medicine in different cases of sickness. The saltwater mussels that they gather which cling to the rocks close to the seashore is an article of food for them, and they gather and eat them while fresh by boiling them. They also dry them and take them up the river to their homes for winter use. In the month of August and a part of September these mussels become poisoned, in some years worse than in others, with phosphorus. Sometimes whole families would get poisoned by eating them out of season, and in this case they use the sugar which is taken from the sugarpine tree, and which is a sure cure if taken in time. This made the Indian prize the sugarpine tree very highly, and put to death even a member of their own tribe who harmed a tree in any way.

The Indians also took the greatest of care of the hazelnut flats, as the nuts are used in many ways. The nuts were gathered and stored away, as they could be kept for a long time and could be pounded into flour, put into warm water and made a good substitute for milk which could be used for weak, sickly children, also in some cases for sick persons that needed nourishment and had weak stomachs. The hazel is used in all of their basketmaking, as the frames of all the baskets are made of hazel sticks. In taking care of the hazel flats, they go out in the dry summer or early in the fall months and burn the hazel brush; then the next spring the young shoots start up from the old roots....

The oak timber they were very careful to preserve, as they gathered the acorns from it late in the fall, October and November. The oak tree furnished them with the staff of life, as it was from the acorn they made all their bread and mush....

All the oak timber was owned by the well-to-do families and was divided off by lines and boundaries as carefully as the whites have got it surveyed today. It can easily be seen by this that the Indians have carefully preserved the oak timber and have never at any time destroyed it.

The Douglas fir timber they say has always encroached on the open prairies and crowded out the other timber; therefore they have continuously burned it and have done all they could to keep it from covering all the open lands.

LUCY THOMPSON, YUROK

People throughout California regularly burned their land. By doing so they created an environment very much to their liking—one that provided the best habitat for game, one that encouraged the growth of favored food and basketry plants. The landscape of old California, in other words—meadows, oak savannahs, "park-like" areas of great boled oaks and clear understory—was not a "natural" landscape. It was a landscape created by people, in many ways as "artificial" as the farmlands of Europe. Thus, when Spaniards and then others first arrived in California a couple of centuries ago, they did not find (as they fondly imagined) a "pristine wilderness." They found what was in many ways a garden, a land very much shaped by thousands of years of human history and adapted to human needs.

Oak trees near present-day Laytonville, showing the large trees and clear understory typical of the old California landscape. *Photo courtesy of Phoebe Apperson Hearst Museum of Anthropology.*

Choosing a Chief

Within each tribal group there was generally a person of pre-eminence—a man (usually) who would in later years be variously called chief, headman, captain, or simply "the big man."

You know how some men are quick and strong and know the things to do, how people like to do things for them, and how they have a gift for getting everybody cheerful? Well, those men were leaders (*kwoxot*). When a man knew he had the power to be a good leader, he told his dreams. If his dreams were good, his plans would be followed, but if they were poor and stupid others would tell him so and he could do nothing. Sometimes men struggled with each other to lead war parties and arrange daily affairs. Then each would try to get more of the people on his side, giving feasts to his friends and encouraging them to speak of his wisdom. But it was not long before we knew who was the better man and he became leader and gave positions to others. If a leader acted stupidly, it meant that his power had deserted him and it was time to have another to decide things. A man did not become *kwoxot* because his father had been *kwoxot,* although some families were more powerful than others and had a lot of good men.

Kwoxot had to feed and look after poor people. He had to get together a big store of food for this. His followers gave him what they could spare, but this was not for his use, only for him to give away to the needy. When there was a death, the family burned its house and almost everything it had. Then they were very poor, without shelter and short of food, but they could go to the *kwoxot* and he would look after them; give them a place to live and food to eat. The *kwoxot* always did this for he was supposed to be kind to everyone, especially to widows. If he needed food for these people, he called on his followers and each gave a share of their stores....

Kwoxot had little to do with arranging ceremonies, he just did his part like anyone else. But he made the best speeches at these times. For it was by his speeches that people knew he had great power and was *kwoxot*.

PATRICK MIGUEL, QUECHAN

Throughout California chiefs had great prestige but little political power. They were not strong leaders, absolute monarchs, or despots in the tradition of other cultures. Far from it. They could persuade but could not give orders, for indeed they had no way of enforcing their decisions. People who did not like their ways generally ignored them. A chief who had lost the confidence of his people might harangue, lecture, or give advice, but people simply walked away. In societies where tradition and restraint were valued, where property and legal rights were deeply accepted, where warfare was limited, and where families were strong and autonomous units, a powerful chief was unnecessary and unwanted.

Early European explorers and commentators, who felt that a proper society required a strong ruler, looked upon Native Californians as living in anarchy. In reality political power was dispersed among family heads whose constant interactions, whose mutual respect for tradition, and whose checks and balances on each other made for a subtle, stable, and in many ways equitable form of government.

Building a Dance House

Life in many of the larger Central California villages centered around a communal building. Such buildings were huge—sometimes up to sixty feet in diameter. They were generally underground or partially underground, and a person passing down the sloping entranceway walked into a world of deep, earthen smells. The temperature was relatively constant throughout the year, the lighting always dim. During the day a narrow shaft of sunlight came through the smoke hole and swept slowly across the floor; a fire flickered at night, casting huge shadows upon the walls. In such dark, cavernous, mysterious places people gathered for ceremonies, public events, and sacred dances. These buildings were variously called "assembly houses," "earth lodges," "roundhouses," or "dance houses."

When they want to build a dance house, all the important men get together in the *elkel* [chief's house] and talk about where they can get the trees. They have all the posts and ribs of the structure named, and the men mention the various logs they have seen that would meet the needs of the different parts. They do not speak of their decision to anyone, but go out and look at the tree that is to form the center pole. They will walk around the tree and examine every detail of it.

Before any further steps are taken, the group goes to the captain of the village and asks his approval of their plan. He will not answer them for a long time, perhaps as much as an hour, and then he may ask them if they are in a position to build a *lut* [dance house]. They will tell him what food they have in store. He will ask, "How do your women feel?" and they will reply that it is all right with them. This procedure is necessary because it is expensive to build a dance house, as they must feed all the neighboring people who assist in the construction and are invited to the dance that follows. The headman can [theoretically] stop the building of a house. Others might object to it, but their only protest is to move to another village.

Having decided to build a house, the men begin to prepare the poles. These are cut down, trimmed, and barked, a fork being left at the top. The

Old-style earth-covered roundhouse at Cortina (Patwin). *Photo courtesy of Phoebe Apperson Hearst Museum of Anthropology.*

cutting of the poles may take a month. The one selected as the center pole is the last pole to be cut. Finally they select a place to dig the hole for the dwelling, and by this time the people have caught on to what is in the air without being told, and those who are next to the important men come to help.

The house is built in one day. The people have gathered and brought what food they could. They all get to work digging out the pit, each person working by digging with his *sen* [club] and carrying the earth out in the conical carrying baskets. Each works in that portion of the excavation toward which his own home lies. By working hard together, they finish the hole in three or four hours. Everyone helps, women, children, and men—all but the menstruant girls.

The important men have meanwhile gone to the location of the center pole and have dressed it as a dancing man with a feather headdress. It is carried to the house pit by six or eight men on a "stretcher" made of grapevine, accompanied by two singers, who sing a "march." They do not set the pole down till they get to the hole, where they set it upright in a special way and tamp it into place.

Next they put the two "brothers" in place and then the other upright posts; then the ribs are put from ground to post and between posts, a man being ready at each joint to do the lashing. Then smaller sticks and finally wormwood are added, each person again working on that portion lying in the direction of his home. After the wormwood is laid over the ribs, the crannies are stuffed with moss, and earth is carried onto the roof and spread over it to a thickness of about three or four inches. It is packed down by constantly walking over it, so that in the end the house is nearly airtight except for the door and smoke hole. At the last the people from the several surrounding villages try to finish their side first, and this work is done in high spirits, the people teasing and making fun of one another. Those first finished raise a great shout and help the others to finish the work.

The house is completed by night, and after this there is either feasting or a "sweat" or both. The hosts are expected to feed their guests for some time, and usually their entire supply of food is exhausted by the occasion.

The dance house belongs to the dancing men and the people, but the chief bosses and uses it, and it is called his. He does not live in it, but has it merely as a meeting house. His own house is the smaller sweat-house called *elkel*.

JEFF JONES, NOMLAKI

The building of the dance house was a joyous, boisterous affair. Men, women, and children crowded onto the site and worked shoulder-to-shoulder, excavating the hole, raising the posts, lashing the beams, and piling the earth onto the roof. Afterwards they feasted and celebrated. What seeming chaos! Yet the confusion was only apparent, as the preceding account suggests. The entire enterprise was well-ordered and carefully planned with the debates and

58

deliberations, the hierarchy of "important" and less "important" men, the division of labor among families, the ritual context of every act.

When completed, the dance house became the center of a village's social and religious activities. In both its construction and in its later use it united the various families into a symbolic whole. During the sacred dances that would be held for years to come, the dance house would continue to unite people with one another—and with the spirit world as well.

Messengers

There were over five hundred autonomous tribal groups in California—little nations, really—most of them numbering no more than a few hundred people. Each group tended to live in its own valley, more or less set apart from neighbors. Each group felt that it, and it alone, was the center of the world— the true "people" who did things the correct way. Others, they would insist (often quarrelsomely), had peculiar habits, spoke strange languages, did things all wrong. Each group was surrounded by "others" who were forever being suspected of treachery and evil magic.

Yet isolation between groups was far from complete. Despite the undercurrent of hostility and tension, each of these small tribal groups needed its neighbors for trade, for marriage partners, for ceremonies, or simply for entertainment. Life in these small, enclosed worlds could be somewhat boring, and a trip to a neighboring group—with different people, different land, games, dances, feasts, the telling of strange tales, and the sound of an alien tongue—was often the most exciting event of the year. After a long winter, when everyone had been kept home too long by rains and muddy trails, the urge to visit and socialize was especially strong.

Our people dance every spring and have all kinds of dances. When everything is all very green, when winter is over and everything is warm and the sun is coming north, when the birds holler *witwitwit,* the people begin to ask, "Why can't we play a little?" Then they send news to their close neighbors that they are going to have a dance....

The messenger who announces the *tami* [dance-feast] to neighboring villages and invites the people has strings with knots in them—one for each day until the dance is to start. One string is given to each headman of a

Knotted message string (Miwok). *Photo courtesy of Phoebe Apperson Hearst Museum of Anthropology.*

village, and every day he unties one knot until they are all untied. The first knot is untied on the day that the messenger delivers it. The people come on the day the last knot is untied. The Indians used to laugh about this custom because now they can just say, "Next Saturday."

Newsboys [messengers] can carry news from Paskenta to Tehama and back between evening and dawn. It is about thirty miles each way. They trot. They have free passage into enemy territory. It is necessary that they eat special kinds of food which is more preserving to the Indian body. The runners have to be careful of their diet. They are from twenty-five to forty years old, for they can't do this work when they are too young. They have to keep their wind. Special ones are picked for this—not just anyone. They try out on the plains—people say that that is the hardest place for runners.

The runner is in a dangerous position. He does no other work, for he must always be ready to go. When he isn't running, he practices. He doesn't hunt or fish, but is well taken care of....

Old blind Martin had been a newsboy. He made trips from Paskenta to Tehama. He said he never shot at a man in his life. He carried news over and back and had to remember every word he heard. After the runner comes back, after he catches his breath, he tells everything that was said. Two fellows repeat what he said, so that everything is heard three times. Everyone listens, and when they are all through they discuss the matter.

JEFF JONES, NOMLAKI

The messenger, as indicated, was chosen not only for his running ability, but for his good memory, for he had to keep even the most complicated and lengthy messages straight. Yet in these worlds that thrived before the introduction of writing, memory was highly developed. It has been noted that Native Californians who had heard an important speech just one time could repeat it twenty years later, the renditions of various listeners being almost identical.

Feast Oration

Feasts and dances allowed neighboring people to get together on a more or less formal and peaceful basis. Among the various Wintu tribal groups the Hesi dances were especially prominent. Hesi ceremonies were held twice yearly, in the fall and again in the spring, to ensure plentiful harvests of acorns, greens, roots, seeds, and berries. They involved four full days of games, feasts, sweating, orations, dances, and other performances. The first day was devoted to preliminary dances. By the second day the sacred pole—twenty-five feet tall and "dressed" in feathers—was ushered out of the dance house and set into its proper place before the dance house entrance. Guests began arriving now, and the master of ceremonies came forth to give his welcoming speech. Because many of the guests were from other groups, there was a potential for trouble. Old grudges might flare up, new hostilities might be generated. The welcoming speech thus developed two major themes: "Enjoy yourselves," and "Don't quarrel." To prevent fights the master of ceremonies implores people to

60

address each other by relationship words, to call each other "niece" and "nephew;" in short, to act like family.

The ritual context of the Hesi dance demanded a formal (rather than casual) welcoming speech—a speech in the full ceremonial manner. To California Indians speech-making was an art, as highly developed and in many ways as abstract as basketry, singing, or dancing. Indeed, speechmaking was governed by a similar esthetic. Thus the Hesi welcoming speech is constructed much like a basket—winding around and around upon itself; creating, developing, and repeating patterns; weaving strong yet simple elements into an effective and urgent whole.

Yes!
Come on! Come on! Come on!
Come on!
Girls come on! Girls come on!
Youths come on!
Children come on!
At eating assembled. At eating assembled.
At this eating.
At this eating assembled.
At this *pinole* [seed-meal] assembled.
At this acorn-soup assembled.
At this acorn-bread assembled.
You say "yes" to one another!
Say "yes" to one another!
Say "yes" to one another!
That is how you will do it!
You will call one another "nephew" or "niece."
At eating that.
At healthy eating assemble.
At eating that assemble. At eating this assemble.
At this pleasant eating assemble.
At this healthy eating assemble.
At that say "yes" to one another's eating!
Say "yes" to one another's eating!
Say "yes" to one another's eating!
Rejoice at one another.
Rejoice, "maternal uncle."
Rejoice, "father."
Rejoice, "younger brother."
Rejoice!
At him who causes you to eat.
At him who gives to you.
At him who gives food.
Who gives this *pinole.*
Who gives this acorn-bread.

Salvador in long cloak dancing about the pole in front of the Cortina dance house during Hesi ceremony, 1906. *Photo by Samuel A. Barrett. Courtesy of Phoebe Apperson Hearst Museum of Anthropology.*

At that be glad.
At that be glad.
So rejoice!
Rejoice for you.
My nephews and nieces, eat!
In this way eat! In this way eat! In this way eat!
You children.
You girls, you youths.
You children.
So eat!
So satisfied.
Satisfied, rejoice!
Satisfied, say "yes!"
Heed his word.
His word, his teaching.
He who teaches you.
So eat! So eat! So eat! So eat!

WINTU

Football Big-Time

Games provided another excuse for people to get together. Larger villages often had areas leveled and cleared for ball games, and each locality throughout the state had its own version of shinny or "soccer." The Nisenan of the Sacramento Valley and Sierra Foothills favored a relay game in which each team tried to kick and carry its ball to a goal and back again to the starting point. The stakes were high (Native Californians loved to gamble) and the play was rough-and-tumble; nevertheless off the playing field restraint and ritual prevailed. Games were interspersed with ceremonial feasting, dancing, and socializing, and good form demanded that the losing team accept even the most crushing defeat with equanimity.

In the early days the Indians had football "big-time." Very early in the morning the other team put up a great deal of money [i.e. many beads]. If they made goals at both ends of the field they won. Then they danced to make fun of us. When we finished we ate breakfast. After breakfast we played football again. At midday we rested, then we ate. When the sun came round to the west we were at it again; we only quit when the sun went down. We danced at night.

When it was dawn we played football again. We did that for two or three days and only quit when we had lost our money, valuables, baskets, clothes, bows. Before we parted we ate, the men of this side treating the other side. Then the men of the other side treated this side. Only then did we go each on his way. That was football "big time."

WILLIAM JOSEPH, NISENAN

How a Dispute Was Settled

For people everywhere the year was marked by feasts, ceremonies, and games. These events served many purposes. They drew people together to celebrate, to laugh, to worship, and at times to make peace. Elsie Allen, the prominent Makahmo Pomo weaver, told about an incident which took place near the present town of Cloverdale before the coming of Europeans.

Mother told me about this; it happened at Makahmo when the people were fishing for salmon. Two families went together, like they were one, to get salmon. One knew how to build a fish dam in the river; the other knew how to fish with the dam. They had good luck fishing and caught many fish, enough to last them a long time. They had a good time; everybody was feeling good. They dug an oven in the gravel bar to bake some of the salmon, and some Indian potatoes and soap plant potatoes too.

Everybody was feeling good. It came time to go home and to divide up the fish. The man who knew about the dam divided up the fish. That other man wanted to do that too, but that dam man, he just took over himself and didn't say anything to the other man. When they finished dividing up the fish, the women counted them to see that they were the same. The pile in front of the dam man's camp had more fish than the other man's pile. There was much talk about that; the other family felt cheated out of their fish. Those with the most fish said that they should get more because they knew all about that dam, where to build it and how to do it; they also helped out in building the dam and with some of the fishing too. It was right that they get more of the fish, they said. They talked and shouted back and forth at each other, but couldn't agree.

They packed up and went home carrying their fish and their bad feelings about each other. The town where they lived had their bad feelings in it too, and it wasn't good for it to be that way. This was so because the relatives of those two families picked up their bad feelings about each other, and they started to feel that way too. This thing carried on until acorn-picking time. After each family had gathered up its acorns, the headman said there was to be a big time and some people from different places had been invited; he had sent out his people to invite those others.

The headman was upset about the bad feelings those two families and their relatives had for each other. He went to the two families and said, "This can't be anymore this way; soon all of the people in the town will feel your way, and then nothing will be right; everything will go wrong. You people must settle this thing before those other people come here. I have talked with everybody; and, they have put up many beads for the women to play for. The family that wins the game has the beads and loses their bad feelings. Those who don't get the beads win their good feelings back, and the other side will give some beads too because they feel good now that everything will be right

64

Pomo fish weir across a stream. The man is holding two woven willow traps. *Photo by H.C. Meredith, 1889-1895. Courtesy of Smithsonian Institution.*

again. It will be this way between you two families." This is what the captain said to those families. He put up a big feed for all of the people after those families gambled and settled their bad feelings for each other. That's how my mother said the captain acted, one of the things he did in those days.

ELSIE ALLEN, POMO

Warfare

Many Native American groups outside California valued warfare: warrior cults and war chiefs played an important part in their tribal life; adolescent boys were expected to kill an enemy or "count coup" before attaining full manhood; bravery and war prowess were qualities for which every self-respecting man strove. By comparison, Native Californians were by and large peaceful—or at least they *valued* peace, even if they did not always attain it. The quarrelsomeness and suspicion between neighboring groups often led to skirmishes; yet war for its own sake was rarely practiced in California, except at the extreme edges of the state—among the Modoc of the Oregon border and among the Colorado River people. Most Californians saw warfare as an evil to be avoided; a "last resort;" an unpleasant act into which "we"—a proper and innocent people—had been forced by the insolent and intolerable behavior of those "others" who lived beyond the next ridge.

Pomo warrior in body armour. *Photo courtesy of Field Museum, Chicago.*

In war times there are arrow carriers, who also carry spears. Normally everyone carries his own, but in tight places they give the extra arrows to these carriers. There is always a lookout on watch when a group of women are gathering seeds. If anyone comes to molest the women, the lookout will yell a war whoop in warning, and the people know what that means. They know by the way the watcher yells that fighting or killing is going on.

People fight at close range. They let their fastest runner use the elkhide. He runs up close and then crouches down. The men come and stand behind this shield. The enemy can't hit the Huta [secret society] members because they dodge the arrows and are good fighters. If a warrior wastes his ten arrows without results, he doesn't fight any more. They never shoot back the enemies' arrows, but they might save them. A man who is being held at bay may shoot back an enemy arrow, however. They quit fighting just at sunset. The peacemaker will yell, "Quit, the sun is down."

It is against the rules to throw rocks at an enemy who is being held at bay hiding under a bush. They won't shoot arrows at such a person unless they actually see him. It is too wasteful of arrows.

They aren't allowed to club one another—they can spear, knife, or shoot. They carry the *sen* [a manzanita burl club], but aren't supposed to use it.

They never talk about wars except among themselves, and then only in a whisper. They don't brag about what they have done except at the place where they have killed the man.

JEFF JONES, NOMLAKI

Throughout California wars were fought, but they were waged with apparent reluctance—indeed, with the same restraint and adherence to tradition that characterized Native California life in general.

The Sweat-house

Virtually every village throughout California had a sweat-house, often several. Typically, these were not the temporary structures erected by people elsewhere—a pole frame covered with hides—but were permanent structures, semi-subterranean, with room for many. This was largely the men's world. It was a place where men would gather after a day of hunting or fishing, where guests from other villages would be put up. The sweat-house was part of a good and proper life, a life (one hoped) that would be filled with pleasant social interaction, good manners, predictable and enjoyable events, camaraderie, and of course, laughter.

My people were in the habit of eating but two meals a day: the first meal or breakfast came about eleven o'clock; and in the evening, after dark, the women prepare the supper, the menu differing according to the season of the year.

As soon as it begins to get cold, the men would go out and get large loads of small limbs and brush, tie it up in a bundle which they placed on their backs and held with both hands; and as they came in, they sang a song for luck in whatever they might wish for, such as making money, good health and many other things. With this wood they made a fire in the sweat-house and the smoke coming out of the crevices would make it look as if the house was afire for a short time, then the wood would burn down to a bed of coals and the smoke all disappeared. And then the men and boys would strip and creep into it, one at a time, and in about thirty or forty minutes would all come crawling out of the small round door, steaming and covered with perspiration, weak and limp, appearing as if they could hardly stand up. After crawling out they lay flat on the stone platform that is fixed for the purpose and sang the same songs, only at this time in a more doleful way.

They lay in this way for thirty or forty minutes, then get up and, still looking weak, start off down to the bank of the river, one at a time, and

Yurok buildings, with sweat-house in the foreground. *Photo courtesy of California Department of Parks and Recreation.*

68

plunge into the cold water and swim and splash for a time. Then all go back to the dwelling-house and go in where the women folks are preparing the evening meal; take their seats around the basement floor, out of the way of the women while they are cooking; and all will join in laughing and talking until the evening meal is over. Then the men and boys go back to the sweat-house for the night and prepare for a big smoke, all laughing and talking about different topics and telling amusing tales. Some of the older ones would discuss points on Indian law; others tell how things are changing, how this and that used to be and is different now, how they fought the other tribes, when they were victorious and when they were defeated; praising one that was the leader or condemning another, one that was a good general; and many other things. And some were very interesting talkers. They talked until they were ready to go to sleep for the night, and then they would place the wooden pillows under their heads. Some of them would not use any kind of covering and would be almost naked, as the sweat-houses would keep very warm for at least twelve hours after a big fire had been built in them.

LUCY THOMPSON, YUROK

The Great Horned Owls

A well-regulated, peaceful, thoroughly domestic world: that is what Native Californians valued most. Each person in this world was expected to perform his or her role properly. The man of the family would hunt and bring home plenty of meat. The wife would collect roots, seeds, and nuts, cook, tend the house, and "keep her baskets right." The child, of course, would obey. Many an exemplary tale extolled this ordered world and warned of the terrible fate that would befall people who deviated from their assigned roles.

A married couple and one child lived at a place called Malkabel. They lived there a long time. They ate food, both acorn mush and deer. The man was always going hunting; he shot many deer at a time and laid them down at home—some he dried. And from the coast, too, he used to gather mussels and abalone, and these he frequently set down at home. The child used to eat; it was a small child, about three or four years old.

Then, one time, he arrived carrying a deer. The mother got everything ready; she cooked acorn mush and deer. "All right, let's eat," she said. The man said, "OK." When the food was ready, they took their mussel-shell spoons and ate the mush. After serving her husband, the wife attended to the child.

She summoned the child. It didn't mind; it failed to heed her; it just sat. "Come eat; you must be starved," said the mother. It didn't obey; it just sat. Then after a while the woman said to her husband, "Let's eat alone."

That man turned out not to be the father—he was the stepfather of the child. Then they ate—they ate for a while. When they had finished their food,

69

they put the rest away. When they did so, the child started to cry. It sat there crying for it hadn't eaten any food. It cried and cried for a long time. Then the man said, "Apparently the crying will never stop. If it keeps crying, I'll push it outside."

Then he arose. His wife tried to stop him, but he shoved her out of the way. He then set the little child outside and tied the door fast so that the mother couldn't pull it open. He held the mother in the house. Because the mother wanted to open the door, the man held her in the house.

The child cried for a long time outside. "Let me in," it said while crying. Then suddenly Great Horned Owls hooted while flying along—two or three perhaps. They were getting closer and closer. Meanwhile the man was holding the mother to prevent her from opening the door. Suddenly the Great Horned Owls carried the child off. The mother heard the crying dying away into the distance.

Now the man went to sleep. The mother just sat there until dawn. When day broke the man arose and again went hunting. When he had gone the mother set out in the direction that she had heard the child's crying.

It turned out to be a long way from the house. She walked along. Suddenly, when she stopped to stand under a big tree, bones were lying under there. The mother gathered all of the bones into a burden basket. She was rushing before the man returned. She laid a fire and poured the bones onto it in order to burn them up. When the fire had burned them all to cinders, they became powder-like. Then, having filled a basket with that, she carried it home. Next she stirred up some acorn mush—a lot of mush. When the acorn mush was cooked, she sprinkled some of that powder into one basket and set it over in the rear of the house, but her own she kept apart.

In the evening, just as the sun was setting, the man arrived and set down a deer. "I'm hungry; is there any acorn mush?" he asked his wife. "Yes, there is some that I have set aside for you," she said. Then she placed the mush before him. When she did so, the man picked up a mussel shell and ate; he ate it all clean.

By that time it was already dark. He stretched himself out—the woman too—but when she lay down she couldn't sleep; she just stayed awake all night. Suddenly when it was approaching daylight, the man wanted to talk with his wife, but he couldn't utter a sound—only his mouth could move. Unexpectedly, after a little while, he died.

When the woman arose, she saw that he had died. He just lay there. Then, having prepared her food, she ate. When she had finished her acorn mush, she got all of her things ready—she filled a finely woven burden basket with her possessions, and with her child's possessions too. But her husband's belongings she just left lying there. When she was ready, she carried the burden basket outside and set it down off by itself.

Then she lay some dry grass against the house and set fire to it. The man was lying in there dead. The house blazed up and burned. When everything else was burned, the man, too, burned. Then the woman set out for another settlement—she packed her belongings along to where her relatives lived.

They asked, "What happened to the child?" She just cried at first. When she did so, the relatives knew what had happened. Then she told, "My child is dead. My husband pushed it outside and the Great Horned Owls carried it away and evidently ate it. When that happened, I burned the bones up, ground them, and sprinkled some on acorn mush. When he ate that mush, he died, and I burned the house and left."

"It is a good thing that you have done, for we would have killed him anyway," her brothers said.

Then she lived there—lived there for a long time. Her brothers fed her now. They lived there for generations.

This my grandmother told us, saying that this old time story was true. This is the end.

HERMAN JAMES, POMO

At the close of the story, the family is established once more; like a chorus it intones the verdict and restores a sense of wholeness to a deeply injured world. The theme is repeated yet again: people suffer and die, the family endures. So is the moral: obey the rules or disaster will follow.

Pomo Tule Houses

Summer shelter along edge of stream, near Upper Lake. *Photo by Edward S. Curtis, 1924. Courtesy of Smithsonian Institution.*

House at Clear Lake, 1917. *Photo courtesy of Bancroft Library.*

Houses with granary in the foreground. Built at the Ukiah Pow-wow, 1922. *Photo courtesy of the Sun House Archive Collection, Grace Hudson Museum.*

IV: Old Age and Death

At the time of death,
When I found there was to be death,
I was very much surprised.
All was failing.
My home,
I was sad to leave it.

I have been looking far,
Sending my spirit north, south, east, and west,
Trying to escape from death,
But could find nothing,
No way of escape.

Song of the Spirit,
José Albañas, Luiseño

The Men I Knew

Throughout California the chief, almost always a moralist, would lecture and harangue the people: be industrious, he would tell them; be moderate, be peaceful, be loyal to family. Everyone shared these values, but of course not everyone lived up to them. (If everyone were perfectly virtuous why would the chief have to harangue?) Personalities within a tribal group varied widely. Some people were kindly, others prone to violence; some foolish and others wise. Thus when a Hupa man talked candidly about his acquaintances, he described not a "typical" Hupa—such a person exists only in the imagination—but rather an amazing range of unique individuals.

Captain John was a good man. He was sort of a religious fellow like a preacher, and he always talked to the people. Old John told them how to act, what to say, and things like that. He was good to everyone. The other people depended on John some. He always was good to them. He knew the laws, and he told others about them. He was always telling young folks what was right and what was wrong. Anything he had, he divided up with others. Sometimes he would get a whole boatload of eels or salmon and give them all away. He gave them to the old people, every one. Old John would give away the last thing he had. He was a good man, but if you got into trouble with him, look out! He didn't stand back for no one....

Captain John's brother was a good man, but sometimes he would get crazy mad. He would get sore at some little thing, and that would start him off. He would beat up his wives and if anyone said anything to him, he would beat them up too. Once he got mad and threw everything in his house in the river. Other times he was a nice fellow, but once in a while he would get on them spells....

S—'s father was the richest man in Hupa. That old man had enough stuff for two dances, a lot of white deerskins and other stuff. He was a good old fellow. Good and generous too. You can't say that for S—. I don't know where he got his ways, but he is sort of selfish, a stingy person. He got all that stuff of his father's that was left. He still got a lot of it, but he's a man who never gives a dance. He's too stingy. If he gave a dance he would have to feed all those people. He lends the stuff to other people who give dances. That's the way he's done all these years. He's good to no one. His father was a different man....

There were some tough fellows in those days. Always getting into trouble. There was a man down on the Klamath named Tipsa Frank [a Yurok] who was bad. If he had anything against a man he would kill him. Everyone was afraid to tackle him. They thought for a while that he had a good dream and couldn't be killed. Finally he did so much someone killed him. I never knew anyone that tough here in Hupa, but there were pretty bad ones sometimes. Rule is they didn't last long. Someone always killed them. When they settled for a man like that, a little pay was good enough. He was better off dead....

Hupa leader, Captain John. *Photo courtesy of Special Collections, Humboldt State University.*

There was an old fellow when I was a boy who had been in a lot of battles. His name was Rennert. He was no man to fool with. He never said much about what he did, but I heard a lot about him from other folks. Once there was a fight down at the Hostler Ranch. There was a little Indian there. Pretty brave man. Rennert and his bunch came down from the side hill and started fighting. That little Hostler Indian kept coming closer. Rennert came closer too. They kept shooting at each other, but they kept dodging the arrows. Rennert wanted to get close enough to him to take after him with a knife. All the others stood back to see what would happen. Then the Hostler people yelled that their fellow was getting too close. He put his arrows in his arrow case and ran back. Rennert pulled out his knife and ran after him. That little fellow ran so fast that Rennert couldn't catch him. A fellow like Rennert has to have confidence in himself to be brave like that....

Some fellows were cowards. They didn't like to fight or get into trouble at all. Fellows like that tried to keep out of the way so they would have no trouble. P— 's father was a coward. I saw men call him down several times. He wouldn't ever fight. Pretty husky fellow, too. Weighed about 180 pounds. Sometimes it is better for a fellow to back down and avoid trouble, but there are times when he has to stand right up to another fellow....

There was a fellow that lived across the river who talked like a woman. He liked to do women's things like sewing. He didn't do what the other men did. I knew another fellow like that at Captain John's Ranch....

I never knew anyone who was bad-crazy. Indians don't get crazy much. When they get that way a doctor [shaman] tries to cure them. I heard a story once about a couple who got crazy, young couple too. Those people got crazy and kept getting worse and worse. They would eat but they never lived in a house. There is a big oak just this side of Miskut Ranch that has a big branch that reaches out over the river. They used to sleep there at night. During the day they just traveled around. All over the valley. They must have eaten something to keep alive. I guess people gave them food. Must have been pretty strong too to be able to keep walking around all the time. They kept going that way for quite a long time. Finally they must have gotten a little better because some people were able to take them over to Redwood where there was a good doctor. She was a Redwood Indian [Whilkut], but a good doctor. That doctor doctored them and they got straightened out. It took a long time, but they got better....

Sometimes there were fellows without much sense. They were harmless, pitiful. People always treated them good and talked to them sort of nice like. There were lots like that in the old days.

HUPA

Strong family and tribal ties did not make the Hupa into a homogeneous assemblage. On the contrary, family and group seem to have provided a tolerant structure in which people had the security to develop their own personalities. After all, no matter how odd or difficult one might be, one was still someone's relative, and part of a family that would—unless pushed to extremes—provide care and companionship and give a sense of belonging. There is a complex paradox here: namely, that tribal societies which value family and "fitting in"—societies that specifically discourage independence—nevertheless often provide a network of support that gives individuals the freedom to become unique.

Old Gambler's Song

The experience of old age varied from one culture to another in California, indeed from one person to another. For some it was lonely and sad.

I am the only one, the only one left.
An old man, I carry the gambling-board;
An old man, I sing the gambling song.
The roots I eat of the valley.
The pepper-ball is round.
The water trickles, trickles.
The water-leaves grow along the river bank.
I rub the hand, I wiggle the tail
I am a doctor, I am a doctor.

KONKOW

The "pepper-ball" was probably the laurel nut, and perhaps the fact that the old gambler was eating roots and laurel nuts (rather than meat, fish, acorn bread, and seed cake) suggests his poverty. "I rub the hand, I wiggle the tail," describes motions made in gambling. The final line, "I am a doctor," is affirmation; despite age and poverty, the gambler declares that he still has the magical powers necessary to let him win.

Grandfather's Prayer

For some people, it is true, old age brought pain, disappointment, even bitterness. For others, however, it brought a deep familiarity with the world, self-acceptance, even wisdom. "Long ago, when I was small," recalled a Wintu woman, "I used to listen to my grandfather when he prayed." The grandfather woke early in the morning, washed his face, and prayed. He prayed to Olelbes, He-Who-Is-Above, the Wintu world creator. He also prayed directly and intimately to the things around him—to the rocks, trees, salmon, acorns, sugar-pine, water, and wood. At the end of his life he talked to the world—sharing his sadness and regret—as one might talk to an old and very trusted friend.

Oh Olelbes, look down on me.
I wash my face in water, for you,

Seeking to remain in health.
I am advancing in old age; I am not capable of anything any more.
You whose nature it is to be eaten [i.e., deer],
You dwell high in the west, on the mountains, high in the east, high in the north, high in the south;
You, salmon, you go about in the water.
Yet I cannot kill you and bring you home.
Neither can I go east down the slope to fetch you, salmon.
When a man is so advanced in age, he is not in full vigor.
If you are rock, look at me; I am advancing in old age.
If you are tree, look at me; I am advancing in old age.
If you are water, look at me; I am advancing in old age.
Acorns, I can never climb up to you again.
You, water, I can never dip you up and fetch you home again.
My legs are advancing in weakness.
Sugar-pine, you sit there; I can never climb you.
In my northward arm, in my southward arm, I am advancing in weakness.
You who are wood, you wood, I cannot carry you home on my shoulder.
For I am falling back into my cradle.
This is what my ancestors told me yesterday, they who have gone, long ago.
May my children fare likewise!

WINTU

The reference to "northward arm" and "southward arm" is typically Wintu, and its usage suggests a cultural wisdom so deep and unconscious that it was embedded in the very structure of language. In English we refer to the right arm and the left arm, and we might describe a certain mountain as being to our right or left, in front or in back of us depending upon which way we are facing at the moment. We use the body—the self—as the point of reference against which we describe the world. The Wintu would never do this, and indeed the Wintu language would not permit it. If a certain mountain was to the north, say, the arm nearest that mountain would be called the northward arm. If the Wintu turned around, the arm that had previously been referred to as the northward arm would now be called the southward arm. In other words, the features of the world remained the constant reference, the sense of self was what changed—a self that continually accommodated and adjusted to a world in which the individual was not the center of all creation.

Crying

People in these small societies were intimately known and closely interconnected. When a person died relatives and close friends began the mourning cry—not an ordinary cry, but the keening or ritualized wail that soon rose up from an entire village.

A nd the first time when I could hardly remember, I think, a person died and my mother was crying. And I was scared. I don't know how old I was, but I was scared. I sure hate to see my mother cry. I think that was the first woman I heard. Maybe I was about five or six years old that time. That was my mother's relation, too, that old man who died. Gee, make me feel so afraid don't know what to do. I was sitting in her lap. And she hold me and crying, and I start to cry too. I can't stop crying, and they had to shake me up.

So my mother hold me in her lap, and I got scared. Never heard her cry before. And my aunt started to cry too, and all the women crying. Women cry, but hardly men cry. They have the tears, but not so loud.

POMO

Death Song

As soon as a person died, messengers were sent to summon distant friends and relatives to the cremation or burial. Widows or widowers singed their hair and covered their faces with pitch and ashes. Women, forlorn and grief-stricken, often beat their breasts with stone pestles and had to be restrained from doing themselves serious harm.

My heart is lost, lost.
My heart sets, sets.
My heart goes to the other world.
My heart goes to the other world.
My heart goes to the ocean foam.
My heart goes to the ocean foam.

CUPEÑO

Burial Oration

In a world in which each person was closely connected to others, death brought deep grief—and also deep fear. The fear was specific: namely that the ghost, cut off from family and friends, would in its terrible loneliness try to capture the souls of the living. Thus throughout California funeral songs and orations urged the spirit of the deceased to go on its way and leave the living behind.

The "spirit trail" (or "flower trail," as it was sometimes called) mentioned in the following oration was the Milky Way, which, according to the Wintu, was the roadway to the land of the dead.

You are dead.
You will go above there to the trail.
That is the spirit trail.

Go there to the beautiful trail.
May it please you not to walk about where I am.
You are dead.
Go there to the beautiful trail above.
That is your way.
Look at the place where you used to wander.
The north trail, the mountains where you used to wander,
      you are leaving.
Listen to me: go there!

WINTU

The Land of the Dead

Images of the afterworld varied from group to group. The Maidu felt that virtuous souls traveled to a paradise of pleasure. Most Native Californians, however, viewed the afterworld as a drab, gloomy place (at least by living people's standards) where everything was the reverse of what it was in the land of the living. In the "Orpheus" story that follows, dead people's days are really years, their deer are beetles, and things are visible only during the darkness of night. Death here is seen not as the absence of life, but rather as the mirror image of life.

A great hunter brought home a wife. They loved each other, and were very happy. But the man's mother hated the young wife, and one day when the husband was out hunting, she put a sharp pointed object in the wife's seat, and the woman sat down upon it and was killed.

The people immediately brought brush and piled it up. They put her body upon it, and burned it, so that when her husband returned that night the body was all consumed.

The man went to the burning-place, and stayed there motionless. Curls of dust rose and whirled about the charred spot. He watched them all day. At night they grew larger, and at last one larger than all the rest whirled round and round the burned spot, and set off down the road. The man followed it. At last when it was quite dark, he saw that it was the figure of his wife that he was following, but she would not speak to him.

She was leading him in the direction of the rock past which all dead people must go. If they have been bad in their lives, the rock falls on them and crushes them. When they came to this rock, she spoke to him. "We are going to the place of dead people," she told him. "I will take you on my back so that you will not be seen and recognized as one of the living."

Thus they went on until they came to the river the dead have to ford. This was very dangerous, because the man was not dead, but the woman kept him on her back, and they came through safely. The woman went directly to her people. She went home to her parents and brothers and sisters who had died before. They were glad to see her, but they did not like the man for he was not dead. The woman pleaded for him, however, and they let him stay. Special food had to be always cooked for him, for he could not eat what dead people live on. Also in the daytime he could see nothing; it was as if he were alone all day long; only in the night could he see.

When the people were going hunting, they said to each other that they ought to take the man along. So they took him, and stationed him on the trail the deer would take. Presently he heard them shouting, "The deer, the deer," and he knew they were shouting to him that the deer were coming in his direction. But he could see nothing. Then he looked again, and he could see two little black beetles; he knocked them over, and these were the deer the dead people hunted. And when all the people had come up, they praised him for his hunting, and after that they did not complain of his being there.

The people were sorry for him. They said, "It is not time for him to die yet. He has a hard time here. The woman ought to go back with him." So they planned that it should be so. They instructed the man and the woman to have nothing to do with each other for three nights after their return to earth; but three nights for the dead meant three years for the living.

So the man and the woman returned to earth, and they were continent for three nights. But they did not know that the dead people meant three years, and when the husband woke on the morning of the fourth day he was alone.

ROSA MARONGO, SERRANO

Cupeño mourning ceremony, 1904. *Photo courtesy of Marjorie Goldschmidt.*

Summons to a Mourning Ceremony

Throughout much of California people held annual mourning ceremonies to honor those who had died during the previous year. Guests were invited from surrounding villages to partake in feasting, dancing, singing, ritual washing and crying, and effigy burning. This was the final ritualized outpouring of grief. Then gifts were exchanged between hosts and guests in ceremonies that bound the living together once again. At the end of the mourning ceremony—which in some places lasted for as long as seven days—relatives of the dead were released from their mourning restrictions. They could wash the ashes and pitch from their faces, let their hair grow long, eat ordinary foods, and perhaps remarry. Life would go on.

On the day of the mourning ceremony, a Miwok chief rouses his people to prepare for the guests. He speaks in the ceremonial manner—a ritualized form of speaking as different from ordinary speech as dancing was from ordinary walking.

Get up! Get up! Get up! Get up! Get up!
Wake up! Wake up! Wake up!
People get up on the south side,
East side, east side, east side, east side,
North side, north side, north side,
Lower side, lower side, lower side!
You folks come here!
Visitors are coming, visitors are coming.
Strike out together!
Hunt deer, squirrels!
And you women, strike out, gather wild onions, wild potatoes!
Gather all you can! Gather all you can!
Pound acorns, pound acorns, pound acorns!
Cook, cook!
Make some bread, make some bread!
So we can eat, so we can eat, so we can eat.
Put it up, and put it up, and put it up!
Make acorn soup so that the people will eat it!
There are many coming.
Come here, come here, come here, come here!
You have to be dry and hungry.
Be for a while.
Got nothing here.
People get up, people around get up!
Wake up!
Wake up so you can cook!
Visitors are here now and all hungry.
Get ready so we can feed them!
Gather up, gather up, and bring it all in, so we can give it to them!

Go ahead and eat!
That's all we have.
Don't talk about starvation, because we never have much!
Eat acorns!
There is nothing to it.
Eat and eat!
Eat! Eat! Eat! Eat!
So that we can get ready to cry.
Everybody get up! Everybody get up!
All here, very sad occasion.
All cry! All cry!
Last time for you to be sad.

CHIEF YANAPAYAK, MIWOK

V: The Aliveness of Things

Plants are thought to be alive, their
juice is their blood, and they grow.
The same is true of trees. All things
die, therefore all things have life.
Because all things have life, gifts
have to be given to all things.

William Ralganal Benson
Pomo

The Pleiades and Their Pursuer

People throughout the world have had stories about heavenly bodies. Stars, planets, or constellations were variously kings, hunters, dragons, lovers, gods, bears—every manner of living thing. To most moderns such stories seem quaint and innocent; stars and planets are held to be inanimate bodies, their motions dictated by certain impersonal, predictable laws of physics. But to Native Californians and others the twinkling of stars, the weaving of planets, the passage of comets, the showers of meteorites, and the stately procession of the zodiac suggested that heavenly bodies were very much alive. Like other living things they had will, intelligence, and history. The Pleiades, moving in a sparkling cluster across the sky, had all the vitality of a flock of birds, a school of fish, or perhaps a group of people.

P aruthvi ("Bright") had a harpoon for killing seals and sea lions, and Kuchachkoshihl (Pleiades) coveted it. But Paruthvi refused to sell it. He kept it hidden in his house, and would not permit anyone to go near it. Then Kuchachkoshihl called his friends together, and they made a plan to steal the harpoon.

In the night they crept up to the house of Paruthvi. Frog slipped inside and crawled up on the beams above the fire, while Mouse gnawed at a board in the wall opposite the place where the harpoon was kept, and Louse tied the hair of the sleepers together. Down on the beach another Mouse gnawed holes in the canoes that were there drawn up. Late in the night a board was gnawed off and holes were gnawed in all the canoes. Then Kuchachkoshihl reached in through the wall, seized the harpoon, and ran.

The women in the house woke and shouted. Someone threw the embers in the fireplace together, but Frog dropped his water on them and put out the fire. Confusion reigned. The people, at last disentangling their hair and tearing themselves apart, ran out and saw a canoe fleeing in the distance. They too launched a canoe, but it filled and sank. They tried another, but it also foundered. So they tried nine. Then they took the last one, and this very one Mouse had overlooked. So Paruthvi and his men gave chase, but they could not overtake the fugitives. And every night they go across the sky, the party of Kuchachkoshihl ahead and that of Paruthvi pursuing, but never overtaking, the thieves.

JERRY JAMES, WIYOT

The story of the Pleiades is not merely an "origin myth"—one that explains how in ancient times living beings got transformed into heavenly bodies. Beyond just providing an understanding of the mythic past, the story describes an ongoing drama. In other words, the Wiyot did not look up at the Pleiades and think, "Once those stars were living beings." For them the stars were *still* living beings; the "origin myth" explained what kind of living beings they were.

The Lunar Eclipse

The moon, according to the Hupa, was also a living being, specifically a man: not an abstract, ethereal, symbolic man—not a *male principle*—but a real, flesh-and-blood, awesomely powerful man. This man had wives and pets, and like men everywhere he hunted deer. The moon's rising and setting, waxing and waning, and especially its eclipses were dramatic, often bloody events in the man's life.

T he one who always travels at night has ten wives in the west and ten wives also where he rises. In the distant west he always comes out to the ocean and hunts the deer which live on the water. He calls them by saying, "wu, wu, wu, wu." He always kills ten and then ten more. Taking ten on his back he carries them to the place where he goes up into the sky. It is there his house is. Then his pets crowd around him, his mountain-lions and his rattlesnakes. He divides the deer among the animals but they are not satisfied with one apiece. They jump on him and eat him besides. They leave only his blood. Then Frog, who stands in the body of her husband, clubs them off and they desist. He goes down in the west, nothing but blood. There his wives brush together the blood and he recovers. He always goes back to the place of rising and there they make him well again.

His pets do not do that way with him every time. Sometimes they get enough and then they quit. When they are not satisfied with the food given them, then they eat him.

McCANN, HUPA

Sun and Moon

Everywhere in California the sun and moon were seen as people. The Maidu pictured them living in a house where they were subject to all the usual domestic inconveniences.

S un and Moon were sister and brother. They did not rise at first. Many different animals were sent to try and see if they could make the two rise, but failed. None of them could get into the house in which the brother and sister lived. This house was of solid stone, and was far away to the east.

At last Gopher and Angle-Worm went. Angle-Worm made a tiny hole, boring down outside, and coming up inside the house. Gopher followed, carrying a bag of fleas. He opened it, and let half of the fleas out. They bit the brother and sister so, that they moved from the floor where they were to the sleeping-platform. Then Gopher let out the rest of the fleas, and these made life so miserable for Sun and Moon, that they decided to leave the house. The sister was afraid to travel by night, so the brother said he would go then, and became the Moon. The sister travelled by day, and became the Sun.

MAIDU

The use of fleas to roust the sun and moon is typical of the Native Californians' religious sensibility. Theirs was a thoroughly domestic world. People seldom ventured more than twenty miles from their birthplace. Their major life experiences took place in a village and family context, and it was village and family that provided them with the metaphors by which they interpreted the workings of the world. Even the most awesome mysteries—the regulation of the sun and moon, for example—were understood basically as domestic dramas.

The Greedy Father

To the California Indian way of thinking, *nothing* was inanimate. Animals, plants, rocks, trees, trails, mountains, springs, manufactured objects and natural objects—indeed all things—were people, fully alive and intelligent, with complex and interconnected histories.

Famine descended, and the people were hungry. A man said, "Tomorrow I'll go fishing." The family went to bed without eating. The next day at dawn he left the house. The sun was rising. It was shining on the water. Suddenly the string attached to the fishnet quivered. A big salmon was in the net. He hauled it out and put it down in back of the fishery.

Then he thought, "Let me cook it! It's because I'm hungry." So he cleaned it. He cut off the tail putting it to one side. Then he cooked the salmon. When he ate it, he devoured it all, and only afterwards did he realize it.

Then he went home. He was carrying just the tail. Some distance from home he was shouting, "Here children, this is the tail! There were a lot of beggars on the way who got the rest."

Then the children ran out. They were shouting, "Hurray, we're going to eat, hurray, we're going to eat."

The next day he went fishing again. Again he caught a big salmon, and he ate it on the spot. Again he shouted, "Here, children, this is the tail! There were a lot of beggars."

Now the woman thought, "He's holding out on us." The next day he went fishing again. She told her children, "You stay here. I'm following him. I think he's holding out on us." When she arrived at the fishery, he had just pulled out a big salmon. He cut off the tail and put it down a little ways off. Then he made a fire and cooked it. He was about to eat it.

The woman ran back upriver. She told her children, "It's really true. He's holding out on us. Let's get started, we're going to leave." They climbed uphill. Then they heard him. He was shouting below them, "Here, children, this is the tail! There were a lot of beggars." It was silent. He shouted again. He ran indoors. There only mice were squeaking. Then he jumped out of the house. He was still shouting like that, "Here, children, this is the tail! There were a lot of beggars." He looked uphill. That is where they had climbed.

His wife shouted, "Eat alone there: that's why you held out on us." He was following them. He got closer. He was still shouting. When he caught

90

up with them, his wife told him, "You're going to be doing nothing but this: you'll be eating only mud in the creeks. But we will be sitting around in front of rich people."

And he thought, "Let me grab the littlest one." He reached out, but the child turned into a bear-lily. He thought, "I'm grabbing the other one." It turned into a hazel-bush. He grabbed his wife: she turned into a pine tree. He, in turn, swooped down there. You will see him like that now. He eats mud on the edge of creeks. [He became a water-ouzel, a small, grey bird called "Moss-eater" by the Karuk.] But his wife and his children, when there is a deerskin dance, are lined up [as baskets] in front of rich people.

LOTTIE BECK, KARUK

When a Karuk woman went out to collect pine roots, hazel stems, and bear-lily for her baskets, she moved in an animate and indeed passionate world. She gathered her basket materials from *people*—from a woman and her children who had once been dreadfully poor. By plucking roots and stems she was not harming these people but rather honoring them, transforming them into beautiful baskets that would be displayed during ceremonies, "sitting in glory before the rich people." The woman was thus helping the roots and stems fulfill their destiny. Her relationship with the pine tree, hazel bush, and bear-lily was one of partnership, friendship, even equality; after all, she and the pine tree were both women, and could thereby understand and help each other very well.

The Stick Husband

To live in a world in which everything was animate and had personhood was to live in a world of endless potentiality. The most common objects around one were filled with power, intelligence, and even sexual desire, making for a thoroughly unpredictable and magical world.

There was a young woman living with her grandmother. The old woman was blind. The girl fetched wood and water, made fires, and prepared food. They lived that way. The girl collected acorns. In the evening she got wood, made the fire, and prepared dinner. They lived that way without a man. Quite a while they lived that way. The girl did all the chores.

The young woman made acorn soup. She went out to pick acorns, pounded acorns, and leached the meal. They lived that way for quite a while.

One day she was out after wood. In picking up wood, she found a pretty little stick, round just as though whittled. She put it in with her firewood. This stick rolled away from the firewood. She did not pay attention to it until she got more wood. She thought she had enough wood to fill the basket. She gathered and piled it and again put the stick with the wood. Again it rolled away. She got the basket full and put the stick in again. Then she went home, threw it down by the door. Again the stick rolled out. She put the wood inside

91

the house, piled it in. The stick of wood she had found kept rolling around, rolling here and there.

She thought: "What is the matter with that stick anyhow?" It kept rolling around. Evening came. She went to bed. That stick rolled into her bed. It lay there. In the morning the stick rolled out and disappeared. After a while the stick rolled back with a dead deer, which it had killed, for the stick was a person.

It rolled around over the deer and the deer was cut up as though by a person. The stick put the meat in the house. The girl was helping. The stick rolled around to the edge of the fire as it cooked meat.

The young woman laid the baskets down for the cooked deer meat. Everything was cooked. She set the acorn mush down. The stick rolled up to the food and away as though eating.

The grandmother did not know about the stick, for the young woman did not tell her. She gave her grandmother some meat on a basket plate. The old lady did not know what to make of it, for they had had no meat before. The girl said: "I did not tell you everything. The other day I was getting wood. I found a stick, a nice pretty little stick. I did not know I had found a man. I picked up the stick not knowing it was a man."

Then they ate the meat. The grandmother said: "Grandchild, you did well."

They lived that way. The stick of wood rolled out when going hunting. After killing deer, it would roll home. When wood was needed, the stick would roll out and all the wood would come to the door. They lived that way. Everything he did, he did by rolling. Every time he hunted he rolled out.

Night would come. They went to bed. The stick would roll around, roll on top of her, roll between her legs, having intercourse. The first thing she knew she had a boy baby.

They lived that way for quite a while. The stick killed deer and got wood and acorns. Pretty soon she was pregnant again. She bore a girl. She thus had two children by the stick.

COAST YUKI

Not only was the stick a *person*, but the story itself was a kind of person as well—a rather fussy person who demanded proper treatment. The narrator dared summon the story only at night and only during the winter; otherwise the story might turn on the narrator and cause him or her to become hunch-backed. If the teller omitted any detail, the story would cause illness. When finished with the telling, the narrator would turn attention away from the audience and address the story directly: "Well, it is done," the narrator would say. "You go back into the rock hole." Like everything else in the world the story was magically alive, possessing will, intelligence, and the power to do good or harm. Like everything else in the world, the story had to be treated respectfully—indeed, like a living person.

The Girl Who Married Rattlesnake

The perception that everything in the world was alive gave commonality to all things. Everything was a person, everything was "kin," and thus nothing in the world was really foreign. Even a rattlesnake was a "brother"—so close to us in nature that he could fall in love with a woman and she with him. Such a love story, inconceivable in our culture, is treated matter-of-factly, with dignity and even tenderness.

At a place called Cobowin there is a large rock with a hole in it and there were many rattlesnakes in this hole. At Kalesima nearby there was a village with four large houses. In one of these large houses which had a center pole there lived a girl. This was in the spring of the year when the clover was just right to eat. This girl went out to gather clover and one of the rattlesnakes watched her. When she had a sufficient amount of this food she took it home and gave it to her mother.

Rattlesnake went to the village and when he had approached very near to the house he transformed himself into a young man with a head-net on his head and fine beads around his neck. He made himself look as handsome as possible. Then he climbed up onto the top of the house and came down the center pole. He went to this girl and told her that he wanted to marry her and he remained there with the family. The following morning he went home again. This he did for four days. On the fifth evening he came back but this time he did not change his form. He simply went into the house and talked just as he had before. The girl's mother said that there was someone over there talking all the time. She made a light and looked over in the place where she heard the sound, and there was Rattlesnake. He shook his head and frightened her terribly. She dropped the light and ran.

On the following morning Rattlesnake took the girl home with him and she remained there. Finally this girl had four children and as they grew up, whenever they saw any of the people from the village, they would say to their mother, "We are going to bite those people." But she would say, "No, you must not do that. Those are your relatives." And the children would do as she told them.

Now these four rattlesnake boys were out playing around one day as they grew a little older. Finally they became curious. They came in and asked their mother, "Why do you not talk the way we do? Why are you so different?"

"I am not a rattlesnake," she replied. "I am a human being. I am different from you and your father."

"Are you not afraid of our father?" asked the boys. "No," she answered.

Then the oldest of the rattlesnake boys said that he had heard the other rattlesnakes talking and that they too thought it strange that she was so different from them and that they were going to investigate and see just why it was that she was so different. They were going to crawl over her body and find out why she was so different from themselves. She was not at all afraid;

93

when the rattlesnakes all came they crawled over her and she was not alarmed in any way.

Then she said to her oldest boy, "It is impossible for you to become a human being and I am not really a human being any longer, so I am going back to my parents and tell them what has happened." She did go home and she said to her parents, "This is the last time that I shall be able to talk to you and the last time that you will be able to talk with me." Her father and mother felt very sad about this, but they said nothing. Then the daughter started to leave, but her mother ran after her and caught her right by the door, brought her back into the house and wept over her because she was so changed. Then the girl shook her body and suddenly she was gone. No one knew how or where she went, but she really went back to Rattlesnake's house where she has lived ever since.

CHARLEY BROWN, POMO

The Man and the Owls

Animals, plants, and objects were *people*, and like people they were thought of as belonging to families that overshadowed individuality. In the Wintu language, for example, one would say, "There is *deerness* on the meadow," whether one deer or a hundred were present. In the Indian mind all the deer in the world comprised a unit of which an individual deer was just a fragment. Every deer was linked to every other deer and shared a common deer consciousness. Thus rather than stalking individual, unconnected deer, the Indian hunter was forever approaching *deerness*: if he mistreated a deer or even a deer carcass it was not an isolated act between him and a solitary deer, but a crime against the entire *deerness* of the world. In the future the *deerness* would withdraw from him, or even injure him.

A man and his wife were traveling. They camped overnight in a cave. They had a fire burning. Then they heard a horned owl (*hutulu*) hoot. The woman said to her husband: "Call in the same way. He will come and you can shoot him. Then we will eat him for supper." The man got his bow and arrows ready and called. The owl answered, coming nearer. At last it sat on a tree near the fire. The man shot. He killed it. Then his wife told him: "Do it again. Another one will come." Again he called and brought an owl and shot it. He said: "It is enough now." But his wife said: "No. Call again. If you call them in the morning they will not come. We have had no meat for a long time. We shall want something to eat tomorrow as well as now." Then the man called. More owls came. There were more and more of them. He shot, but more came. The air was full of owls. All his arrows were gone. The owls came closer and attacked them. The man took sticks from the fire and fought them off. He covered the woman with a basket and kept on fighting. More and more owls came. At last they killed both the man and the woman.

YOKUTS

94

According to California Indian thought, people, plants, animals, and objects were basically equals. The relationship between people and animals was not one of exploitation, but of reciprocity. People had to respect animals and perform certain rites for them; animals on their part provided people with food and skins. People and animals lived in balance, and to maintain that balance demanded mutual restraint. Animals acted benevolently toward people despite the animals' extraordinary physical and spiritual powers. People did not slaughter needlessly or humiliate the carcass of a slain animal despite humanity's great hunting prowess. To reach beyond reciprocity and demand more than one's due was to upset the balance and ultimately bring punishment.

Many Relatives

To modern people, educated in European modes of thought, competition is what defines relationships. People, plants, and animals compete, both with their own kind and with other species, for scarce resources, evolving over millenia in a harsh world that rewards the fittest with survival, punishes the weak with extinction. Modern political, economic, psychological, educational, and biological sciences are all to a huge extent based on the idea that competition lies at the basis of life.

California Indians, and most other traditional people, certainly recognized that competition existed, and that it was important. But they did not elevate it to the status of prime cause. Rather, they felt, in a world in which everything was alive, in which everything had a place and a role ordained from the beginning of time, it was not the competition between beings but rather their interrelatedness that underlay the functioning of the world.

We had many relatives and... we all had to live together; so we'd better learn how to get along with each other. She [my mother] said it wasn't too hard to do. It was just like taking care of your younger brother or sister. You got to know them, find out what they like and what made them cry, so you'd know what to do. If you took good care of them you didn't have to work as hard. Sounds like it's not true, but it is. When that baby gets to be a man or woman they're going to help you out.

You know, I thought she was talking about us Indians and how we are supposed to get along. I found out later by my older sister that mother wasn't just talking about Indians, but the plants, animals, birds—everything on this earth. They are our relatives and we better know how to act around them or they'll get after us.

LUCY SMITH, DRY CREEK POMO

Dancers and Their Regalia

Dancers in white deerskin ceremony, Hupa. The man the on the left is William Quimby, the first Indian police officer at Hoopa. On the right is Arthur Saxon. *Photo by H.C. Meredith, ca. 1890. Courtesy of Phoebe Apperson Hearst Museum of Anthropology.*

RIGHT: Pomo man from Lakeport in dance regalia with bird bone whistle in mouth. *Photo by Jaime de Angulo, 1931. Courtesy of Phoebe Apperson Hearst Museum of Anthropology.*

BELOW: Kumeyaay man, Manuel Duro, from Mesa Grande. *Photo by T.T. Waterman, 1907. Courtesy of Phoebe Apperson Hearst Museum of Anthropology.*

Prayer for Good Fortune

The feeling that everything was alive also gave a sacred quality to the world, at times a mystical sense of one's presence in it. A Yokuts prayer ends this way:

My words are tied in one
With the great mountains,
With the great rocks,
With the great trees,
In one with my body
And my heart.
Do you all help me
With supernatural power,
And you, day,
And you, night!
All of you see me
One with this world!

YOKUTS

Initiation Song

The sense of the aliveness and personhood of everything made for an apparently anarchistic world—one in which trees, bows, or pestles might either favor one or hate one. "These mountains, these rivers hear what you say, and if you are mean they will punish you," a Modoc woman recalled her parents saying. To function well in a world of dispersed power demanded attentiveness, spiritual knowledge, and outright luck.

There was more to the religious sensibility than what is referred to as "animism," however. Often, a Native Californian prayer or statement suggests that beyond the apparent anarchy people perceived a mystically unifying force. When a Yuki shaman led initiates around the tribal boundaries to point out prominent landmarks, he chanted:

This rock did not come here by itself.
This tree does not stand here of itself.
There is one who made all this,
Who shows us everything.

YUKI

VI: Getting Power

To the edge of the earth
To the edge of the earth
To the edge of the earth
Snap all the people!
Snap all the people!
To the edge of the earth
To the edge of the earth.

Poisoning shaman's song,
Fanny Brown, Wintu

My Mountain

Trees, rocks, animals, mountain, springs, and other objects were not only alive, but they also had immense power. People sought that power by forming spiritual friendships and alliances with objects of great strength. An animal might approach a person in a dream and offer to share its power. Or a spring might approach. Or a ghost. Or a rock. Or even a mountain.

When I was still a young man, I saw Birch Mountain in a dream. It said to me: "You will always be well and strong. Nothing can hurt you and you will live to an old age." After this, Birch Mountain came and spoke to me whenever I was in trouble and told me that I would be all right. That is why nothing has happened to me and why I am so old now.

Not long after this, when I was bewitched, my power helped me out. I had been visiting one of the villages at Pitana Patu and had started back home to Tovowahamatu when I met a man who invited me to his house to have something to eat. It happened that a witch doctor lived in this vicinity, but thinking little of this, I ate a big meal of boiled meat and then went toward home. After walking a few miles, I became very ill and had a passage of blood. I went on, but became weaker and weaker, and when I reached the hot springs, a few miles north of Big Pine, I lay down under a bush. For a long time I lay there, and when it was nearly dark I got up and said to my soul, "Since my mountain has spoken and told me that I shall not die, why should I die here?" I went on to Tovowahamatu and made my camp just outside the village. The next day I entered the village.

A "stick doctor," who was my cousin and lived at Pitana Patu, was called. He arrived that night and came to my bed. He said: "How are you? Are you still there?" I was desperately sick by now and had hardly any strength to answer, "I am almost gone." Then the doctor began to work. He twirled his fire drill until the end was hot and put it to my stomach until it burned me. Then he worked over my body with his hands. This felt good. But he did not sing; stick doctors do not do this. After a while he said: "Soon the morning star will rise up, and after that there will be a star brighter than the morning star. You will feel better then." It happened as the doctor said. When the bright star arose, I felt better and soon I was entirely well. This man, this doctor, probably helped me some, but it was my own power, Birch Mountain, which saved me....

Once, I became so sick that I gave myself up for dead. My soul admitted that I would have to die. I died and my soul started southward, toward Tupusi Witu. While I was traveling, I looked down and my soul saw a stick in the ground not quite as tall as a man. I went to the stick and dug my foot into the ground about ankle deep. Then I turned to the stick and said, "This is the *muguavada* ["soul stick"]. I seized the stick and looked back toward my mountain, which was my power. I knew then that I would be all right and live forever, for whenever a soul going south sees the "soul stick," it knows that it will come back.

My soul then came back to Tovowahamatu, and the next day I set about doctoring myself. I went into the mountains and gathered roots which I boiled and put on my sores. Soon I recovered....

My power from Birch Mountain helped me just as much in hunting as in sickness. My favorite deer-hunting ground was in the Sierra Nevada, west of Tovowahamatu, in the vicinity of my mountain. It often happened that after I had seen deer and tried to sneak up on them they caught wind of me and started toward my mountain. I would say: "My mountain, I want you to help me get some of these deer. They are yours and live upon you." After this I always overtook one and killed him while he was lying under a mountain mahogany tree or some other shelter on the mountain side. This happened many times. After such a killing, I remained overnight on the mountain and treated myself to a feast of deer meat. The next day I returned to the valley. I distributed the meat to my people and sold the upper part which belongs to the hunter.

Once when I started up Big Pine creek toward the foot of my mountain, I asked my power to make it easier for me to hunt deer. I said to it: "Now, great mountain, I wish that you would give me some of your deer to eat. You have so many on you. If you would give me some, I wish you would give them at your foot, not far up." Soon I came upon a group of deer at the very foot of the mountain as I asked, and killed one. As I was packing it back to my village, I saw a herd of mountain sheep. I stopped and hid to watch them, and as I waited one came toward me. I killed it with little trouble and went on to the valley, carrying both animals. I distributed and sold them when I got home. My mountain is always good to me.

The deer and mountain sheep were a heavy load, for I had packed them both at once down to the valley. But when I was a young man nothing was too heavy for me. I enjoyed carrying a large, heavy load. Didn't my power come from the mountain upon whose back are rocks which never hurt it? It is this way with me. Once I proved my strength carrying a stump which no one had been able to move. My soul had told me that no mountain would be too high for me to climb, nor any place too far away for me to go to. That is why I have always been able to get to every place for which I have started.

I had two calls to be a doctor. In early manhood I had my first chance. My mountain spoke to me in a dream and asked me to become a doctor. It told me how I should cure. I would not have to dance, it told me. I should sit by my patient all night, holding my hands on him and singing. When the morning star should rise, I should get up and dance a few rounds, and then hold out my hand, when something like snow would appear in my palm. I should place this in my patient's mouth and blow. But my soul refused this power, for I knew that sometime in my old age it would fail me and I would die. I knew the work was dangerous. I had had another dream and saw blood on a rock, meaning that I should be killed if I were to become a doctor. I refused the power because I wished to live to be a very old man. All I had to do was refuse....

A transvestite Tolowa shaman (note, for example, the woman's basket cap).
He wears dentalia through his nose and in strings around his neck. *Photo
courtesy of the Del Norte County Historical Museum.*

Whenever I dream, especially if it is a bad dream which means trouble, I talk to something in the darkness. I talk to my power. That is why I have lived so long. If I had not called upon my power, accident or disaster would have overtaken me long ago. Even when I have sex dreams, I talk to the night, because if I should pay no attention to them, they would continue and lead to fits....

When I die, my soul will go south to the land of the dead. It will stay there by the ocean and I will have nothing to do but enjoy myself.

JACK STEWART, OWENS VALLEY PAIUTE

The Long Snake

People throughout California quested after power by seeking alliances with plants, animals, objects, and spirit-world figures. It was felt that a person needed such power to gamble well, stay healthy, fend off enemies and achieve success in hunting, love-making, or other endeavors. Yet quests for power were filled with danger. The "allies" from whom one sought help were not all-wise, beneficent gods, but rather a kind of *people*. Like people everywhere they were often impetuous and unpredictable, a mixture of good and evil, capable of betrayal as well as friendship.

Long ago a person of Saivari thought: "I'll go swimming." When he got to the river's edge, he looked around, and behold an egg was lying there on the sand. He thought: "What a nice-looking egg." He had heard for a long time what a Long Snake egg looks like, and that it is medicine, is luck. He picked it up. He carried it upslope to the living house. Then he put it on the bench above the *yoram* [back wall], he put it in a trunk. They claim that wealth will come to such an egg. He thought: "I think it is a Long Snake egg." He fixed it up good. He knew what it was, and he thought: "How good." He was winning a lot of money all the time, he was lucky.

Then after a while one morning he looked at the egg. Behold it was hatched out. Behold there was sitting a baby snake in the trunk. Behold a little snake, that was his pet. He used to say: "He is good, he is good, my pet," when he was gambling. That snake was his money whenever they bet on the other side.

Then after a while he bought a woman. The snake was already getting big. It was coiled on the *yoram* bench, coiled up in a trunk. It ate lots of food, salmon too, they fed it deer meat too. That snake was already getting big. Then after a while his wife gave birth to a baby. The snake lived there a long time. The snake was getting bigger all the time, every day it was bigger. It lived in the *yoram*. After a while they got to hate it. It was getting too big. It helped itself to the food, to the dried salmon in the house it helped itself.

Then one morning the little girl was asleep, she was asleep in the baby basket. The woman thought: "I'll go and get water." The baby was asleep.

103

She stood the baby basket up by the fireplace and left the house. The man was in the sweat-house. She hurried along fast, she hurried. All at once it was like there was a noise, she had not got back yet, she was coming back close below the house. Then she glanced down toward the river. Behold the snake was going downslope. Behold only the top hoop of the baby basket was sticking out of its mouth. Then there was a booming noise heard afar as it jumped into the river, downslope of Saivari. The woman ran downslope. She thought: "Maybe the baby fell back out by the river." The snake made a big booming sound as it jumped in. It had swallowed the baby. That was the last of it, the snake went to its home in the river. It was getting big. And it could have eaten up all the people in the house. They had made a pet out of it, out of that Long Snake.

PHOEBE MADDUX, KARUK

A Doctor Acquires Power

Almost everyone in California sought power to a greater or lesser degree. Shamans differed from ordinary people in that they pursued power more vigorously than others or, in many cases, power pursued them; they cultivated friendships with particularly dangerous allies; they underwent a long, formal training under the tutelage of other shamans; and they put their power up for hire by others.

Among the Yurok and other northwestern California people, shamans were almost always women. An apprentice shaman—generally a woman from a family of shamans—underwent a prolonged and at times terror-ridden training in which she would dance, fast, and devote herself to ritual until eventually, in a dream or trance, she attained a vision. An ally would appear in the vision—generally the ghost of a dead person, a monster, or an animal spirit—and give the woman a "pain" (telogel). The pain was an object—a physical manifestation of power, something like an amulet. In the weeks following the vision the woman struggled to gain control over the pain, to learn how to swallow it and regurgitate it at will. Once she succeeded, she could summon the pain whenever she needed it and draw out of it the power of her dream ally. As her training proceeded she acquired other pains from still other allies, and likewise gained control over them. Sometimes an ally, instead of giving her a pain, would give her a song which could also be used as an amulet to call forth power.

T his is how Fanny Flounder of Espeu became a doctor. She told me the story herself, at various times. For several summers she danced at Wogelotek, on a peak perhaps three miles from Espeu north of the creek. It looks out over the ocean. Then at last while she was sleeping here she dreamed she saw the sky rising and blood dripping off its edge. She heard the drops go "ts, ts" as they struck the ocean. She thought it must be *Wesona olego*, where the sky moves up and down, and the blood was hanging from it like icicles. Then she saw a woman standing in a doctor's maple-bark dress

104

with her hair tied like a doctor. Fanny did not know her nor whether she was alive or dead, but thought she must be a doctor. The woman reached up as the edge of the sky went higher and picked off one of the icicles of blood. "Here, take it," she said, and put it into Fanny's mouth. It was icy cold.

Then Fanny knew nothing more. When she came to her senses she found she was in the wash of the breakers on the beach at Espeu with several men holding her. They took her back to the sweat-house to dance. But she could not: her feet turned under her as if there were no bones in them. Then the men took turns carrying her on their backs and dancing with her. Word was sent to her father and mother, who were spearing salmon on Prairie Creek. But her mother would not come. "She will not be a doctor, " she said. Most of Fanny's sisters had become doctors before this. Her mother was a doctor, and her mother's mother also, but her mother had lost faith in her getting the power.

Now, after five days of dancing in the sweat-house, she was resting in the house. Then she felt a craving for crabmeat; so an old kinswoman, also a doctor, went along the beach until she found a washed-up claw. She brought this back, roasted it in the ashes, and offered it to Fanny. At the first morsel Fanny was nauseated. The old woman said, "Let it come out," and held a basket under her mouth. As soon as she saw the vomit she cried, "Eya," because she saw the *telogel* in it. Then everyone in Espeu heard the cry and came running and sang in the sweat-house, and Fanny danced there. She danced with strength as soon as the *telogel* was out of her body. And her mother and father were notified and came as fast as they could. Then her mother said, "Stretch out your hands [as if to reach for the pain] and suck in your saliva like this: hlrr." Fanny did this and at last the pain flew into her again.

This pain was of blood. When she held it in her hands in the spittle in which it was enveloped you could see the blood dripping between her fingers. When I saw it in later years it was a black *telogel* tipped red at the larger end. This, her first, is also her strongest pair of pains. About it other doctors might say, "*Skui ketsemin kel*" (Your pain is good). They say that sort of thing to each other when one doctor has seen a pain in a patient but has been unable to remove it and the next doctor succeeds in sucking it out. The words of Fanny's song when she sucks out blood with her strongest power are: "*Kitelkel wesona-olego kithonoksem*" (Where the sky moves up and down you are traveling in the air).

Now after a time an old kinsman at Espeu was sick in his knee. The other doctors there, who were also his kin, said, "Let the new doctor treat him." Her mother wanted her to undertake it but warned her not to try to sing in curing until she told her to. So she treated the old man without singing; and then she took on other light cases. Altogether she doctored seven times before she sang. Then her mother told her to try to sing, and the song came to her of itself.

Next summer she was at the same place on the hill, again dancing for more power. She was stretching out her hands in different directions when she saw a *tspegyi* [Cooper's hawk] soaring overhead. She became drowsy, lay down, and dreamed. She saw the hawk alight and turn into a person about as tall as a ten-year old boy, with a marten skin slung on his back. He said, "I saw you and came to help you. Take this." And he reached over his shoulder, took something out of his marten skin, and gave her something which she could not see; but she swallowed it. At once she became unconscious.

At Espeu they heard her coming downhill singing. As she ran past the sweat-house the people seized her and put her into it and she danced and came to her senses again. This *telogel* took her less long to learn to control. It is her second strongest pain. After she had taken it out and reswallowed it she saw that it looked like a dentalium.

Now when she is called on to doctor, if she sees a hawk overhead while she is on her way she knows she will be able to cure, even if she has not seen the patient. If she does not see the hawk the case is serious and the patient may die.

The song she got from the hawk is also about the ocean or something near it. When she is not in the trance state she can hardly remember the song, but when in a trance she sings it without knowing it.

When Fanny first told me about her power, she told me only about the hawk. She was saving out how she got her first and strongest pain. That is the way doctors do: they do not give it all away. Nevertheless, other doctors soon find out that a doctor has additional pains, from what they see she can do and they cannot.

All her other pains came to her later and are smaller and weaker. She did not have to dance at Wogelotek for these; she dreamed and got them at home. That is the way it is with all doctors.

ROBERT SPOTT, YUROK

How I Got My Powers

A shaman's training was strenuous, dangerous, and prolonged. As an inducement to persevere, an apprentice shaman from northwestern California keeps visualizing the money (dentalia shells) she will receive when she becomes a full-fledged doctor.

All that winter I went daily high up on the ridge to gather sweat-house wood and each night I spent in the sweat-house. All this time I drank no water. Sometimes I walked along the river, put pebbles into my mouth and spat them out. Then I said to myself, "When I am a doctor I shall suck and the pains will come into my mouth as cool as these stones. I shall be paid for that." When day broke I would face the door of the sweat-house and say: "A long dentalium is looking in at me." When I went up to gather wood, I kept saying: "The dentalium has gone before me; I see its tracks." When I had filled my basket with wood, I said: "That large dentalium, the one I am carrying, is very heavy." When I swept the platform before the sweat-house clean with a branch, I said: "I see dentalia. I see dentalia. I am sweeping them to both sides of me." So whatever I did I spoke of money constantly....

In my dancing I could see various pains flying above the heads of the people. Then I became beyond control trying to catch them. Some of the pains were very hard to drive away. They kept coming back, hovering over certain men. Such men were likely to be sick soon. Gradually I obtained more control of my pains, until finally I could take them out of myself, lay them in a basket, set this at the opposite end of the sweat-house, and then swallow them from where I stood. All this time I drank no water, gathered firewood for the sweat-house, slept in this, and constantly spoke to myself of dentalium money. Thus I did for nearly two years. Then I began to be ready to cure. I worked hard and long at my training because I wished to be the best doctor of all. During all this time, if I slept in the house at all, I put angelica root at the four corners of the fireplace and also threw it into the blaze. I would say: "This angelica comes from the middle of the sky. There the dentalia and woodpecker scalps eat its leaves. That is why it is so withered." Then I inhaled the smoke of the burning root. Thus the dentalia would come to the house in which I was. My sweating and refraining from water were not for the entire two years, but only for ten days at a time again and again. At such periods I would also gash myself and rub in young fern fronds....

When I am summoned to a patient I smoke and say to myself: "I wish you to become well because I like what they are paying me." If the patient dies, I must return the payment. Then I begin to doctor. After I have danced a long time I can see all the pains in the sick person's body. Sometimes there are things like bulbs growing in a man, and they sprout and flower. These I can see but cannot extract. Sometimes there are other pains which I cannot remove. Then I refer the sick person to another doctor. But the other doctor may say: "Why does she not suck them out herself? Perhaps she wishes you to die." Sometimes a doctor really wishes to kill people. Then she blows her pains out through her pipe, sending them into the person that she hates.

MERIP OKEGEI, YUROK

Dentalia wrapped in the skin of the "money snake." Photo courtesy of Phoebe Apperson Hearst Museum of Anthropology.

"Pains," to repeat, are physical manifestations of power. Good pains are those which the shaman learns to control and which, once mastered, enable her to cure disease. Bad pains are manifestations of malignant power, and these are the ones seen hovering about patients' heads.

The shaman, like all Yurok, appears obsessed with money, but money had a different meaning for the Yurok than it has for us. Money was dentalia shells, and dentalium (like everything else in the world) was a living being. A person could thus talk to money, plead with it, cultivate an acquaintance with it. Yet dentalium—no matter how ardently it was wooed—was not very easy to get along with; it was seen as fastidious, even snobbish. It preferred to keep company only with proper and successful people, those who had fulfilled their social obligations and who had high standing in the community. Thus the shaman's constant visualizing of money was more than just greed. It was, in effect, a whole-hearted, single-minded wishing to be a skillful and highly respected doctor—to be someone worthy of dentalium. Such desire was as necessary a part of Yurok shamanism as the mystical visions and ecstatic experiences.

Portrait of a Poisoner

Illness—or at least one class of illness—was generally seen as a physical object (variously called a "pain," "poison," or "bad medicine") which had been magically shot into the body by an enemy or by a shaman who had been hired for the deed. Once the disease lodged in the body another shaman had to be engaged to find it and suck it out.

A man's father, when he begins to make him a poison shaman, places a crystal on the left hand of his son. After placing it there, he makes him eat the root of a plant with poisonous properties. The father takes his son into the brush, he does not eat anything for a day. He gives him porcupine quills, and he sticks a feather into the ground at a distance.

"Hit that!" he says, "Hit that!" giving him the porcupine quills. He shoots the feather with the porcupine quills. Then he scatters earth upon it, and he calls the feather by name, as he scatters earth upon it....

[A man who is a poisoner] must live far away from everyone. He must go out there near the place where he is living, and when he gets there he rolls a log about. He shouts, he hates to let his poison go. The poison is like fire. He calls the name of the one he is poisoning. He commands the poison, "Go to his head!" he says. Sometimes he says: "Go to his breast!" To whatever place is mentioned, there goes the poison.

After poisoning and killing someone, he cries for the man more than anyone, he grieves for the one he kills.

TOM WILLIAMS, MIWOK

Poisoning shamans were feared and hated, yet they were also accepted as a necessary and inevitable part of life. The poisoning shamans' skills were for hire, and in these small societies that stressed obedience, moderation, and accomodation sorcery was the last resort of people who felt themselves badly treated.

The idea that illness was caused by enemies tended to make people wary of each other—especially of strangers—and it gave many Native Californians a cautious and suspicious cast of mind. Yet fear of being poisoned also encouraged people to be courteous and to keep social commitments, since any person whom one had inadvertently insulted could take vengeance by hiring a poisoning shaman. Sickness, in other words—like one's very identity—was seen largely as a social condition; to maintain good health required that one maintain good relationships with other people—a powerful and pervasive impetus to virtuous behavior.

A Fearful Encounter

While common diseases were the result of "poisons" that had been purposefully shot into the body, there were other illnesses—especially shock—that resulted from hapless encounters with the spirit world. Shamans tended to specialize in one or the other kind of sickness. Among the Kato, sucking doctors cured "inside" illnesses that had been caused by the penetration of a "poison." Dancing and singing doctors attended to "outside" (or fright) sickness brought on by confrontation with spirit beings.

W e were killing lizards. I was carrying the sack. We had many of them. The sack was full. My companion killed a small one. Its mother ran off and lay nearby.

"Where is the big one lying?" he asked me.

"There it is," I said.

He was about to shoot it.

"Do not kill me. Already you have killed my little one. I would live," she said.

Fire burst out of its mouth. I dropped the load in the sack and ran up the hill. I was sick. They doctored me. I didn't know anything because I had died. I heard my mother when she cried and said, "My little boy." It was very dark. My father and mother were standing there. I was standing at the base of the rock behind a bush.

From the north something flew there. It spit over me.

"Your feathers will grow. You will fly up in the sky. There are flowers there. It is a good place. There is sunshine. It is a good land."

Again, a large one flew there.

"Have you fixed him already?" he asked.

"Yes, I fixed him some time ago. Why have not the feathers come out?"

"Listen, two are doctoring him. Well, we must have him. Make him fly up now."

I fell back because I did not know how to fly. I did not go anywhere. I was senseless right there. That is all.

BILL RAY, KATO

109

Searching After a Soul

Another major kind of illness was caused by ghosts—*halyatsxamn huthao* (soul-taking), as the Quechan called it, when the ghosts of dead relatives tried to steal the soul of a living person. In many parts of California shamans specialized in the diagnosis and cure of the much-dreaded ghost diseases.

I t sometimes happens that a man drops down dead [unconscious] and may be in that condition for days. The soul has been taken away by that of a relative who wants it with him in the spirit world. I remember it happening when I was a young man. They got a ghost-doctor because the man had not been sick at all.

The doctor came about midday and stretched the body out in the open with the head lying to the east. He built four little hills of sand in a line stretching away from his feet to the west. He stood near the westernmost hill and took out of his bag cane tubes with tobacco in them. Carrying these he walked in a wide circle around the man, singing as he went. He stopped where he had begun and laid the tubes at his feet. Then he picked up one, lit it and smoked. In one whiff all the tobacco had gone. But no smoke came out of his mouth. In a minute the smoke began to come out of the hill nearest to the dead. He repeated this four times, walking around, singing, smoking and making smoke come out of the hills one after another. When he had finished he waited awhile and then said that the dead man's soul could not be found in the spirit world, that no one knew about it. He said that the spirits had not taken it, and perhaps the cause of the illness was witchcraft.

PATRICK MIGUEL, QUECHAN

The Rainmaker

Aside from curing, shamans had a variety of other powers. The rainmaking shaman was especially prominent among the farming groups of the Colorado River. Generally these people depended upon the river's spring floods. The water subsided throughout the summer, laying down a thick, rich blanket of mud in which people planted corn, beans, pumpkins, melons, and native grains. In most years the crops grew prodigiously under the hot desert sun. Sometimes, however, the river failed to rise sufficiently; people looked anxiously to the sky for rain—and, ultimately, they looked to the rainmaker.

T he last rainmaker we had was an old man named Silutha-up who belonged to the Liots Kwestamuts [clan]. It was a very religious clan and its members had very powerful dreams. People said it was different from the other clans because in the old days it treated the dead in a different way. Instead of cremating, a special shelter was built. The dead man was put with his back against one of the center posts in a sitting position and the body was left there to rot.

I remember a time when there was no rain for two years and the flood was very low. There was very little overflow. Everybody got very worried and all the men got together. They decided to send for this old man who was living out to the west at the foot of the mesa. He sent a message telling them to place four bamboo tubes filled with tobacco in the middle of the big shelter where the meeting was held; to build a fire close by them and let it die away into embers.

When he came to the place hundreds of people had gathered around. He picked up the tubes one at a time and smoked them very quickly. He made a short speech, saying that it was the spirit Turtle (*Kupet*) that had given him the power on the mountain Amyxape. The spirit had shown him exactly what to do and had told him to think of the Turtle and name him when he performed the ritual. He commanded the people to follow him out of the shelter and run in a body towards the north, raising as much dust as possible. This they did and the old man went off home. Before he had gone very far there were patches of cloud all over the sky and rain had fallen in several places. In less than an hour a heavy downpour had begun which lasted about four days.

JOE HOMER, QUECHAN

The Rattlesnake Shaman

For the Kumeyaay who lived in the extreme southern part of California and in northern Mexico, rattlesnakes were a fearsome, ever-present threat. The mountains and deserts of the Kumeyaay world held no fewer than five distinct species of rattlesnake: the sidewinder, the western diamondback, the speckled, the red diamond, and the Pacific. In a world such as this the rattlesnake shaman was a figure of considerable importance.

A rattlesnake shaman is called *wikwisiyai*. I knew an old man, Tcipalai, who was sitting, with his two sons, at Snauyuke. He said, "There goes an old man with a basket hat on his head" [a cryptic reference to a snake]. His son said, "You lie; there is nothing there. We are going to look." Tcipalai said, "All right; go and see. Go close to the bush by the draw." They went where he directed them and saw a snake. They were frightened: one ran off, the other ran back. This man was owner of the snakes and could cure their bites. He was a snake. He could talk with them. A snake would come to him to say that he was going off to borrow something. He really meant he was going to bite someone. But Tcipalai would say, "No: you will put me to a lot of work [to cure the patient]."

Once I was hunting with him. His wife prepared a quantity of acorn mush. We hunted all day but found nothing, neither rabbits nor rats. When we returned to within a mile from home, we reached a large rock, with a hollow under it, standing near the trail. He said to me, "I have a great deal of mush at the house, but nothing to eat with it. I am going around this rock to get

111

some game: you remain here." He went to the other side of the rock, rapped on it four times with his hand, stamped around it several times, until snakes began to come out of the hollow in numbers. He killed some with a dry stick. I stood by, very much afraid, until I was invited around the rock to see. I saw a great heap of snakes of all descriptions there. Then, when he had taken what he wanted, he told the others to return under the rock. I saw him wring their heads off, wrap them in tanglefoot grass, and tie the bundle with his breech clout to carry home. There he boiled them all in a big pot filled with water. I refused to eat because it was rattlesnake, but the man said it was not; it was another species. But still I refused. Rattlesnakes are not food, so I think that man must be a snake himself to deal with them.

From infancy this man dreamed of curing rattlesnake bites. The faculty grew in him. He remained continent until he was an adult. Then, when a rattlesnake bit a man, he told the people that all his life he had dreamed of curing such bites, that now he was going to try in secret. He cured him. Then he took a wife and continued his vocation. No one ever doubted him, because he always effected a cure when he announced his intention.

When I was young I saw him cure a man at Snauyuke. The stricken man was carried to a spot distant from a house (such patients are never treated near houses), and Tcipalai was sent for. Others wanted to watch him, but he forbade them saying that they had been with their women. Menstruating women were also warned away, for such would kill a patient. Before he reached the patient, he rubbed himself liberally with dust. He sang and danced, circling about the man lying on the ground. He had a thick bundle of white sage in each hand. The man could not see: his vision was darkened. Each time the shaman fanned his own eyes with the sage, first with one hand, then the other, the patient's vision cleared. As he circled he kicked the prostrate man; first on the feet. Then he blew over his entire body. He sat there gazing at him a short time, then he turned him face down, applied his lips to the small of his back, and sucked out some yellow matter, the snake poison. He instructed the others to turn the man face up. He sucked just below the navel and brought out more yellow matter and blood, spitting it out. He repeated the sucking at the base of the sternum. There was no sign of a wound [incision] where he sucked; perhaps the poison comes out through the pores. He told the man to get up and take a wife: he was cured. Then the shaman went home. The man sat up immediately. He never even swelled from the poison. Eventually he died of old age: he was never ill again.

JIM McCARTHY, KUMEYAAY

Rattlesnake Ceremony Song

Rattlesnake shamans were also prominent among the Yokuts of the San Joaquin Valley and surrounding foothills. Such shamans gained the power to cure and prevent snake bites by cultivating dream communications with the rattlesnakes. The shamans also acted together to conduct public ceremonies which were among the most dramatic events in California. In order to protect people against snake bite the shamans collected and handled live rattlesnakes, often teasing the snakes and allowing themselves to be bitten as proof of their powers. Then they led the entire populace in rituals, songs, and dances. Toward the end of the ceremony the snakes were put into a small hole. Community members approached the hole with sticks, threatening to kill the snakes. The shamans, however, came to the aid of their "darlings." They pleaded with the people and even paid them not to harm the snakes. The people relented, and now the entire community filed past the hole, each person touching it with the right foot. This completed the communication between people and rattlesnakes; in gratitude for having been spared, the rattlesnakes would not strike blindly at people for the next year, but would rattle a warning whenever a person approached.

The following chant was sung during the rattlesnake ceremony. It repeats the mythic words which King Snake used against Rattlesnake in ages past to gain immunity from Rattlesnake's bite. By reciting King Snake's words, people too would become immune.

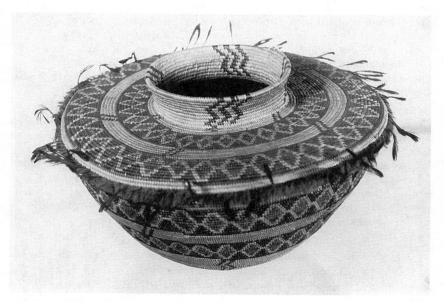

Yokuts basket with rattlesnake pattern. *Photo courtesy of Southwest Museum.*

113

The King Snake said to the Rattlesnake:
Do not touch me!
You can do nothing with me
Lying with your belly full,
Rattlesnake of the rock pile,
Do not touch me!
There is nothing you can do,
You Rattlesnake with your belly full,
Lying where the ground-squirrel holes are thick.
Do not touch me!
What can you do to me?
Rattlesnake in the tree clump,
Stretched in the shade,
You can do nothing;
Do not touch me!
Rattlesnake of the plains,
You whose white eye
The sun shines on,
Do not touch me!

YOKUTS

The Shaman and the Clown

On certain occasions, especially at annual mourning ceremonies, shamans gave public demonstrations of their powers. Among the Maidu, for example, shamans battled each other in contests of magic. Stronger shamans caused seizures and bleeding in the weaker members of the profession, and as the action reached its climax, native witnesses reported seeing flames and lights dancing about the victorious shamans, lizards and mice materializing in the air and disappearing.

Among the Sierra Miwok the contest was between a shaman and a clown. The clown was a major ceremonial figure in Miwok rituals. He was introduced properly into the most sacred of dances where he shouted, "Woo!" (whence his name, *Woochi*), and with hilarious and obscene gestures he parodied the dancers and even the master of ceremonies. His body was painted white, and he was said to have had the character of Coyote: tricky, gluttonous, greedy, foolish, lascivious—and unkillable: a ridiculous figure, yet protected by sacred powers. Who else but such a clown would have dared subject himself to the terrible powers of the shaman?

The one on the far side is the poison shaman, the other is the clown. Dancing as they go, they come to meet each other, early in the morning, they leap and dodge each other as they shoot with bow and arrow. As he dodges, the shaman scatters earth and throws it at the clown. He makes him bleed at the nose and mouth, makes him die under the hot sky.

114

He dances for him, he runs about, he, the one doing the poisoning, looking at the sun. When the sun is getting low, he brings him to consciousness, with his cane he draws him back to life—the one that died.

The one doing the poisoning laughs, as he brings the other back, as he coughs up the poison. He laughs at him, laughs at him, as he comes back to life. He has come to life for good.

The two walk about together, they are partners, they dance together.

TOM WILLIAMS, MIWOK

At the end of the performance the shaman would have paid the clown for his sufferings; they were indeed "partners."

A Great and Wise Shaman

Today we hear tales of shamanistic powers that perplex the modern mind; we hear of shamans who achieved remarkable clairvoyance and augury, who could eat glowing embers, influence the weather, transport themselves instantaneously over long distances, cure the sick, resurrect the dead, kill by pointing a finger or a wand, command owls, beach whales, turn themselves into grizzly bears, summon monsters, and do all kinds of astounding things.

Jakalunus was the greatest, wisest, and most patient of Indian doctors. Once when Warm Springs warriors came to Modoc country and killed a few men this great doctor sent his spirits to combat them. The invaders wondered why their men died without an observable cause.

Once war broke out with the Snake Paiute. They killed women and children but this doctor's spirits killed all of the Paiutes but two or three who were left to go home with the news.

I don't know what would have happened to the whites if he had been living then.

Jakalunus always brushed his hair at noon with a porcupine brush; in that way he knew if anyone was coming. In his house he had strands of small round plaques, several rows of eagle feathers and red-headed woodpecker feathers, and also stuffed jack rabbits. When anything unusual happened one of these would jump around as if it were alive.

He had the largest pipe ever seen. After he filled it with tobacco it would light itself. A Klamath doctor wanted to trade for the pipe. He was told that the pipe wouldn't stay with him but he was confident of his ability and the trade was made. When the Modoc man returned home the pipe was there. Later the Klamath doctor called and inquired about it. The Modoc said, "I gave it to you. What did you do with it?" "It disappeared." "Well, it got to my house before I did. Here it is. You should have listened to me. Even if you held this pipe in your hand it would leave and come to me. My spirits do that."

115

"Why can't it serve me in the same way?" the Klamath inquired.

"I don't know," the Modoc answered. "My spirits determine that."

A few days later the Klamath shaman died. Jakalunus' spirit had caused it. The Klamath people wanted the Modoc to kill Jakalunus. They offered many furs and blankets.

An old woman was once buried alive by her children because they didn't want to take care of her any more. Jakalunus immediately went out to dig her up; his spirits had told him about it. While he was busy the Klamath came and filled him full of arrows. He didn't die right away. First he killed many Klamath by snapping his right index finger at each of them. They dropped and died almost immediately.

JENNY CLINTON, MODOC

Accounts of shamanistic magic puzzle and disturb the modern mind. They run counter to our understanding of how the world works, and many modern people tend to dismiss shamanistic powers as mere sleight-of-hand—deception perpetrated upon the populace by crafty shamans. But Native Californians did not feel that way, and indeed shamans themselves apparently believed in their own and their colleagues' powers. A shaman who fell ill would generally call upon another shaman for a cure, and most shamans seemed authentically fearful and respectful of each other. Among Native Californians the power of shamans was taken for granted—a basic and necessary part of a fundamentally spiritual world.

Porcupine-tail hairbrush (Northern Paiute). *Photo courtesy of Phoebe Apperson Hearst Museum of Anthropology*

VII: Dream Time

I dream of you,
I dream of you jumping.
Rabbit,
Jackrabbit,
Quail.

Ohlone song

117

Dance of the Spirits

Shamans, and ordinary people too, saw their dreams as passageways into the spirit world—a world where not only power awaited them, but truths as well.

W hen it was time to gather acorns, all the people of Kamak left their houses empty and went up on Palomar Mountain. An old man named Pautovak came up from the neighboring village of Ahoya, and stopped at Kamak. Finding the village deserted, he decided he would stay all night and go on in the morning. He took one of the enormous storage baskets, *mushkwanish*, that was empty, inverted it over himself for shelter, and went to sleep.

Early during the night he heard the people call out the summons to a dance. He lay and listened. There were children among the people, little boys, and they came near the granary basket. The basket had a rip through which the toes of the old man were sticking out. "A spirit," yelled the boys, and ran away.

The old man could recognize the voices of men and women who had died long ago. He could hear the spirits talk and hear them laugh. One was Exwanyawish, the woman that was turned into a rock, and Piyevla, the man that scooped the rock with his fingers. Piyevla sang that night all the songs that had been his when alive.

The old man could hear the women's songs as they danced. He lay awake all night and listened; till at last, just before dawn, he could not wait any longer, but determined to see them for himself; so suddenly throwing off the basket, he said, "Hai, are you there?" and immediately all the spirits turned into a flock of birds and flew away; and the turtle-shell rattle they had used all night for the dancing he found where they had left it, but now it was nothing but a piece of soaproot.

SALVADOR CUEVAS, LUISEÑO

House of Silver-Fox

For most modern people, waking thoughts and perceptions are the only valid measures of "reality;" dreaming is considered less trustworthy, less accurate. To say, "I dreamed it," is to imply that something is false or fantastical.

To Native Californians, however, dream events were at least as valid as waking events. If a man dreamed that someone had insulted him, he would assume that indeed such a person *had* insulted him. To dream of a dead person was to be visited by a ghost. Dreaming, in other words, did not take place entirely within one's own mind; rather it was an act of communication, an important way of gaining knowledge—in some ways even more important than ordinary seeing or hearing because in dreams one came into close contact with the spirit world. Through dreams people met spirit helpers who gave them advice, sacred songs, and extraordinary powers. Courageous shamans might

118

travel great distances in their dreams, associate with the most powerful and dangerous spirits, and see the most awesome and terrifying of sights.

When Silver-Fox left this world, he said to his sweat-house, "Nobody shall ever come in here," and he left a strong wind there to guard the place. No one dares go near this place, for a whirlwind blows up out of it and makes a noise like thunder. Only shamans can approach it; but whoever enters is immediately turned to stone inside. Wolf and Silver-Fox left their power of wind there. Even now, wolves will catch people that come near; and whoever gets inside turns to white rock.

Once a great shaman dreamed of a wolf that was in that sweat-house. He went in. As soon as he got inside, the wind stopped. He went around inside and vomited blood. He said it was an immense sweat-house, as much as a mile across inside. When he came out, he fell down nearly dead. Another shaman cured him. He had seen nothing inside but men turned to stone. Next night this shaman's hair turned as white as snow.

ACHUMAWI

A Shaman's Dreams

A thousand years ago the Mohave River flowed full and strong, nourishing at least two large freshwater lakes in what is now "The Mohave Sink." The water table was much higher then, the vegetation lusher, and many people lived throughout the area. They supported themselves by gathering wild plants and freshwater mussels, catching fish and wild game, and farming small plots of land. Then the climate changed, an exceptionally dry period became firmly established, and by 1400 A.D. the area was a desert—virtually uninhabited and uninhabitable. Civilization retreated to the banks of the Colorado River—a magnificent river 1,700 miles long, fed throughout the summer by the melting snows on the continental divide in western Colorado. Here in the jungle-like growth of willow, cottonwood, sycamore, and arrowweed the Mohave, Quechan, Halchidhoma, and other river people cleared farmland and formed an utterly distinctive civilization. Their passions were warfare, travel—and especially dreaming. Mohave dreams in particular were noted for their haunting strangeness and their deep poetic beauty.

Homyavre, the bug who causes the mirage, came to me one night when I was a small child, and said to me: "I will give you my breath; my breath is cold, my breath is warm, my breath is hot. I will give you my breath, that you may be able to cure sickness."

A female bug came to me and said: "I am the one who made the sun, the moon, the stars. I will give you something. My breath is blue, my breath is green, my breath is red. I give you my breath to cure sickness." This was Mastamho, the creator, speaking through the bug, for Mastamho never speaks to men himself.

A buzzard came; but his color was not the color of a buzzard, for he was brown. He sang this song to me: "I blow my breath at the darkness, and it disappears like a mist before the sun, and day comes. When you sing this song and blow your breath at the darkness of disease, it will disappear."

In a dream I went to the mountains and built a house. There came a tarantula with a great long beard. It pulled some of the hair from its body and laid it on the ground to represent a sick man. Then it sang: "Come and stand beside me, boy, and I will teach you how to cure sickness. I blow my breath over the sick one, and he is well."

AHWEYAMA, MOHAVE

A dream such as this, like many other Mohave dreams, is striking for its simplicity and elegance of structure, its balance and complexity of symbol. Dreams like this are possible only among a people for whom dreaming was more than a random and uncontrolled activity of the mind; for whom it was an important and well-cultivated art.

Deserted Mohave dwellings. *Photo courtesy of California Department of Parks and Recreation.*

Visit to Kumastamho

Dreaming—important throughout California—reached its highest development along the Colorado River. Good dreams were necessary for all endeavors. Dream interpreters were highly respected and oversaw the planting of crops, the forming of alliances, the undertaking of journeys, and the waging of wars. A song or myth was not considered known until it had been properly dreamed.

Before I was born I would sometimes steal out of my mother's womb while she was sleeping, but it was dark and I did not go far. Every good doctor begins to understand before he is born. When I was a little boy, I took

Avekwame Mountain seen from the south. *Photo by James Bennyhoff.*
Courtesy of Phoebe Apperson Hearst Museum of Anthropology.

a trip to Avekwame Mountain [in a dream] and slept at its base. I felt of my body with my two hands, but found it was not there. It took me four days and nights to go there. Later I became able to approach even the top of the mountain. At last I reached the willow-shade in front of the darkhouse there. Kumastamho [the Creator] was within. It was so dark that I could hardly see him. He was naked and very large. Only a few great doctors were in there with him, but a crowd of men stood under the shade before the house.

I now have power to go to Kumastamho any time. I lie down and try, and soon I am up there again with the crowd. He teaches me to cure by spitting [i.e., by blowing frothy saliva] and sucking. One night Kumastamho spat up blood. He told me: "Come here, little boy, and suck my chest." I placed my hands on his ribs and sucked his sickness out. Then he said: "You are a consumption dreamer. When anybody has consumption lay your hands on him and suck the pain out continually, and in four months he will be well."

It takes four days to tell [the origin myth] about Kwikumat and Kumastamho. I was present from the very beginning, and saw and heard all. I dreamed a little of it at a time. I would then tell it to my friends. The old men would say: "That is right! I was there and heard it myself." Or they would say: "You have dreamed badly. That is not right." And they would tell me right. So at last I learned the whole of it right.

QUECHAN

In dreams the distinction between past and present was erased. In dreams one could talk directly to the Maker of the universe; one could stand witness to the very creation of the world.

To modern people dreaming is clearly set off from waking, but not for the Quechan. As a person grew older he or she often could no longer distinguish between what had been learned in a dream and what had been learned from other people or from direct, sensory experience. To the Quechan the unconscious dream world—timeless and fluid—merged seamlessly with the conscious waking world.

121

VIII: Mythic Time

Cottontail lived at Black Rock. He decided that the sun was too hot. With his bow and arrow he lay in wait for it one morning in his little cave in the rocks. He lay there, and just as the sun came up, he shot it and brought it down. Then he took a piece of liver, which he cut thin, and put it over the sun. Since then the sun has not been so bright.

A myth
Tom Stone, Owens Valley Paiute

Birth of the World-Makers

At the furthest reaches of mythic time, perhaps even beyond the deepest of dreams, lay the void, the infinite darkness, the spanless sweep of time before the world was formed.

I n the beginning, there was no earth or sky or anything or anybody; only a dense darkness in space. This darkness seemed alive. Something like lightnings seemed to pass through it and meet each other once in a while. Two substances which looked like the white of an egg came from these lightnings. They lay side by side in the stomach of darkness, which resembled a spider web. These substances disappeared. They were then produced again, and again they disappeared. This was called the miscarriage of the darkness. The third time they appeared, they remained, hanging there in this web in the darkness. The substances began to grow and soon were two very large eggs. When they began to hatch, they broke at the top first. Two heads came out, then shoulders, hips, knees, ankles, toes; then the shell was all gone. Two boys emerged: Mukat and Tamaioit. They were grown men from the first, and could talk right away. As they lay there, both at the same time heard a noise like a bee buzzing. It was the song of their mother, Darkness.

CAHUILLA

So begins the Cahuilla creation epic. The creation epic was one of several Cahuilla song cycles recited by an official ceremonial singer, the *hawaynik*.

Cahuilla ceremonial house and enclosure. *Photo by Edward S. Curtis, 1921. Courtesy of Smithsonian Institution.*

124

Some of the song cycles lasted as long as twelve hours, and the *hawaynik* had to perform flawlessly. He trained hard, studied long, and underwent dietary and other religious proscriptions before a performance. Each *hawaynik* had under him a company of dancers and assistant singers, as well as several apprentices who were learning the song cycles. The Cahuilla treated the *hawaynik* with lifelong honor, even veneration; for within his songs the sacred knowledge of the people was preserved.

The idea of two creators, while not universal, was widespread in California. Often a being called "World-Maker" was matched with another potent being sometimes called "Coyote." To the extent that they represented abstract principles, they embodied not so much "good" and "evil," although in later years they would become associated with God and Satan, but rather something closer to the "ideal" and the "practical." World-Maker generally argued for a perfect world, one in which there would be no death, where childbirth would be easy, where food would be always ample. His opposite argued for a world of difficulty and struggle, and it would be through the tension between the two of them that the world we live in would emerge.

The Creation

Different Maidu communities seem to have had widely differing versions of how the world was made. There was no dogmatic orthodoxy, and the idea that war might be waged over matters of belief was simply ridiculous. "This is how we tell it; they tell it differently," is a sentence still heard in many Indian communities.

The version of the creation epic that follows begins with a vision of the world covered with water. A raft with two beings floats out from the north. A feathered rope drops from the sky, and Earth-Initiate climbs down into the raft. Who made the water, the raft, the trinity of Earth-Creators? Like many California creation epics, the Maidu account seems to begin in the middle of the story. Mysteriously, elements of the world seem to have always been present, their existence apparently beyond question or speculation.

I n the beginning there was no sun, no moon, no stars. All was dark, and everywhere there was only water. A raft came floating on the water. It came from the north, and in it were two persons—Turtle and Pehe-ipe. The stream flowed very rapidly. Then from the sky a rope of feathers, called *Pokelma*, was let down, and down it came Earth-Initiate. When he reached the end of the rope, he tied it to the bow of the raft, and stepped in. His face was covered and was never seen, but his body shone like the sun. He sat down, and for a long time said nothing.

At last Turtle said, "Where do you come from?" and Earth Initiate answered, "I come from above." Then Turtle said, "Brother, can you not make for me some good dry land, so that I may sometimes come up out of the water?" Then he asked another time, "Are there going to be any people in the world?" Earth-Initiate thought awhile, and then said, "Yes." Turtle asked, "How long before you are going to make people?" Earth-Initiate replied, "I don't know. You want to have some dry land: well, how am I going to get any earth to make it of?" Turtle answered, "If you will tie a rock about my left arm, I'll dive for some." Earth-Initiate did as Turtle asked, and then, reaching around, took the end of a rope from somewhere, and tied it to Turtle. When Earth-Initiate came to the raft, there was no rope there: he just reached out and found one. Turtle said, "If the rope is not long enough, I'll jerk it once, and you must haul me up; if it is long enough, I'll give two jerks, and then you must pull me up quickly, as I shall have all the earth that I can carry." Just as Turtle went over the side of the boat, Pehe-ipe began to shout loudly.

Turtle was gone a long time. He was gone six years; and when he came up, he was covered with green slime, he had been down so long. When he reached the top of the water, the only earth he had was a very little under his nails: the rest had all washed away. Earth-Initiate took with his right hand a stone knife from under his left armpit, and carefully scraped the earth out from under Turtle's nails. He put the earth in the palm of his hand, and rolled it about till it was round; it was as large as a small pebble. He laid it on the stern of the raft. By and by he went to look at it: it had not grown at all. The third time that he went to look at it, it had grown so that it could not be spanned by the arms. The fourth time he looked, it was as big as the world, the raft was aground, and all around were mountains as far as he could see. The raft came ashore at Tadoiko, and the place can be seen today.

MAIDU

"As in a dream," is perhaps the best way to describe the Maidu creation myth. Motives and actions are suffused with dreamlike indetermination and vagueness. Even Earth-Initiate seems oddly befuddled. "I don't know," he answers when asked when people will be created, and his making the world out of mud seems a rather homey and spur-of the-moment affair. The Maidu earth-makers were far from omniscient and omnipotent. They appear, in fact, rather tentative and at times confused—as figures in a dream tend to be.

As for Pehe-ipe who shares the creation raft, throughout all of creation he remains uninvolved—a witness to this most awesome of events, never a participant. His name literally means "Father-of-the-Secret-Society." During Secret Society dances a Pehe-ipe impersonator appeared and played a major role: curiously, that of the clown!

Marumda and Kuksu Make the World

Today when we read an ancient myth we ask ourselves, "What does it mean?"—for meaning is virtually all that most translations convey. But for the original audiences myth-telling was a rich sensual event as well. On winter nights when myths could be told, people crowded around the assembly house fire, the myth-teller cleared his throat, and ordinary language—the language of cooking, hunting, child-rearing, fishing, and basket-making—became transformed by poetry and music into the sacred rhythms of myth. In the Pomo creation myth that follows, one catches a hint of the original music that transported its listeners into the realm of the gods. The night was long, and the myth proceeds at a slow, stately, measured pace.

He lived in the north, the Old Man, his name was Marumda. He lived in a cloud-house, a house that looked like snow, like ice. And he thought of making the world. "I will ask my older brother who lives in the south," thus he said, the Old Man Marumda. "Wah! What shall I do?" thus he said. "Eh!" thus he said.

Then he pulled out four of his hairs. He held out the hairs. "Lead me to my brother!" thus he said, Marumda the Old Man. Then he held the hairs to the east; after that he held the hairs to the north; after that he held them to the west; after that he held them to the south, and he watched.

Then the hairs started to float around, they floated around, and floated toward the south, and left a streak of fire behind, they left a streak of fire, and following it floated the cloud-house, and Marumda rode in it.

He sat smoking. He quit smoking. And then he went to sleep. He was lying asleep, sleeping..., sleeping..., sleeping..., sleeping.... Then he awoke. He got up and put tobacco into his pipe. He smoked, and smoked, and smoked, and then he put the pipe back into the sack.

That was his first camp, they say, and then he lay down to sleep. Four times he lay down to sleep, and then he floated to his elder brother's house. His name was Kuksu. This Kuksu was the elder brother of Marumda.

The Kuksu, his house was like a cloud, like snow, like ice, his house. Around it they floated, four times they floated around it the hairs, and then through a hole they floated into the house, and following them the Marumda entered the house.

"Around the east side!" said the Kuksu. Then around the east side he entered the house, and he sat down, he sat, and he took off the little sack hung around his neck. He took out his pipe and filled it with tobacco, he laid a coal on it, and he blew, he blew, and then he blew it afire. Then he removed the coal and put it back into his little sack. After that he smoked, four times he put the pipe to his mouth. After that he offered it to his older brother the Kuksu.

Then Kuksu received it. "Hyoh!" he said, the Kuksu. "Hyoh! Good will be our knowledge, good will end our speech! Hyoh! May it happen! Our knowledge will not be interfered with! May it happen! Our knowledge will go smoothly. May it happen! Our speech will not hesitate. May it happen! Our speech will stretch out well. The knowledge we have planned, the knowledge we have laid, it will succeed, it will go smoothly, our knowledge! Yoh ooo, hee ooo, hee ooo, hee ooo, hee ooo! May it happen!" Thus he said, the Kuksu, and now he quit smoking....

Then Kuksu poked Marumda with the pipe, and Marumda received the pipe, he received it and put it back in his little dried-up sack. Then the Marumda scraped himself in the armpits, he scraped himself and got out some of the armpit wax. He gave the armpit wax to the Kuksu. Then Kuksu received it, he received it, and stuck it between his big toe and the next. And then he also scraped himself in the armpits, he scraped himself, and rolled the armpit wax into a ball. His own armpit wax he then stuck between Marumda's toes.

Then Marumda removed it and blew on it, four times he blew on it. Then Kuksu also removed the armpit wax and blew on it four times, and after that he sat down. Then Marumda went around the Kuksu four times, and then he sat down. And then the Kuksu, he got up, he got up, and four times around the Marumda he went. Then they both stood still.

Now they mixed together their balls of armpit wax. And Kuksu mixed some of his hair with it. And then Marumda also mixed some of his hair with the armpit wax.

After that they stood up; facing south, and then facing east, and then facing north, and then facing west, and then facing the zenith, and then facing the nadir: "These words are to be right and thus everything will be. People are going to be according to this plan. There is going to be food according to this plan. There will be food from the water. There will be food from the land. There will be food from under the ground. There will be food from the air. There will be all kinds of food whereby the people will be healthy. These people will have good intentions. Their villages will be good. They will plan many things. They will be full of knowledge. There will be many of them on this earth, and their intentions will be good.

"We are going to make in the sky the traveling-fire. With it they will ripen their food. We are going to make that with which they will cook their food overnight. The traveling-fires in the sky, their name will be Sun. The one who is Fire, his name will be Daytime-Sun. The one who gives light in the night, her name will be Night-Sun. These words are right. This plan is sound. Everything according to this plan is going to be right!" Thus he spoke, the Kuksu.

And now the Marumda made a speech. Holding the armpit wax, holding it to the south, he made a wish: "These words are right!" Thus he said, the Marumda. And then he held it to the east, and then he held it to the north, and then he held it to the west, and then he held it to the zenith, and then he held it to the nadir: "According to this plan, people are going to be. There are going to be people on this earth. On this earth there will be plenty of food for the people! According to this plan there will be many different kinds of food for the people! Clover in plenty will grow, grain, acorns, nuts!" Thus he spoke, the Marumda.

And then he blew tobacco-smoke in the four directions. Then he turned around to the left four times. Then he put the armpit-wax into his little dried-up sack. After that he informed the Kuksu: "I guess I'll go back, now!" Thus he said, and then he asked the Kuksu: "Sing your song, brother!" And then the Kuksu sang [in an archaic language]: "Hoya, hoha, yuginwe, hoya,...etc....etc."

After that Marumda floated away to the north, singing the while a wishing song [also in an archaic language]: "Hinaa ma hani ma...etc...etc..." Thus he sang, the Marumda.

With this song he traveled north, the Marumda, riding in his house, in his cloud-house. He was singing along, holding the armpit-wax in his hand and singing the song. Then he tied a string to the ball of armpit-wax, passed the string through his own ear-hole and made it fast. Then he went to sleep.

He was lying asleep, when suddenly the string jerked his ear. He sat up and looked around but he did not see anything, and he lay down again to sleep. It went on like that for eight days, it went on for eight days, and then it became the earth. The armpit-wax grew large while Marumda was sound asleep, and the string jerked his ear. At last Marumda sat up, he sits up, and he untied the string from his ear-hole. Then he threw the earth out into space.

WILLIAM RALGANAL BENSON, POMO

Marumda and Kuksu are strange beings. Far from abstract or ethereal gods, they seem very real, very concrete—right down to their toes, ear lobes, and armpits. The ambience in which they function, however, is utterly magical, saturated with number-ritual, rites, and mystery. Strange yet concrete figures in a magical ambience—the material that myths are made of is very close indeed to the material dreams are made of.

The use of a vulgar, even laughable material—in this case armpit wax—to make the world is typically Californian. Perhaps the use of such lowly matter emphasizes the immense power of the gods. More than that, however, it suggests that even the grossest of substances has sacred potential. Sacredness, in other words, did not reside just in distant, rare, or "heavenly" materials. The most common, mundane things of the body, the village, the earth—these too, in the Indian mind, were suffused with a history of sacredness and power.

Remaking the World

California Indian religious belief systems often include a sense of a prior world—a world generally inhabited by monsters and sometimes subject to great floods. Evidence for this world was apparent. Fossil bones of monstrous animals—mammoths, camels, and other strange and unknown beasts—abound in California, and could hardly have escaped the attention of the native peoples. Seashells and petrified ripple marks give evidence that even the highest ridgetops were once covered with water. Clearly there was a world, or even worlds, that existed before the present.

In the following myth, a bygone world is dimly seen and mysteriously described. The sense of dreaming is exceptionally strong here. Creation and destruction seem to happen by themselves; indeed the dreamer of the old world and the maker of the new world seem passive witnesses rather than active creators, staring open-eyed, amazed, and even helpless as the grand processes unfold around them.

M any people came into existence somewhere. They dwelt long ago and no one knows what they did. And then one of them dreamed. So he said, "I dreamed; of a whirlwind I dreamed." And they said, "You have dreamed something bad."

Then they all dwelt there a long, long time. And after that it blew, and the wind increased. They had an earth lodge, so they said, "Let us go into the earth lodge. The world is going bad." So they all went in. And they said, "Let all the people together enter the earth lodge; the world is going bad."

So at noon they all entered the earth lodge. Then it blew. It blew terribly. Every kind of tree fell down westward. And the one who had dreamed, that man who had dreamed, stood outside and did not come into the earth lodge. Standing outside he spoke, "It is raining, O you people, and the trees are falling westward all at once." And he went on speaking, "The water is coming, the earth will be destroyed."

And all the houses outside were blown away; none remained. Then, coming into the earth lodge, he said, "It must be that my dream is coming true. I dreamed of wind and I must have been right about the destruction of the world." He stood alone, leaning against the post of the earth lodge. And all the people went. He remained thus for a while and then the post he was leaning on came loose. Then this person went; the one who had dreamed went last after all the people were gone. So the world was destroyed and water alone was left.

Thus it was for some time, and then Olelbes [He-Who-Is-Above] looked down from the north. He looked for a long time everywhere, west, and east, and south; he looked all around in a circle. And in the north, right in the middle of the water, something was barely visible. Then while he was looking, it moved to the west and to the east. He could scarcely see it. Then it seemed to him as if it swam around a little. It was lying there before him on the bedrock. He-Who-Is-Above knew. It was a lamprey eel which lay there all alone. That lamprey had come first into existence, and lay there alone. In the meanwhile, there on the rocks, lay a little mud. The water lay there long, very long, no one knows how long it lay there, and then finally the water began to recede, to go down south, and as it receded it turned into a multitude of creeks. Then at last there lay a little earth that had come into being, and that earth turned into all kinds of trees.

This is all. It has been transformed.

JENNY CURL, WINTU

Woman's Love Medicine

Throughout California the time between the making of the world and the creation of present-day people was viewed as a separate epoch. A race of creator-beings, often much like ordinary people but possessed of exceptional powers, lived in the world and partook in momentous events; the adjustment of the sun and moon; the molding of the landscape; the rescue of deer, salmon, fire, and other valuables from evil captors; the establishment of all human rituals, clans, and institutions. At the end of this epoch the race of creator-beings either withdrew from the world or became transformed into present-day animals, plants, or geographic entities. *Kixunai* is what the Hupa called these creator-beings.

The young men of the Kixunai used to come to a certain rock that stands in the ocean at the mouth of the Klamath. They used to hold there their sports and shooting matches. But notwithstanding all the attractions, a modest woman lived there who never went out of her house. Once, while she was sitting working on her baskets, a beam of sunlight fell on her without cause. "What is going to happen?" she thought. As she was going on with her weaving, she noticed a person coming toward her. "The Kixunai who live around here never come in this house," she said. "Up there is the place they go in."

The one who came in, came intending to be the woman's husband. He lived there for a time. Then he went away and never returned. She heard no longer the sound of the games and the talk of the Kixunai.

Mink came to her one time and said, "You won't see again the one who used to come here. Across the ocean to the south he has two wives. One lies in each of his arms." When she found this out, she was more lonesome than ever. She went outside. "When Indians come," she thought, "they will do this way." She went outside. She looked for the herb with which she was to make the medicine. She looked all over the world for it, but in vain.

Once she was surprised to see that as the lonesomeness fell upon her, the herb grew. It came into the world with lonesomeness. She looked at the ground and saw the herb growing there. She pulled off part of it and took it into the house with her. She bathed her arms and legs with it, and when it was night lay down with some of it in her hand and a bundle of it behind her. In the middle of the night she took the bundle up and put it in front of her.

Then speaking to it she said, "If ten times his heart goes from me to other women, finally it will come back to me. I hope he may be crazy. How many soever women he likes, even if they lie in his arms, this medicine will come to him. Among how many soever of them he goes, thus my heart will find him."

The noise of the Kixunai was quiet. She did not hear their talk. "This way it will be," she thought. "You will hate the one you used to like. Before all others you will think about me. It will be this way in the Indian world, if they do this." When she got up in the morning, she put the bundle of medicine toward the north. The sun shone upon her. "This way it will be," she thought, "if Indians when they come make medicine. But there will not be many who will make it," she thought. "I have made it good," she thought. "This way it will be."

The medicine went to him, and he came back to her. It was the moon who discarded her.

EMMA LEWIS, HUPA

Hupa woman. *Photo by Edward S. Curtis, 1923. Courtesy of Smithsonian Institution.*

The story of the love potion took place in mythic time; but the energy of that event stretched into the present, filling the herb with meaning and magic. A woman who gathered the medicine and performed the rites would draw upon the power of this ancient and mythic event, would feel in effect the rhythms of the sacred era. There was not, then, an impenetrable boundary that separated a "mythic" past from a "mundane" present. Objects and rites of the everyday world were still filled with the power of mythic time; the world of myth was still manifest, alive, and very much accessible through actions and rituals in the present.

He-Lives-in-the-South

The following story is about ordinary things: a woman, a boat, a pestle, a sea stack, a flock of gulls. The emotions—maternal love, jealousy, and anger—are equally commonplace. But the story takes place in mythic time and in a dreamlike ambience. The characters are the *Kixunai*—the ones who lived before the present age. And these common objects and emotions become linked together in utterly wondrous relationships.

At Orleans Bar there lived a maiden. She always brought wood for her fire in the morning before breakfast. The rest of the day she used to spend making baskets. One morning when she was after wood she heard a baby rolling about in a hollow tree. Without stopping to gather the wood for which she had come, she took the baby and carried it home. There she cared for it as if it were her own. When the umbilical cord fell off she considered where she should put it. She decided to throw it into the river.

Soon the boy was large enough to run about. She made a bow for him and put a mark in the house for him to shoot at. She did not go for wood as she had formerly done. She kept the door shut and never allowed the boy to go out for fear she should lose him. Whenever she was obliged to go out she closed the door with great care. After a time he became a good-sized boy.

At a village below Orleans there lived another maiden, who noticed that her neighbor did not go out as she had been in the habit of doing and suspected there must be some cause for it. One day when the foster mother was gone after wood this girl came and sat down by the house to watch. Soon she saw a straw fall and stick up in the ground like an arrow. Watching carefully she saw another one come out of the smoke-hole. Running up on the roof of the house she looked in. She was surprised to see a boy inside. She opened the door, picked him up, and ran away with him. When she got back to her own house she took a little canoe out of the house, put water in it, and stretched it until it became a full-sized canoe. She also took from the house a small storage basket, which contained her treasures. Placing the boy in the stern of the boat she started down the river. They went on down past Weitchpec until they came to the mouth of the Klamath.

When the foster mother came back she saw that the door was not just as she had left it. She went in and found the boy was gone. She looked for him

The rock, Oregos, at the mouth of the Klamath River. *Photo courtesy of Phoebe Apperson Hearst Museum of Anthropology.*

everywhere but could not even find his tracks. She searched for him in the neighboring mountains in vain. "Somebody has taken him away from me," she thought. Taking her stone pestle with her she climbed the mountain on the south side of the river. From its top she saw with surprise a boat going along on the ocean toward the south. "I am going to kill him," she thought, and threw the pestle at him with all her might. The girl had taken a head-dress from the storage basket and put it on the boy. The pestle just hit the end of this and knocked the feathers off. These feathers flew away as gulls and other sea-birds. The pestle stuck up in the water and stands there yet. They went on to the end of the world at the south where they are still living.

EMMA LEWIS, HUPA

Pounding acorns was a woman's daily task—tedious and mundane—and the pestle was her most basic and ordinary implement. Yet it too was alive, possessed of sacred powers and a complex mythic history. Once, the woman might think to herself, in the hands of the *Kixunai*, it had been transformed into a sea stack. Who could tell what might happen to it next? To the Hupa

134

woman even the lowliest of implements was a living part of a sacred and magical world in which anything might happen.

Yet along with the familiarity and domesticity, there is something of the exotic as well. The story takes place in a distant world, a world of long ago, before Indians arrived in the area. The maiden who found the infant lived at Orleans Bar, in Karuk territory. The flight through Weitchpec to the mouth of the Klamath is entirely through Yurok territory. The youth himself, as his name indicates, now lives in the south. The entire story, then, takes place in a time before the present, in places just beyond the well-known world of the Hupa. Perhaps it is this mixture of the utterly familiar with the exotic that gives these stories such gripping power.

Yurok houses at Weitchpec. *Photo courtesy of Phoebe Apperson Hearst Museum of Anthropology.*

The Tar Woman

Indian people in other parts of North America, notably the Southwest, the Great Plains, and Mexico, often had poetic and highly symbolic mythologies. The origin of the hallucinogenic mescal, for example, might—depending upon the tribe—involve the four cardinal directions, the winds, rainbows, magical

135

numbers, the hierarchy of colors, and an array of allegorical gods and goddesses. When the Salinan described the creation of mescal, however, it was with a much different sensibility.

I n former times there was an old woman known as Chahe. Her stomach was a basket full of boiling tar which she carried on her shoulder. She would entice people to approach her and then throw them into the boiling tar where they were digested.

One day she was seated on a hill waiting for someone to pass by. There came Prairie-Falcon accompanied by his uncle Raven. They saw Chahe, and Prairie-Falcon said, "Have you got your flute?" "Yes," said Raven. "What charms have you?" For both of the friends possessed magic flutes which aided them in everything they undertook.

When Chahe saw them she said, ingratiatingly, "Nephews, you have a long journey to go. Better get up on my shoulder and let me carry you." So they flew up on their flutes and sat on her shoulder. She was very tall. Then she sang:

Wayawaye! Hesekola!

It is crying, that which I am going to kill!

Then they stood up on their flutes, but Raven missed his balance and fell into the basket of tar. That is the reason he is so black; before this Raven was as colorful as Prairie-Falcon. But the latter reached down and caught Raven by one feather and hauled him out and revived him. Then they pulled out their fire drills and set fire to the tar. Chahe jumped as the fire touched her and cried out, "Oh, grandfather!" Her skin began to peel off and she ran about furiously. She ran into the earth in her endeavor to extinguish the fire, and then came out again. "I am burning up!" she cried.

All over the earth she ran leaving drops of burning tar, and every place where the tar fell there sprouted the mescal. Her course finally ended in the north where she still is heard running in circles. And so she will continue all her life to the end of the world, dropping seeds of mescal. There is still the old woman in the north.

My story is ended.

MARIA OCARPIA, SALINAN

The image of Chahe, an old woman with a burden basket, could hardly be more domestic and concrete. But the dreamlike, sometimes violent workings of the mythic imagination make transformations. The woman becomes a monster and the basket—full of boiling tar—is her stomach. The other characters in the myth, Raven and Prairie-Falcon, seem straightforward at first, but upon close consideration they turn out to be as polymorphous as dream figures. They must have had hands and fingers, for example, in order to play the flute and use the fire drill. Yet we are told that they possessed feathers and could fly, which would suggest wings. Did they have hands or did they have wings? Were they birds or were they people? In this age before the present age they were both at the same time. The rational mind balks at this apparent contradiction, but the dream mind understands.

Time also has a dreamlike boundlessness in the *Tar Woman* story. The events described happened a long time ago; they are happening in the present; and they will continue to happen "to the end of the world," in the timelessness of myth, the timelessness of dream.

A Pomo flute. *Photo courtesy of Phoebe Apperson Hearst Museum of Anthropology.*

IX: Coyote Tales

A long time ago, when I was a little girl, I used to go around with my grandmothers and grandfather. I used to go along when they went to the mountains, and I used to watch while they panned gold. Then, when it got dark, we all used to sleep in a little house, built Indian style. Then, the children would all be bedded down and my late grandfather would tell tales of Coyote. He would say to us, "Listen well." Afterwards, with his elderberry flute, he used to sing Indian songs. "All of you listen very closely," he would say to us, "I am talking in the ancient manner." Then he would talk and tell us many things of long ago.

From the reminiscenses of
Maym Hannah Gallagher,
Maidu

Illustration by Harry Fonseca.

Coyote and Spider

Humans first appeared in California 12,000, or 20,000, or perhaps 30,000 or more years ago. They hunted with spears, for the bow and arrow had not yet been invented. Without knowing how to make mortars and pestles they could not pound seeds or acorns into flour, but survived by gathering roots, greens, and berries. We know almost nothing about how they lived or what languages they spoke. Yet it is quite probable that many of their stories featured the "Trickster."

The trickster figure was widespread throughout North America and the Old World, ancient beyond calculation and enormously complex. He is at the same time good and evil, crafty and foolish, godlike and scroungy. He is both the prankster and the dupe. He seems to exist in the free and wild area of the mind beyond duality—beyond the trick of intellect that divides things into good or bad, smart or stupid, winner or loser, allowable or forbidden. The trickster is everything at once. He dies, is dismembered, decays, and then is pulled back together again to continue his journey. He exists in an undifferentiated, boundless, intensely creative world.

The specific embodiment of the trickster varies from people to people across North America. Sometimes he is human, sometimes animal, often both at once. He was variously called Manabozho, The Foolish One, The Great Rabbit, Glooscap, Sweet-Medicine, Wakdjunkaga, Hare, or Raven. In California, the Southwest, and in much of Mexico the trickster generally took his name from the sly dog-like animal who skulked around the outskirts of villages, hunting gophers, scavenging the refuse piles, and occasionally stealing salmon and deer meat from the drying racks.

In a typical Coyote story the "hero" sets off on a foolish mission and gets into trouble, as he falls victim to his own irrepressible curiosity and compulsions.

Coyote had a baby and put him in the sun. The sun was so hot that the baby died. Coyote stalked the sun every morning. He went up and up, hunting for the sun, and he wanted to get down. He saw everything at a distance under him. He did not know how to get down. He spit down and the spit fell and fell and fell and Coyote did not know how to get down that far.

Spider came along. He told Coyote he would let him down with his rope if he would not look up and would not laugh. Spider let him down and down, but Coyote looked up and he laughed because Spider's behind looked so funny, you know how it works when he makes rope. Spider was angry and he drew him up, drew him up, drew him up. Coyote promised not to do it again, so Spider let him down again, but Coyote looked up again and he could not help but laugh because Spider looked so funny. Spider drew him up, drew him up, drew him up. He was angry. Coyote promised not to laugh again, so Spider let him down again. Coyote laughed again because Spider looked so funny. Spider broke the rope and Coyote fell and fell and fell down and hit the ground and broke all to pieces. He broke every bone. He was all mashed up. Two girls came along and said, "That looks like Coyote!" One kicked the bones, and Coyote came to life again.

BEAR RIVER

Coyote and the Acorns

Those who know Coyote stories only from books can only dimly imagine the performance. Family and close friends have crowded into a dwelling or assembly house and are gathered around a masterful storyteller. The storyteller begins, voice full of laughter and vitality. Now he takes on the character of Coyote, alternately whining, pleading, posturing, importuning, or demanding. He assumes the roles of other characters, he imitates and mimics, he breaks into song. His voice drops to a confidential whisper, then bursts out into a loud and amazing harangue. He ranges freely and widely, opening the darkest fears and most forbidden subjects to laughter. Coyote wallops his grandmother. Coyote makes love to his own daughter. Coyote's penis falls off. Coyote is squashed, eaten by maggots, and comes back to life. The stories are absurd, deeply ludicrous, so profound that they provoke thought among the elders, at the same time so simple that they draw laughter from the youngest child. Everyone—young and old, man and woman, rich person and poor—is laughing together. Coyote stories had morals and deep meaning; but the dominant experience of listening to Coyote stories was the longed-for feeling of being united with others in laughter, everyone liberated and joyful.

Coyote lived with his grandmother. Once he went away on a visit. They fed him sour acorns. He liked them and asked, "How do you make sour acorns?" So they told him how to prepare them. "You put a little water on them and press them down and about two days later you look at them." But Coyote would not believe that this was how one did it. He said, "I think you do it some other way." They said, "No, that is the way we do it." But Coyote would not believe them; he kept asking them how sour acorns were really made. After a while they got tired of his always asking about a different way and said to him, "We take the acorns down to the river and put them in a canoe." Then he said, "I knew you did it some other way." "After you load them into a canoe, you tip it over and drown the acorns." "I knew," Coyote said, "you did it some other way!" "And after a while you walk along the river and you find lots of acorns again."

Coyote believed them and ran to his grandmother to tell her about the sour acorns that he liked. The old woman said, "Yes, you damp them a little and press them hard. That is how they get sour." But Coyote said, "No, I know a different way to sour them. You take the acorns to the river and put them in a canoe and drown them." My! That old woman was angry. Coyote took all those acorns down to the river. He was going to put them into a canoe. The old woman hid some of the acorns.

Coyote drowned his acorns. After he had drowned them he went along the river, thinking that he would find them, but he never found them. He went to his grandmother afterwards and told her about it. The old woman was angry. Coyote nearly starved. Whenever he went somewhere the old woman pounded acorns and soaked them. She had acorns ready now, but she would not feed him.

Coyote made a fire in the sweat-house. The old woman thought, "He's in the sweat-house, I'm going to cook those acorns." And she cooked the acorns. Coyote smelled them from the sweat-house. He ran out. The old woman heard someone coming as the acorns were boiling. She threw blankets on top of the basket and sat down on it. She was not going to let him eat. Coyote came in. "What are you cooking, grandma?" "Nothing." "I smell acorns." "Yes, you have lots of acorns!" He stood around. "I hear something boiling under your buttocks." "No," said the old woman, "I pooped." "No," he said, "I hear something boiling." "I pooped," she said again. But Coyote seized her and lifted her up. He found the acorns. He ate them, for he was almost starved.

MRS. HAYDOM, YUROK

Coyote's Journey

The Karuk, like many other California groups, viewed Coyote as a benefactor of the human race. It was Coyote, for example, who dispersed acorns and salmon throughout the world for human use. The other side of his character—his foolishness, lechery, and utter scrounginess—was also present and the subject of many tales, most notably among them a long, loosely put-together series of stories about Coyote's abortive journey to gather shell-money at Klamath Falls.

People who have studied the Karuk language have praised it greatly. "Copious, sonorous, and rich in new combination," noted the nineteenth century ethnographer, Stephen Powers. John P. Harrington felt that, "Karuk literature, when its syllables are analyzed and the exquisite force and balance of the elements appreciated, ranks well with the literature of any language." To express the vitality of the Karuk oral tradition, the linguist, William Bright, has translated the Coyote saga into verse form. The following is excerpted from a much longer retelling.

A man lived there,
    he had many strings of shell-money
        Coyote saw him there,
            he saw him measuring shell-money,
                that person there.
And then Coyote said,
    "Where do you find it,
        that money?"
And then that person said,
    "At Klamath Falls."
And then Coyote
    he went home.
And then he thought,
    I'll make some string!

"I have to go to Klamath Falls!
"I'll go get that money,
        I like it so much."
And he made a lot of it,
        that string.
So he tied it in a bundle,
        that string.
And then he thought,
        "Now I'll start out!"....

Coyote went on upstream,
        there had been a big brushfire.
And he looked around,
        there were lots of roasted grasshoppers.
"I won't eat them."
Finally he went a little ways.
And he thought,
        "I'll just gather a few of them,
                those roasted grasshoppers."
There he was going to gather them.
And then he thought,
        "I wonder why it is,
                I'm not getting full."
And he thought,
        "I think they're coming out my rear,
                while I'm eating them."
And he thought,
        "I'll plug up my ass!"
So he gathered pitch,
        and he plugged up his ass with it.
And he thought, "There,
        now I'll get full.
I've plugged up my ass."
So he ate them—
        but there had been a BIG brushfire.
And he was sticking his butt all around there.
And he thought,
        "I think I'm getting there,
                to Klamath Falls"—
                        he heard it,
                                the thundering,
                                        he heard it like that,
                                                it sort of said HUHUHUHUHU.

143

And he thought,
      "I'm getting there,
            to Klamath Falls"—
                  all he could hear was the HUHUHUHUHU.
It was really his ass,
      there it was burning.
It was really the pitch,
      what he had plugged it with,
            there it was burning.
What could he do?
He slid all around there,
      on the ground, in the sand.
And he was just saying ATUHTUHTUHTUHTUH!"
So finally his ass stopped burning.
And he thought,
      "Now I'll never eat them again,
            those roasted grasshoppers.
That's enough, I won't eat them." ....

And then he looked downriver.
There were young women downriver leaching flour,
      on the shore.
And then he said,
      "I'll turn into some pretty driftwood!"
And then he turned into some pretty driftwood.
And then he floated down from upstream,
      he watched them close by,
            while they were leaching flour.
And he said,
      "I'll float to the shore,
            I'll float to the shore!
I'll keep floating in circles just downslope from them."
And then one girl looked downslope to the river.
And she said, "Look, my dear!
      Oh, look how pretty,
            downslope,
                  that driftwood!"
"All right!"
So they ran downslope,
      they went to look at it,
            where it was floating in circles.
And one said, "Come on, my dear,
      Where's a little stick?
We'll hook it out with that."

144

And so they hooked it out.
And oh! they took a liking to it.
Oh, how pretty it was,
    the driftwood,
        they took a liking to it!
And then one threw it to another,
    they played with it,
        that driftwood,
            the pretty little stick.
And then one girl said, "Ugh,"
    she said, "Ugh! Maybe it's Coyote,
        they said he drowned in the river, upstream."
And then they threw it back in the river,
    that driftwood.
And they took it up,
    their acorn mush,
        what they were leaching.
Sure enough, in a while, they both were pregnant.
There Coyote floated downstream,
    then he floated ashore downriver from them.
And then he traveled on,
    Coyote did,
        he turned back into a person,
            he turned back into himself....

Coyote wandered around there,
    there was a sweat-house standing.
And he looked inside,
    he saw nobody at all.
And Coyote crawled in.
And when he got inside,
    when he looked around,
        all the chairs were made of pure grease,
            their headrests too were of grease,
                and their stepladder too was of grease.
And Coyote was hungry.
And he thought,
    "I'll just taste them,
        those headrests."
And when he took a taste,
    they were very delicious.
Finally he ate them all up,
    he ate up their stepladder too.
Then suddenly he sort of heard something.

And he thought,
     "I'd better hide."
And he lay down there behind the woodpile.
And when the men came back in the sweathouse in the evening,
          as each man crawled in,
                    he fell down. [Because the stepladder was eaten.]
And they said,
     "I'm thinking,
          Coyote's wandering around here.
"That's who did it,
     he ate them all up,
          our headrests."
He just lay there,
     he heard them,
          when they were talking about him.
And then they said,
     "Let's spend the night away from home,
          at Long Pond."
And then he thought,
     Coyote thought,
          "They're talking about my country."
And he jumped out—
     "Nephew, my nephews,
          "I'll go along!"...

So Coyote went with them.
And finally he kept his eyes closed for a long ways.
Suddenly they paddled ashore.
And they said,
     "We've arrived."
And then he jumped up,
     Coyote did.
And then he said,
     "My country!"
And he kicked dirt out into the river.
And he kicked it out from Camp Creek,
     he kicked it out from Kattiphirak,
          he kicked it out from Ullathorne Creek,
               Coyote was so happy,
                    when he returned,
                         back to his country.
That's why he kicked it out.

Kupannakanakana!

146

Young brodiaea plant,
　　you must come up quickly,
　　　　hurry to me!
Spring salmon,
　　shine upriver quickly,
　　　　hurry to me!
My back has become like a mountain ridge,
　　so thin,
　　　　so hungry.

KARUK

Among the Karuk each storyteller had his or her own version of Coyote's Journey, and even the versions were not fixed. On a given night a storyteller might expand certain incidents and delete others, depending upon the mood of the audience or the flow of the story. Yet while there was considerable freedom in telling the story, the closing invocation was ritualistic, and always the same—a prayer for the end of winter and the quick arrival of spring with its edible brodiaea bulbs and salmon.

Throughout California it was generally forbidden to tell Coyote tales during the summer; to do so would bring illness or bad luck to the storyteller and listener alike. Coyote tales were winter tales, reserved for the time when days had become short, leaves had dropped from the trees, rainy days brought gloom and chill, food was limited, and wet trails made travel difficult. At this time people gathered together in cramped quarters to await the arrival of spring; social tensions built up inside houses and assembly lodges. In this atmosphere of constriction nightly fires were lit and people gathered around the storyteller to enter once again the immortal, wild, boundless world of Coyote—fool and benefactor, idiot and god, the one who is killed again and again but keeps rising back to life.

Coyote and His Grandmother

Foremost among Coyote's traits is his insatiable sexuality. He is forever traveling about the world, humping whatever he can find—ludicrously and everlastingly horny. Of questionable taste, he seldom makes love "the right way." Sometimes he fails to figure out the facts of life and is forced into far-fetched experimentation. Sometimes he meets monster-women whose toothed vaginas impel him to take special defensive measures. Sometimes he forces himself upon his daughter or grandmother or indulges his taste for a variety of bizarre (and in some cases impossible) perversities.

Coyote often seems to be a victim of his own urges. In many stories his penis appears as a separate, independent character with a mind and voice of its own. It drives Coyote to distraction with its endless insistence, its mindless lust for difficult adventures. It habitually gets Coyote into trouble and then—how the original audience must have laughed at this typically male predicament!—often betrays or deserts him.

Grandmother told Coyote to go out and hunt fawn. He went away and he saw new Indian potatoes. He stopped and asked his testicles if he should tell his grandmother there were plenty of potatoes and take her back there with the digging stick so he could catch her and rape her. His testicles told him that he could do that, so he went back and told her there were many new potatoes. She took her digging stick and went with him and began digging.

Coyote said, "Dig down deeper." So she dug deeper and deeper until her behind stuck up out of the ground. Coyote then grabbed her and stuck her head down in the sand so she could not see and he copulated with her. Then he ran so she could not see who did it, but she knew it was Coyote.

She called out, "I know you now, you are Coyote." He said, "No, grandmother, I did not do that to you. I'm going to ask my testicles and penis if I did that to you and they will tell you." So he sat down and asked his testicles and they did not answer, so he asked his penis and it said, "Yes, that is what you asked me."

Grandmother said, "I knew that, I know it now. It is a good thing that I'm an old woman or I would be having lots of little coyotes." She quit digging and went home. Coyote was so angry at his penis for telling on him that he was going to mash it on a rock. He sat down and started to hit it with a rock, but the penis drew back. Coyote pulled it out again and tried to hit it again, but it pulled back every time and Coyote never succeeded in mashing it.

BEAR RIVER

Two Coyote Adventures

Many Coyote stories are dirty jokes—good dirty jokes at that—but they are also much more. A sense of awe pervades even the raunchiest tale. Among some people, such as the Ohlone of the San Francisco and Monterey Bay areas, it was Coyote's mating that was responsible for the very creation of the human race. Coyote's horniness, perverse and ridiculous as it might be, is also full of powerful joy and creativity—as in these two Maidu tales recently translated into English with a freshness, clarity, and obvious delight that catches, much of the original vitality.

Coyote went along until he saw a place where a whole lot of women were staying.
When he was still a little way off from there,
he made magic again:
"Let some old kind of pack-basket appear,
and a sifting tray, and also a worn-out cradleboard."
And the things appeared.

He mashed up a *lókbom* root.
When it was all pounded and mashed up fine,
he shaped it into a woman's what-you-may-call-it
and attached it to himself.

148

He made a woman's bark skirt—
an old and frazzled one—
one that wouldn't cover him completely.
Then he bound his pisser into the cradleboard
and shoved it into the pack-basket.
He picked up the basket, took a staff,
and, walking all bent over the way very old people do,
he went down among the women.
Just at dusk, he came to where they were.

"Well, now," said one of the women,
"I think I see a very old woman coming along."
She took a careful look at the child.
"That doesn't look much like a child," she said.

"I'm so weak that when I took him out of the cradle
I dropped him and he hit the ground with a bump.
That's why he's so swollen up that he doesn't look like himself," said Coyote.
"It makes me feel so sad when he calls for his father."

"Ylbyl, ylbyl, ylbyl," said the child.

"That's the way he calls," said Coyote,
"and it makes me feel so sad!"
Coyote was talking like a woman.
"I'm so pitiful, sad and weak that I let him hit with a bump."

Now, though his what-you-may-call-it was covered by the bark apron,
the women could see through the raggedy holes.
They all took a peek.

"How un-childlike that child looks!"
said two of the women who were in the back.
"No, it is certainly a child," said another one.
"She says it got a bump on the head.
That's why it looks so swollen."

"That thing there has the head of a pisser!" said the two women.
"That's why bumping swells it up like that!"

Just those two were wary.
All the others believed Coyote.
"Look at her," they said.
"She looks just like an old woman.
Don't you see? Her thing-a-ma-jig looks just like it should!"

Illustration by Harry Fonseca.

"Maybe so," the two women said.
They all had supper.

After darkness fell, the forest was frightening.
The women told Coyote:
"You'd better sleep here, between us.
You might get cold."
So they put him in between a couple of them
and everyone went to sleep close by—
everyone but the two women who were wary.

Then, in the dark, Coyote took out his magic sleeping powder.
He sprinkled it all around, over the women,
casting them into deeper slumber.
Then he threw off his disguise and thrust into the women—
all but the two suspicious ones.
He kept at it through the night;
then, just before dawn, he sneaked away.

What noisy, crying litters of children the women had next morning!

But Coyote got away.
He went down along the river for a while....

Now he had just set out again
when he came to the house where Cottontail lived.
And Cottontail told him:

"There are some women who have dances,
but I don't go to watch them."

"Well, then," said Coyote, "let's the two of us go dance."

"All right. We'll go when it gets dark," said Cottontail.

After nightfall, the dancing and singing sounded wonderful.
So the two of them went.

When they had gone on a little way, Coyote said:
"Stop right where you are! I'll tell you what.
You'd better wait here."

"All right," said Cottontail.

"And keep this here with you," said Coyote, handing him his cock.
"Women are very wary of me when I'm wearing it.
If these women go for me, I'll whistle.
When you hear me, come and bring it with you."

So, Cottontail stayed back
while Coyote went on to where the women were dancing and hollering.
They sounded fine.
As he got there,
he could see that there were some good-looking women dancing.
Two really beautiful ones took that Coyote fellow
and led him away.
He went along with them,
and they all wandered off, holding hands.

When they got to where Coyote had left Cottontail,
they all sat down.

Coyote whistled
The place was deserted.
He whistled again.

"What's the matter with you?" asked one of the women.

"I'm just kidding around," said Coyote.
"I must say, it makes me feel fine,
going around with two women like you.
It makes me feel wonderful!"

The women laughed,
threw their legs across him and hugged and kissed him.
It was a sight to behold!

"Wooeeee," said Coyote.
"Wait right here, you two!"

He ran up to where he'd left Cottontail,
and, when he got there, he whistled.
He didn't hear anything.
He was really angry.
He searched all around but he saw no sign of Cottontail,
so he went back to where he had left the women.

"What are you looking for?" they asked.

"Oh, nothing," said Coyote.
"I'm just fooling around."

Then they all lay down,
and the two women put him in the middle,
hugging him and tickling him.

He jumped up again and scouted around,
going over the same old ground,
but he still saw no one.
He was very, very angry.

Now, when Coyote had left Cottontail to go to the dance,
a couple of Star Women came and led Cottontail away.
By and by, Cottontail entered the woman who was a little older.
He made her gasp until she cried out.

The younger woman said:
"How can a fellow like that make you almost cry out?
No little pipsqueak could do that to me!"
So he entered *her* and made *her* cry out.
She was gasping so hard it sounded really frightening.

Meanwhile,
Coyote bedded down with the other women until daybreak.
Then he left them and went to Cottontail's house.
Cottontail was there.
Coyote rushed up and glared at him in a rage.

"I just feel like I want to kill you," he said.
"What did you do with that thing I left with you?"
He was furious.

"Two women came and led me away by the hand," said Cottontail.

"And then what?" demanded Coyote.

"I just went ahead and screwed them with your thing," said Cottontail.

"Oho!" said Coyote.
"I really made those two women cry," said Cottontail.

"Mm *hmm*!" said Coyote.
"That thing *will* make little women cry!"

He felt very much as if *he'd* been screwing.
He quickly got over being angry.
When Cottontail handed it back to him,
he washed it in the creek and put it away.
"This thing is a good one," he said.
"It's more than enough, even for big women."

He didn't dance that day,
but he stayed the night
and, the next morning, feeling good,
he set off down the trail.

HANC'IBYJIM (TOM YOUNG), MAIDU/ATSUGEWI

Coyote and Bullfish

Coyote, at his most absurd, is driven by obsessions, by single-minded compulsions, by relentlessly insistent urges. More than a passive victim of misfortune, he is a talented, never-tiring creator of his own downfall.

Coyote was going up the river to visit someone. He was very well dressed. He had his quiver, bow and arrows, moccasins, and beads. He looked very fine. It was a hot summer day. He came to a nice stretch of sand. He saw Bullfish sunning himself. He was black as charcoal. Coyote said, "What are you doing there?"

Bullfish didn't say a word. Coyote talked and talked but Bullfish never answered. At last Coyote said, "You are pretty small. You are too little to do anything. I'll bet you can't swallow my toe," and at the same time he thrust his toe in front of Bullfish's mouth. Bullfish just turned his head away.

Then Coyote said, "I'll give you my bow and arrows if you bite me." He teased Bullfish that way for a long time. Finally Bullfish nipped Coyote's toe. Coyote did not pay any attention to him; he only continued to taunt him. Soon Bullfish had swallowed Coyote's leg; Coyote became frightened and begged for mercy, but Bullfish ignored him and kept on swallowing him. Coyote offered him all his fine things, but Bullfish just swallowed him entirely and swam off under a rock in the riffle.

The people missed Coyote. They hunted for him and found his valuables on the sand and saw the track where he had been dragged in. So they asked a doctor to find out where he was. The doctor went into a trance and about in the middle of the night said that he was under the water, that Bullfish had swallowed him, but that he was not yet dead.

Then Bullfish made the water muddy so the people could not find him. Otter, Raccoon, everyone hunted for Coyote but they could not find him. At last Mud-Spear [a water bird] climbed a tree and looked. He said, "I see a tail under a rock in the riffle. I am going to try to spear him." So he took a spear pole, aimed carefully, and speared Bullfish right above the tail. The people pulled him out and cut open his abdomen. Coyote jumped out and said, "Nephew, I have been sleeping."

JO BENDER, WINTU

Coyote and Trap

Ordinary people struggle to avoid trouble, but Coyote works hard and imaginatively to bring trouble upon himself—and often upon the world. It was thought throughout much of California, for example, that the world was created without death, until Coyote insisted that death would be a good idea: after all, it would generate colorful and dramatic mourning ceremonies. Coyote was also often responsible for hunger, difficult childbirth, and other evils of the world. In the following tale Coyote's insistence is strictly comical and self-defeating, but it had deeper overtones for the original audience. For within Coyote's mindless and perverse intransigence lay the explanation for much of the cruelty of what might otherwise have been a more beneficent world.

Coyote had a brother-in-law who was Trap. One day Coyote was near Trap. He began to feel around with his foot to find him. He felt all around, and said, "I wonder where that fellow is?" He felt around some more. All at once he stepped right into Trap. Trap caught him and he could not get loose.

Coyote began to plead. He said, "Let me go, Trap. I will not come around any more to bother you." Trap would not let him go. Coyote begged, "Brother-in-law, won't you let me go? I'll stay away from you after this." "No," said Trap, "I am not supposed to do that. I'll get into trouble." Coyote went on begging, and finally Trap said, "Well, I'll let you go just this once. But you must not come back again. If you do come back, I shall not be able to let you go." Coyote said, "No, I promise I won't come around any more. I will go far off and stay there."

Trap let Coyote go. After he had gone off a little way, he began to call Trap all kinds of names. He called him all the mean things he could think of. Trap said, "Brother-in-law, I want you to come around and see me again sometime." Coyote said, "No, I won't come back again. I am going far off now and I won't be back to see you any more." He called Trap more bad names and went away.

As Coyote went along, he worried. Trap had told him to come back and see him, and Coyote could not get that out of his mind. He said, "That Trap asked me to come back and see him. I must find some way to forget about him, and then I shall be all right. I will go to sleep and forget all about it. When I wake up in the morning I shall be all right."

Coyote lay down to sleep. He had a long sleep. But in the morning when he woke up, the first thing he thought was, "My brother-in-law asked me to come back sometime. He said I must come back to see him. I must not do that. I must find some way to forget about it." Coyote went along trying to forget about Trap, but this thing was on his mind. He said, "I will kill myself and then I shall forget about it. I will go and drown myself."

Coyote ran to a big lake and jumped into it. He swam far out and drowned himself. But after a long time, he came back to life and swam to shore. The thing was still on his mind. "My brother-in-law, Trap, said I must come back to see him sometime," thought Coyote. "I'll have to forget about that. I shall have to kill myself." Coyote went along trying to think of some way to forget about Trap. "I'll run myself to death," he said.

He started out to run with all his might. He ran as fast as he could over hills and mountains until he was all out of breath and fell down exhausted. When Coyote came to life again, he thought, "My brother-in-law wants me to come back to see him. I guess I'll have to go back and pay him a visit."

Coyote went back to where Trap was. When he got near the place, he said, "Where are you, Trap? You said I must come back to see you sometime. I did not intend to be mean to you. I have come back to see you. Where are you, brother-in-law?" He could not see Trap, and he felt around for him with his foot. Pretty soon he stepped right into Trap. Trap caught him and held him fast.

TOM STONE, OWENS VALLEY PAIUTE

Among the Paiute there was no correct way of telling a Coyote tale. Every storyteller had a unique and personal rendition. If challenged with the fact that others had different versions, the storyteller would reply simply: "Some people tell it differently." Paiute Coyote tales, it seems, were as mercurial yet persistent as was the character of Coyote himself.

Coyote Steals Fire

Along with his sheer ridiculousness, Coyote was also—at least for many groups—the benefactor of the human race, using his trickery for the good of people.

A t first there was no fire. Turtle had all the fire in the entire world. He sat on top of it and covered it all up. Turtle lived far up in the east in the mountains. Coyote went there to search for fire. When he neared Turtle's house, he lay down like a piece of wood. The people who lived with Turtle came by and saw him. They picked Coyote up, took him home, and put him in the fire. Coyote pried his way underneath Turtle. Turtle said, "Stop pushing me," but Coyote squirmed onward. He caught on fire. Then he ran downhill westward into this country, where it was icy cold. He caught a quail and with its fat he made the fire blaze up. Now for the first time the people began to get warm. The Mono lived far back in the hills; the Chukchansi Yokuts were in the middle; the Pohonichi Miwoks were the ones who received the fire. That is why the Mono cannot speak well; it is too cold where they live.

MIWOK

Coyote and Falcon Create People

For many groups Coyote was the creator or co-creator of the world.

F alcon proposed that Coyote create human beings. Coyote replied that it would mean a great deal of work, but Falcon insisted that it be done. Coyote finally told Falcon how they must proceed.

Accordingly Coyote went out and threw himself upon the ground, simulating a dead body. Presently a large flock of crows and buzzards gathered about and commenced to peck at Coyote's rump. He kept perfectly still until the birds had eaten a large hole in one side and were within. He then caused the hole to close very suddenly and caught a considerable number of them. He took them home and Falcon plucked them. "Now," said Coyote, "we will go out in the country and put these feathers in every direction." On each hill they placed one buzzard and one crow feather. The crow feathers became the common people and the buzzard feathers, the chiefs. As Coyote deposited the feathers he named each place, and on the following day there were people living in all these localities.

Coyote then said to Falcon, "Now that there is a new people, we shall have to become animals. I shall be coyote; no one will miss me. You shall be falcon, and everyone shall know you as chief." Straightway all of the then-existing animal people were transmuted and became birds and mammals as Coyote directed.

MIWOK

In many non-Indian religions, the Creator is all-knowing, all-powerful, in a word, perfect; evil and folly are attributes of a separate being. Coyote, however, rises above—or perhaps has not yet reached—dichotomy. Within this ancient figure the majesty and messiness of the world, the good and the evil, the wise and the foolish, the joyful and the tragic are combined in a complex and intensely creative whole. Captured within these tales, passed down from one generation to the next for thousands upon thousands of years, is the figure of Coyote the all-inclusive, Coyote the incomprehensible, Coyote the ineffable, Coyote the divine, Coyote the holy fool.

X: The Coming of the Whites

My grandpa, before white people came, had a dream.
He was so old he was all doubled up.
Knees to chin, and eyes like indigo.
Grown son carry him in great basket on his back, every place.
My grandpa say: "White Rabbit"—he mean white people—
"gonta devour our grass, our seed, our living.
We won't have nothing more, this world."

Lucy Young, Lassik/Wintun

The Portolá expedition, 1769, was the first European land expedition into California. While the Spaniards were making diary entries about the native population and the landscape, the Indians of the area were noting the arrival of the newcomers. Here men on horseback appear at a Chumash rock art site. *Photo courtesy of Santa Barbara Museum of Natural History.*

The Death of Father Quintana

The year was 1769. Columbus's first voyage nearly three hundred years before was already ancient history. Mexico had been under Spanish rule for well over two centuries. Boston, New York, and Philadelphia were centers of commerce and culture. In Scotland James Watt was working on the steam engine. The modern age was dawning. Yet as far as Europeans were concerned, California was still *terra incognita*. Only a handful of ship captains had touched upon its coast, the interior had never been explored or even penetrated, and prominent landmarks such as San Francisco Bay, the Sacramento River, Mount Shasta, and Yosemite Valley were unknown to the world at large.

In 1769 a small party of Spaniards arrived in present-day San Diego. In the next half century twenty-one missions—and with them *presidios* (forts), *pueblos* (towns), and *ranchos*—spread along the coast and throughout the coastal valleys as far north as Sonoma County. Over 50,000 Indians were drawn into these missions, baptized as Catholics and taught—to a greater or lesser degree—European ways. By 1836 the missions were "secularized" and mostly abandoned. Thus Anglo settlers who would arrive decades later found not working missions, but rather picturesque ruins, and from those ruins they would invent a romantic and idealized image of mission life—an image in which devout Franciscan fathers strode peacefully through ample mission gardens, smiling lovingly upon their innocent, industrious, and appreciative Indian flock.

The few outsiders—often European sea-captains—who actually witnessed mission life, however, tended to paint another picture. LaPérouse, who visited Mission Carmel in 1786, compared it emphatically to the slave plantations of the Caribbean. Louis Choris said of the Indians at Mission Dolores in San Francisco: "I have never seen one laugh, I have never seen one look one in the face. They look as though they are interested in nothing." Another early visitor, Otto von Kotzebue, likewise noted of the Indians that, "a deep melancholy always clouds their faces, and their eyes are constantly fixed upon the ground."

The following account, taken in 1877 from a man who had been born at Mission Santa Cruz, captures something of the fear-soaked, perverse, nightmarish quality that pervaded this and, one suspects, other missions.

160

The following story which I shall convey was told to me by my dear father in 1818. He was a neophyte of the Mission of Santa Cruz. He was one of the original founders of that mission. He was an Indian from the rancheria of *Asar* on the *Jarro* coast, up beyond Santa Cruz. He was one of the first neophytes baptized at the founding, being about 20 years of age. He was called Venancio Asar, and was the gardener of the Mission of Santa Cruz.

My father was a witness to the happenings which follow. He was one of the conspirators who planned to kill Father Quintana. When the conspirators were planning to kill Father Quintana, they gathered in the house of Julian the gardener (the one who made the pretense of being ill). The man who worked inside the plaza of the mission, named Donato, was punished by Father Quintana with a whip with wire. With each blow it cut his buttocks. Then the same man, Donato, wanted vengeance. He was the one who organized a gathering of 14 men, among them were the cook and the pages serving the Father. The cook was named Antonio, the eldest page named Lino, the others named Vicente and Miguel Antonio. All of them gathered in the house of Julian to plan how they could avoid the cruel punishments of Father Quintana. One man present, Lino, who was more capable and wiser than the others, said, "The first thing we should do today is to see that the Padre no longer punishes the people in that manner. We aren't animals. He [Quintana] says in his sermons that God does not command these [punishments]—but only examples and doctrine. Tell me now, what shall we do with the Padre? We cannot chase him away, nor accuse him before the judge, because we do not know who commands him to do with us as he does." To this Andrés, father of Lino the page, answered, "Let's kill the Padre without anyone being aware, not the servants, nor anyone, except us that are here present." (This Lino was pure-blooded Indian, but as white as a Spaniard and man of natural abilities.) And then Julian the gardener said, "What shall we do in order to kill him?" His wife responded, "You, who are always getting sick—only this way can it be possible—think if it is good this way." Lino approved the plan and asked that all present also approve it. "In that case, we shall do it tomorrow night." That was Saturday. It should be noted that the Padre wished all the people to gather in the plaza on the following Sunday in order to test the whip that he had made with pieces of wire to see if it was to his liking.

All of the conspirators present at the meeting concurred that it should be done as Lino had recommended.

On the evening of Saturday at about six o'clock [October 12] of 1812, they went to tell the Padre that the gardener was dying. The Indians were already posted between two trees on both sides so that they could grab Father when he passed. The Padre arrived at the house of Julian, who pretended to be in agony. The Padre helped him, thinking that he was really sick and about to die. When the Padre was returning to his house, he passed close to where the Indians were posted. They didn't have the courage to grab him and they allowed him to pass. The moribund gardener was behind him,

161

but the Padre arrived at his house. Within an hour the wife of Julian arrived [again] to tell him [the Father] that her husband was dying. With this news the Padre returned to the orchard, the woman following behind crying and lamenting. He saw that the sick man was dying. The Padre took the man's hand in order to take his pulse. He felt the pulse and could find nothing amiss. The pulse showed there was nothing wrong with Julian. Not knowing what it could be, the Padre returned to pray for him. It was night when the Padre left. Julian arose and washed away the sacraments [oil] that he [the Padre] had administered, and he followed behind to join the others and see what his companions had done. Upon arriving at the place where they were stationed, Lino lifted his head and looked in all directions to see if they were coming out to grab the Father. The Father passed and they didn't take him. The Father arrived at his house.

Later, when the Father was at his table dining, the conspirators had already gathered at the house of the alleged sick man to ascertain why they hadn't seized Father Quintana. Julian complained that the Padre had placed herbs on his ears, and because of them, now he was really going to die. Then the wife of Julian said, "Yes, you all did not carry through with your promised plans; I am going to accuse you all, and I will not go back to the house." They all answered her, "All right, now, in this trip go and speak to the Father." The woman again left to fetch Father Quintana, who was at supper. He got up immediately and went where he found the supposedly sick man. This time he took with him three pages, two who walked ahead lighting his way with lanterns and behind him followed his Mayordomo Lino. The other two were Vicente and Miguel Antonio. The Father arrived at the gardener's house and found him unconscious. He couldn't speak. The Father prayed the last orations without administering the oils, and said to the wife, "Now your husband is prepared to live or die. Don't come to look for me again." Then the Father left with his pages to return to his house. Julian followed him. Arriving at the place where the two trees were (since the Father was not paying attention to his surroundings, but only in the path in front of him), Lino grabbed him from behind saying these words, "Stop here, Father, you must speak for a moment." When the other two pages who carried the lanterns turned around and saw the other men come out to attack the Father, they fled with their lanterns. The Father said to Lino, "Oh, my Son, what are you going to do to me?" Lino anwered, "Your assassins will tell you."

"What have I done to you children, for which you would kill me?"

"Because you have made a *cuarta de hierro* [a horse whip tipped with iron]...," Andrés answered him. The the Father retorted, "Oh, children, leave me, so that I can go from here now, at this moment." Andrés asked him why he had made this *cuarta de hierro*. Quintana said that it was only for transgressors. Then someone shouted, "Well, you are in the hands of those evil ones, make your peace with God." Many of those present (seeing the Father in his affliction) cried and pitied his fate, but could do nothing to help him because they were themselves compromised. He pleaded much, promising to leave the mission immediately if they would only let him.

"Now you won't be going to any part of the earth from here, Father, you are going to heaven." This was the last plea of the Father. Some of them, not having been able to lay hands on Father, reprimanded the others because they talked too much, demanding that they kill him immediately. They then covered the Father's mouth with his own cape to strangle him.

LORENZO ASISARA, OHLONE

The Arrival of Whites

For the Native Californians, the arrival of the Spaniards meant disruption, virtual enslavement, diseases, and death. Diseases such as smallpox, measles, and syphilis spread through the mission population and beyond, sweeping even those parts of California that remained unexplored by the Spaniards. By 1845 the Indian population in the state had fallen from an estimated 310,000 people to 150,000.

The years between 1845 and 1855 brought a flood of Anglos who penetrated into even the most remote valleys and mountains in search of gold, timber, and land. The confrontation between Anglos and Indians was ugly and brutal, and in a mere ten years the Indian population plummeted from 150,000 to 50,000, the result of disease, starvation, and outright murder. Throughout the state native people were engulfed in pain, suffering, and annihilation—in an unspeakable, almost inconceivable tragedy.

We had a man at Thomas Creek that had power given to him. He was young. He sang all the time. He drank water and ate once a month. He ate a little of everything, then took one swallow of water and smoked. He stayed in the sweat-house all the time.

Now our captain [chief] used to get out early every morning on top of the sweat-house and, calling everybody by name, would tell them what to do.

This fortuneteller from Thomas Creek would tell the people just how much game they would get and whether any mishaps would fall. He lived across from our present reservation at Paskenta. One day he said, "There are some people from across the ocean who are going to come to this country." He looked for them for three years. "They have some kind of boat [tco'ltci] with which they can cross, and they will make it. They are on the way." Finally he said that they were on the land and that they were coming now. He said that they had fire at night and lots to eat. "They cook the same as we do; they smoke after meals, and they have a language of their own. They talk, laugh, and sing, just as we do. Besides, they have five fingers and toes; they are built like we are, only they are light." He said their blood was awfully light.

"They have a four-legged animal which some are riding and some are packing. They haven't any wives, any of them. They all are single. They are bringing some kind of sickness."

163

So everybody was notified. The night watch and day watch were kept. He said that they had something long which shoots little round things a long distance. They have something short that shoots just the same.

Finally the whites came in at Orland; many of them. When they came in they started shooting. There were thousands of Indians in the hills who went to fighting the whites. The Indians went after them but they couldn't do anything to them. Finally they got to Newville, and the man who was telling these fortunes said the whites were going to be there. The Indians were ready for them. The whites came by Oakes' place and down the flat at one o'clock in the morning. They killed the first Indian that showed himself. The captain told the others to stay in the house and get their bows and arrows ready.

The captain [chief] yelled to the whites that he was ready inside the house. He told his men, "When you get ready, run out and crowd into it." The captain sent them to fight at close range. He said, "We are dead anyway." The whites couldn't load their muzzleloaders, so they used revolvers. The captain told his men to spear them. They fought from morning till afternoon. The Indians had come all the way from Colusa. They killed all those whites. The Indians were afraid of gray horses. They killed the horses. They examined everything. They divided everything up. One old man from south of the Tapscott place took away a lot of their money. His children used to take the money and play with it. Finally he took it up the canyon and hid it. The whites are looking for that money today but can't find it.

Another group of whites came to Mountain House [*lopom*]. They killed many of the Indians. White people hit women and children in the head. One Indian shouted from a rock when the white men started back. The whites came up there, and that Indian went into the rock cave, and they shot one white man from there. But the whites threw fire into the cave and killed all the Indians in there.

They had been hiding in the hills. Indians couldn't get to the salt. They got very weak—they say salt keeps a person fit. There was no rain for three years, and fighting going on every day. No clover, no acorn, juniper berries, or peppergrass. Nothing for three years. Very little rain.

Finally the Indians got smallpox, and the Indian doctor couldn't cure them. They died by the thousands. Gonorrhea came amongst the Indians. That killed a lot of them. My grandfather said that if he had fought he would have been killed too. But he went up to Yolla Bolly Mountain with about six hundred others and stayed three years. On the third winter there was a heavy snowstorm. The snow was over his head. He said women can stand more starvation than men. They singed the hair off a deerhide shoulder strap and ate it.

Men died every day from starvation. That was in Camp of Dark Canyon in the winter. Women would find a little bunch of grass and eat it and would bring a handful back for their husbands. The women would have to chew it for the men. The man was too weak to swallow it. She would take a mouthful of water and pour it into his mouth. That was the way they saved a lot of them.

One man and his brother were lying among the rocks. They wanted to steal something. They saw six riders with forty head of cattle. The Indians lay there and watched them. The riders left after they corralled the cattle. The two Indians got a long willow sprout and made a whip. They tore the fence down and drove the cattle up the creek. They killed one of the steers. First they shot it with an arrow and then hit it in the head with a rock. Then they cut its throat. They skinned it and divided the meat among the people. They had a big feast and they had to make soup for the weak people. They heated water in a basket. Then they put meat in the basket. That saved the people.

After that the whites began to gather up the Indians. They made the Nome Lackee Reservation in Tehama County. They take a tame Indian along when they bring Indians together on a reservation. They worked the Indians on the reservation. Old Martin was given a saddle mule and clothes. He wouldn't wear anything but the shirt—the overalls hurt his legs. He was a kind of foreman. Every Saturday they killed four or five beef and divided it among the Indians. They ground wheat and made biscuits. The women shocked hay. They had to examine all the men and women for disease.

Garland on the present Oakes' place wouldn't let them take the Indians off of his land, and that's what saved them. When they took the Indians to Covelo [in Round Valley, on the Nome Cult Reserve] they drove them like stock. Indians had to carry their own food. Some of the old people began to give out when they got to the hills. They shot the old people who couldn't make the trip. They would shoot children who were getting tired. Finally they got the Indians to Covelo. They killed all who tried to get away and wouldn't return to Covelo.

ANDREW FREEMAN, NOMLAKI

The Massacre at Needle Rock

The Sinkyone were one of several Athapaskan-speaking peoples who inhabited southern Humboldt County and the extreme northwestern part of Mendocino County. Some fifty Sinkyone villages were spread along the lower course of the Eel River, and nearly twenty others dotted the coastal area near present-day Shelter Cove. Before goldrush days the Sinkyone numbered over 4,000 people. By the end of the 1860s they were almost totally wiped out.

Disease contributed to the annihilation. So did starvation, as native people were displaced from their villages, salmon creeks were choked with logging and mining debris, and as fences and property "rights" of white settlers kept native people from hunting, fishing, and gathering in their accustomed places. But a large part of the destruction of the Sinkyone was the result of murder. Supported by a community fearful of the "Indian menace" and greedy for Indian land, legitimized by newspapers that extolled the "manifest destiny" of the white race, groups of men throughout northwestern California formed "volunteer armies" that swooped down upon Indian villages, killing men, women, and children indiscriminately. After such raids the men—often a ragtag group of unemployed miners—would present expense vouchers to the state and federal governments for actions against "hostile Indians." In 1851 and 1852 California authorized over one million dollars for such excursions. It was nothing short of subsidized murder.

My grandfather and all of my family—my mother, my father, and me—were around the house and not hurting anyone. Soon, about ten o'clock in the morning, some white men came. They killed my grandfather and my mother and my father. I saw them do it. I was a big girl at that time. Then they killed my baby sister and cut her heart out and threw it in the brush where I ran and hid. My little sister was a baby, just crawling around. I didn't know what to do. I was so scared that I guess I just hid there a long time with my little sister's heart in my hands. I felt so bad and I was so scared that I just couldn't do anything else. Then I ran into the woods and hid there for a long time. I lived there a long time with a few other people who had got away. We lived on berries and roots and we didn't dare build a fire because the white men might come back after us. So we ate anything we could get. We didn't have clothes after a while, and we had to sleep under logs and in hollow trees because we didn't have anything to cover ourselves with, and it was cold then—in the spring. After a long time, maybe two, three months, I don't know just how long, but sometime in the summer, my brother found me and took me to some white folks who kept me until I was grown and married.

SALLY BELL, SINKYONE

The Stone and Kelsey Massacre

Under Spanish and Mexican rule the Indians had a place—a miserable place to be sure, but at least there was some accomodation for them in the social and political structure. They were neophytes at the missions, domestics and laborers in the towns, *vaqueros* at the ranches. Spanish soldiers often married Indian women, and their offspring were socially accepted. Indians who adopted Catholic ways might (in theory and sometimes in practice) receive land to farm.

Under the Anglos, however, Indians had no place in the social order, and indeed they were scarcely considered human. Atrocities against the Native Californians were not just the result of a few demented individuals; atrocities were built into the social structure, even written into the laws. Under early California code, for example, an Indian could not bear witness against a white in court; thus whites who entered Indian villages and committed rape, mayhem, and murder could not be prosecuted on the witness of Indians alone. Also, on the statement of any white an Indian could be declared a vagrant and bound over to a white landowner to work for subsistence—in other words, to be a slave. Other laws gave whites custody over Indian minors, leading to an active kidnapping industry wherein youngsters—especially young girls—were stolen from their villages and sold to white farmers and ranchers. All this happened in the 1850s when, it is helpful to remember, slavery was a legal and reputable institution in much of America.

The following narrative describes conditions on a ranch at Clear Lake where Indians were held as virtual slaves by two white men, Andy Kelsey (after whom Kelseyville has been named) and his partner, Stone. In 1849, pushed to desperation by the sadistic treatment they were subjected to, a small group of men rose up and killed both ranchers. A military expedition was sent by the federal government to avenge the killings. According to the official tally sixty Indian people were slaughtered on the island in Clear Lake, another seventy-five were killed along the Russian River.

The narrator, William Ralganal Benson, was born in 1862 and learned about these events directly from those who took part. Having spoken only a Pomo language as a youth and never having attended school, Benson nevertheless taught himself to read and write English. His manuscript is presented here in its entirety—unedited and with his spelling and punctuation preserved.

The Facts Of Stone and Kelsey Massacre. in Lake County California. As it was stated to me by the five indians who went to stone and kelseys house purpose to kill the two white men. after debateing all night. Shuk and Xasis. these two men were the instigators of the massacre. it was not because Shuk and Xasis had any Ill feeling torge the two white men. there were two indian villages, one on west side and one on the east side. the indians in both of these camps were starveing. stone or kelsey would not let them go out hunting or fishing. Shuk and Xasis was stone and kelsey headriders looking out for stock. cattle horses and hogs. the horses and cattle were all along the lake on the west side and some in bachelors valley. also in upper lake. so it took 18 indian herdsman to look after the stock in these places. Shuk and Xasis was foremans for the herds. and only those herders got anything to eat. each one of these herders got 4 cups of wheat for a days work. this cup would hold about one and ahalf pint of water. the wheat was boiled before it was given to the herders. and the herders shire with thir famlys. the herders who had large famlys were also starveing. about 20 old people died during the winter from starvetion. from severe whipping 4 died. a nephew of an indian lady who were liveing with stone was shoot to deth by stone. the mother of this yong man was sick and starveing. this sick woman told her son to go over to stones wife or the sick womans sister. tell your aunt that iam starveing and sick tell her that i would like to have a handfull of wheat. the yong man lost no time going to stones house. the young man told the aunt what his mother said. the lady then gave the young man 5 cups of wheat and tied it up in her apron and the young man started for the camp. stone came about that time and called the young man back. the young man stoped stone who was horse back. rode up to the young man took the wheat from him and then shoot him. the young man died two days after. such as whipping and tieing thier hands togather with rope. the rope then thrown over a limb of a tree and then drawn up untell the indians toes barly touchs the ground and let them hang there for hours. this was common punishment. when a father or mother of young girl. was asked to bring the girl to his house. by stone or kelsey. if this order was not obeyed. he or her would be whipped or hung by the hands. such punishment occurred two or three times a week. and many of the old men and women died from fear and starvetion.

167

these two white men had the indians to build a high fence around thir villages. and the head riders were to see that no indian went out side of this fence after dark. if any one was caught out side of this fence after dark was taken to stones and kelseys house and there was tied both hands and feet and placed in a room and kept there all night. the next day was taken to a tree and was tied down. then the strongs man was chosen to whippe the prisoner. the village on the west side was the Qu-Lah-Na-Poh tribes the village on the east side. Xa-Bah-Na-Poh. tribes.

the starvetion of the indians was the cause of the massacre of stone and kelsey. the indians who was starving hired a man by the name of Shuk and a nother man by the name of Xasis. to kill a beef for them. Shuk and Xasis agreed to go out and kill a beef for them. the two men then plan to go out that nigth and kill a beef for them. thir plan then was to take the best horsses in the barn. stones horse which was the best lasso horse. so between the two men. they agreed to take both stones and kelseys horses. so the two men went to stone and kelseys house to see if they had went to bed. it was raining a little. moonligth now and then they found stone and kelsey had went to bed so they went to the barn and took stone and kelseys horses and saddles. Shuk wanted to do the job in the day time but Xasis said stone or kelsey would sure find them and would kill the both of them. Shuk said then somebody is going to get killed on this job. so any how they went out west they knew where a larg band was feeding they soon rounded the band up and Shuk was to make the first lasso Xasis was good on lassing the foot of anox so he was to do the foot lassing. Shuk said to Xasis get redy i see large one hear hurry and come on. Shuk got a chance and threwed the rope on the large ox Xasis came as quick as he could the band began to stampede. the ox also started with the band. the ground was wet and slippery and raining. and before Xasis could get his rope on. Shuks horse fell to the ground. the horse and the ox got away. Xasis tried to lass the horse but could not get near it to throw the rope on. the horse soon found the other horses and it was then much harder to get the horse. so the chase was given up. the two went back to the camp and reported to the peopel who hired them. told them the bad luck they had. Xasis then took the horse he had back to the barn which was kelseys horse. all the men who hired Shuk and Xasis was gathered in Xasiss house. here they debated all night. Shuk and Xasis wanted to kill stone and kelsey. they said stone and kelsey would kill them as soon as they would find out that the horses was taken with out them known; one man got up and suggested that the tribe give stone and kelsey forty sticks of beades which means 16000 beads or 100 dollars. no one agreed. another man suggested that he or Shuk. tell stoneor kelsey that the horse was stolen. no one agreed. and another man suggested that the other horse should be turned out and tell stone and kelsey both horses were stlen. no one agreed. every thing looks bad for Shuk and Xasis. no one agreed with Shuk and Xasis to kill the two white men. at daylight one man agreed to go with Shuk and Xasis. his indian name. Ba-Tus. was known by the whites as Busi. and alittle while later Kra-nas agreed. and as the four men started out another man joind the Shuk and Xasis band: Ma-Laxa-Qe-Tu. while this Debateing was going on the hired or servants boys and girls of stones and kelseys were told by Shuk and Xasis to carrie out allthe guns. bows and arrows. knives and every thing like weapon was taken out of the house by these girls and boys so the two white men was helpless in defense. so Shuk and Xasis knew the white man, did not have any thing to defen themselfs with and they were sure of their victims.

so the five men went to the house where stone and kelsey were liveing. at daylight were to the place where stone always built a fire under a large pot in which he boiled wheat for the indian herders. about 16 of them. these five men waited around this pot untell stone came out to build the fire. Stone came out with pot full of fire which was taken from the fireplace. and said to the indians. whats the matter boys you came Early this morning. some thing rong; the indians said. O nothing me hungry thats all. Qka-Nas: or cayote Jim as he was known by the whites: Qka-Nas said to the men. I thought you men came to kill this man; give me these arrows and bow. He jerk the bow and the arrows away from Shuk and drew it and as he did Stone rose quickly and turned to Qka-Nas and said what are you trying to do Jim, and as Stone said it. the indian cut loose. the arrow struck the victim pith of the stomach. the victim mediately pull the arrow out and ran for the house. fighting his way. he broke one mans arm with the pot he had. and succeeded in getting in the house and locked the door after him. little later Kelsey came and opened the door and noticed the blood on the doorstep. the indians advanced. Kelsey seen that the indians ment business. he said to them. no matar kelsey. kelsey bueno hombre para vosotros. the indians charged and two of the indians caught kelsey and the fight began. in this fight kelsey was stabed twice in the back. kelsey managed to brake loose. he ran for the creek and the indians after him. a man by the name of Xa-sis or blind Jose as he was known by the whites. who was in pursuit. shot kelsey in the back. kelsey manage to pull the arrow out jest as he got to the creek and jumped in the water and dove under and came out on the other side of the creek. where several indians were waiting. there was one man kelsey knew well. he thought who would save him. this man was Joe sefeis. indian name. Ju-Luh. he beged Joe to save him. Joe he could not save him from being killed. Joe said to kelsey. its too late kelsey; if I attempt to save you. I allso will be killed. I can not save you kelsey; kelsey was geting weak from loss of blood. Big Jim and Joe had kelsey by the arms. Big Jim said to his wife. this is a man who killed our son. take this spear. now you have the chance to take revenge. Big Jim's wife took the spear and stabed the white man in the hart. this womans name was Da-Pi-Tauo. the body was left laying there for the cayotes.

this hapend on the east side of the creek, while this was going on. Xasis and Qra-Nas was trailing the blood up stairs and for a hour allmost. Qra-

169

Nas said they crawled up stairs breathless thinking that stone was yet alive. they opend the door of a wheat bend and saw stones foot Qra-Nas drew his arrow across the bow. redy to cut loose. for a moment they watch the lifeless body. Xa-sis discovered that the body was dead. they then took the body and threw it out the window. and then they called all the people to come and take what wheat and corn they could pack and go to-a hiding place. where they could not be found by the whites. so the indian of both villages came and took all the wheat and corn they could gather in the place. and then went to hide themselfs. some went to Fishels point and somewent to scotts valley. the men went out to kill cattle for their use and every man who was able to ride caught himself a horse. in around the valley and upper lake and bachelor valley. there was about one thousand head of horses and about four thousand head of cattles. so the indians lived fat for a while. Qra-Nas and Ma-Laq-Qe-Tou was chosen to watch the trail that came in from lower lake. and Shuk and Xasis was watching the trail on the west side of the valley. yom-mey-nah and ge-we-leh were watching the trail that came from eight mile valley. two—or three weeks had pass. no white man were seen on eather trail. one day. Qra-nas and ma-Laq-Qe-Tou seen two white men on horse back came over the hill. they stoped on top of the hill. they saw nothing staring around stone and kelseys place. no indians in the village. Qra-nas and Ma-Laq-Qe-Tou . went around behind a small hill to cut the white man off. the white man saw the indians trying to go around behind them. the whites turned and went back before the indians got in back of them. so three or four days went by. no more white man was seen.

one day the lake watchers saw a boat came around the point. som news coming they said to each others. two of the men went to the landing. to see what the news were. they were told that the white warriors had came to kill all the indians around the lake. so hide the best you can. the whites are making boats and with that they are coming up the lake. so we are told by the people down there. so they had two men go up on top of uncle sam mountain. the north peak. from there they watch the lower lake. for three days they watch the lake. one morning they saw a long boat came up the lake with pole on the bow with red cloth. and several of them came. every one of the boats had ten to fifteen men. the smoke signal was given by the two watchmen. every indian around the lake knew the soldiers were coming up the lake. and how many of them. and those who were watching the trail saw the infantrys coming over the hill from lower lake. these two men were watching from ash hill. they went to stones and kelseys house. from there the horsemen went down torge the lake and the soldiers went across the valley torge lakeport. they went on to scotts valley. shoot afew shoots with their big gun and went on to upper lake and camped on Emmerson hill. from there they saw the indian camp on the island. the next morning the white warriors went across in their long dugouts. the indians said they would met them in peace. so when the whites landed the indians went to wellcome them. but the

170

Rattlesnake Island on Clear Lake. *Photo courtesy of Phoebe Apperson Hearst Museum of Anthropology.*

white man was determined to kill them. Ge-We-Lih said he threw up his hands and said no harm me good man. but the white man fired and shoot him in the arm and another shoot came and hit a man staning along side of him and was killed. so they had to run and fight back; as they ran back in the tules and hed under the water; four or five of them gave alittle battle and another man was shoot in the shoulder. some of them jumped in the water and hed in the tuleys. many women and children were killed on around this island. one old lady a (indian) told about what she saw while hiding under abank, in under aover hanging tuleys. she said she saw two white man coming with their guns up in the air and on their guns hung a little girl. they brought it to the creek and threw it in the water. and alittle while later, two more men came in the same manner. this time they had alittle boy on the end of their guns and also threw it in the water. alittle ways from her she, said layed awoman shoot through the shoulder. she held her little baby in her arms. two white men came running torge the woman and baby, they stabed the woman and the baby and, and threw both of them over the bank in to the water. she said she heared the woman say, O my baby; she said when they gathered the dead, they found all the little ones were killed by being stabed, and many of the woman were also killed stabing. she said it took them four or five days to gather up the dead. and the dead were all burnt on the east side the creek. they called it the siland creek. (Ba-Don-Bi-Da-Meh). this old lady also told about the whites hung aman on Emerson siland this indian was met by the soldiers while marching from scotts valley to upper lake. the indian was hung and alarge fire built under the hanging indian. and another indian was caught near Emerson hill. this one was tied to atree and burnt to death.

the next morning the solders started for mendocino county. and there killed many indians. the camp was on the ranch now known as Ed Howell ranch. the solders made camp a little ways below, bout one half mile from the indian camp. the indians wanted to surrender, but the solders did not give them time, the solders went in the camp and shoot them down as tho they were dogs. som of them escaped by going down a little creek leading to the river. and som of them hed in the brush. and those who hed in the brush most of them were killed. and those who hed in the water was over looked. they killed mostly woman and children.

the solders caught two boys age about 14 or 15. the solders took them to lower lake, and then turnd them loose, when the solders started the two boys back, they loded them with meat and hard bread, one said as soon as they got out of site, they threw the meat away and som of the bread also. he said they went on a dog trot for dear life. thinking all the time that the solders would follow them and kill them. he said they would side tract once and awhile and get up on a high peak to see if the solders were coming he said when they got back that night they could nothing but crying. he said all the dead had been taken across to a large dance house had been and was cremated. wetness, Bo-Dom or Jeo Beatti, and Krao Lah, indian name. an old lady said her further dug a large hole in abank of the river and they hed in the hole. one old man said that he was aboy at the time he said the solders shoot his mother, she fell to the ground with her baby in her arms, he said his mother told him to climb high up in the tree, so he did and from there he said he could see the solders runing about the camp and shooting the men and woman and stabing boys and girls. he said mother was not yet dead and was telling him to keep quit. two of the solders heard her talking and ran up to her and stabed her and child. and a little ways from his mother, he said laid a man dieing, holding his boy in his arms the solders also stabed him, but did not kill the boy, they took the boy to the camp, crying, they gave it evry thing they could find in camp but the little boy did not quit crying. it was aboy about three years of age, when the solders were geting redy to move camp, they raped the boy up in ablanket and lief the little boy seting by the fire raped up in a blanked and was stell crying, and that boy is alive today, his name is bill ball, now lives in boonville; One Old man told me about the solders killing the indiuns in this same camp. he said young man from the description he gave. He must have been about 18 or 20 years of age. he said he and another boy about the same age was taken by the soldurs and he said there were two solders in charge of them. one would walk ahead and one behind them. he said the solders took him and the other boy. they both were bearfooted he said when they began to climb the mountain between mendocino and lake county. he said they were made to keep up with the solders. thir feet were geting sore but they had to keep up with the solders. when they were climbing over the bottlerock mountain. thir feet were cutup by the rocks and thir feet were bleeding and they could not walk up with the solders. the man behind would jab them with the sharp knife fixed on the end of the gun. he said one of the solders came and looked at thir feet and went to abox opened it took acup and diped something out of asack and brought it to them and told them both of them to hold their foots on a log near by. the solder took ahand of the stuff and rubed it in the cuts on the bottom of thir feet. he said he noticed that the stuff the solder put on their feet look like salt. sure enough it was salt. the solder tied clouth over their feet and told them not to take them off. he said the tears were roling down his cheeks. he said all the solders came and stood around them laughing. he said they roled and twested for about two hours. and they also rubed salt in the wounds on their seats and backs wher they jabed them with the solders big knife. as he call it. two or three days later the chife solder told them they could go back. they was then gaven meat and bread, all they could pack. he said they started on thir back journey. he said it was all most difficult for them to walk but raped alot of cloth around thir feet and by doing so made thir way all right. he said the meat and bread got too heavy for fast traveling so they threw the meat and some of the bread away. looking back all the time thinking that the solders would follow them and kill them. now and then they would side tract. and look back to see if the solders were following them. after seen no solders following them they would start out for another run. he said they traveled in such manner untell they got to thir home. he said to himself. hear I am not to see my mother and sister but to see thir blood scattered over the ground like water and thir bodys for coyotes to devour. he said he sat down under a tree and cryed all day.

WILLIAM RALGANAL BENSON, POMO

Refuge

In order to settle the "Indian problem" in California, the federal government in Washington sent three commissioners, McKee, Wozencraft, and Barbour, to negotiate peace treaties with the native people of California. Between March 19, 1851 and January 7, 1852, these commissioners covered virtually the entire state, signing eighteen separate treaties with 139 Indian "chiefs" or signatories. In these treaties the Indians agreed to cede their land and to live within the laws of the United States. In exchange they were allowed to reserve certain portions of their land (i.e., reservations) upon which they could live, and they would be accorded certain other rights and benefits as well. The eighteen reservations totalled some seven million acres of land.

When the commissioners left, the Indians who had signed these treaties assumed they were now at least partially protected. Years later they discovered that when the commissioners presented the treaties to Congress, the senators from California lobbied against them. The eighteen treaties were never ratified.

Meanwhile, the slaughter of Indians increased as more Anglo settlers swept into California. In 1854, the superintendent of Indian affairs, in cooperation with the U.S. military, authorized the establishment of seven hastily constituted reservations, in part to protect Indians from settlers, in part to control them. Since these reservations were not established by treaty with the Indians, those who lived on them had few rights. In some ways they functioned more as refugee camps in this period of bloodshed than as reservations.

The outlined areas represent land ceded by Indians in the treaties of 1851. The dark areas represent territories reserved to Indians by those treaties.

This [Sacramento Valley] was a place where the People lived. There was water, good hunting, plenty of wild fruit and berries. It was the home of the Concow, a small branch of the Maidu.

For many years they lived here in relative peace and harmony with nature and other tribes. There were always rumors about the strange white men that were seen about, but no one thought they would ever see one.

But then the rumors became fact. They were there, and they were not very good people. They stole food, they ran off the game, and worst of all they stole the young girls. Some they sent back to the tribes—after they were through with them—but others were sold to other people. This created bad feelings for the whites, and there were killings. Many young men were killed—the warriors.

The land was good, and white families wanted to build homes and start farms. The Indian was in the way. A problem had to be solved.

One day the soldiers came. Everyone was rounded up: men, women, old people, children. In these times all the People had learned to live with the knowledge that they would have to leave their homes, sometimes in the middle of the night. So they were always packed, their food baskets and blanket roll ready. The women and children would have on all the clothes they owned—ready!

They came in the early morning, many soldiers. Everyone was rounded up in the middle of the village and told they were going to a better place. So they started walking. Along the way many old ones and many babies died. When someone tried to run away, they were killed.

Somewhere between the mountains and the Pacific Ocean they came upon some Indians who told them that to the south was a valley where there were soldiers and white people, but also many Indians of all tribes—some taken there by soldiers, some there on their own.

A young girl listened to all this and wondered if this was where they were going. She discussed it with her friend and decided they could make it there somehow.

But, instead, they finally got to the ocean and they were all amazed at the amount of water, so much more than any of them could even imagine. Then the soldiers started running them, hitting and shooting anyone who didn't run, right up to and over the edge of a high cliff, down into the water.

The two young girls swam for a long time. When the smaller one got tired, the bigger one put her on her back and swam with her. In time they made it to the other side, for, you see, it was a bay—Humboldt Bay. Many people died that day.

Army post at Round Valley. *Photo taken 1901 or 1902. Courtesy of Phoebe Apperson Hearst Museum of Anthropology.*

After they got out of the water, they started walking south to what the people called the Valley. They ate berries and wild vegetables, and sometimes the bigger girl would again have to carry the smaller one. But eventually they arrived in the Valley. It was beautiful. A prison, yes, but with more freedom than they had otherwise.

They spoke only the Concow language, but they went to the fort and asked for work. They were strong and growing and were soon maids at Fort Wright. The older one worked for a major and his wife.

And that's how Mary Major came to Round Valley.

EVELENE MOTA, MAIDU

We Had to Move Again

As years passed, more reservations were established, often tiny, barren tracts of land set aside for "homeless Indians." Altogether over a hundred reservations (or *rancherias*, as the smaller reservations are often called) were created, scattered throughout the state. Yet only a portion of the native population ever benefitted from them. While some people eventually drifted into the cities or lived on the outskirts of towns, most native people found seasonal work on farms and ranches, often squatting on vacant land, living in old-style dwellings, supplementing their income by hunting, fishing, or gathering wild foods in their ancestral territory.

Meanwhile, strangers kept pouring into California. At first they came by wagon or by ship, later by transcontinental railroad, automobile, bus, and airplane. They tended to settle in valleys and along rivers, often on the sites of older Indian villages. Their numbers were beyond belief, their greed for land and resources beyond imagining. Each decade saw still more land fenced for cattle, given over to orchards and farms, degraded by water diversions, set aside as parks or wilderness preserves, and later built into cities and suburbs. Indian people found themselves trespassers in the land of their birth, exiles in the land in which their ancestors had lived for milennia.

The following selection describes the way of life of a refugee band of Kumeyaay people who did not get even a modicum of land reserved for them. The narrator, Delfina Cuero, was born around 1900; most of the incidents she describes occurred in a period within the memory of people still alive today.

My father and mother left Mission Valley, they told me, when a lot of Chinese and Americans came into the Valley and told them that they had to leave. They did not own the land that their families and ancestors had always lived upon. They moved east into ʔewi· ka·kap (Mission Gorge). There were many Kumǝya·y villages all through that way, up the canyon, and in Lakeside and El Cajon valleys. There was a big xa·tu·piʔ [Padre Dam, built by the Mission Fathers] that they talked about where there was a village also. My mother and father went to one village, and then the next one, and on and on. After they had to leave their own place, they lived around wherever there was work or wild food to be gathered. They lived in El Cajon,

176

than Jamacha. That's where I was born. Later we lived in *xamu·ł* (Jamul) and then *səmu·xu·* (Cottonwood or Barrett). We just worked at a place and then my father would tell me we had to move again....

The Indians didn't speak English in those days. The men they worked for never told them their names. But there was one old timer, a pretty old man who lived in Barrett that we worked for longer than most. I remember his name was Maxfield. He might still remember us if he is living, but I doubt it. He was pretty old then. I was very young but the whole family was working for him, my father, mother, grandfather, grandmother, and I. All doing some kind of work. I can remember, we cleared a lot of land. The men cut trees and they did many other things while we carried, piled and burned the brush. Other times while the men worked, my mother, grandmother and I used to go all over looking for wild cherries at the right time of year, or wild wheat, or different kinds of Indian food. That's what we used to eat. We lived on those things we gathered when I was little. This old man gave us some food too. The ranchers that my people worked for gave us some food or sometimes some old clothes for the work. They never gave the Indians money. We didn't know what money was in those days.

The Indian women never worked for the ranchers' wives where my family was. I heard they did it other places. We worked with the men sometimes. Most of the time we hunted for wild food, greens, honey, and things.

Maxfield gave us a little place where we could stay while we worked for him, a place to build our *səmay ʔewa·* [little Indian house of willows and other brush]. The men put up two posts and tied a beam between them with fibers stripped from yucca leaves. The reeds or brush were tied to the beam. It looked kind of like a small [pup] tent. We used *tamu·* (reeds) when we could get it otherwise we used *xatamu· [Haplopappus* sp., brush]. Then the men put four posts to make a square and on them we made a ramada beside the house.

I remember my father used to work all around El Cajon and Jamul and many places. He did ranch work. We just camped as close as we could most times. We never lived in a house. We just lived out away from the ranch houses in the brush of some small canyon. My father would pick a place where the wind couldn't hit us. In those days there was water in places that are dry now.

The Indians had to move around from place to place to hunt and gather food, so we knew lots of places to camp. Later on white people kept moving into more and more of the places and we couldn't camp around those places anymore. We went farther and farther from San Diego looking for places where nobody chased us away....

When the Indians were told to leave a place, they generally just headed farther into the mountains. Pretty soon they would tell me we had to move again. We would pack up everything we had, a few *sa·kay* (ollas) and baskets of dried food if we had been lucky and found enough to dry for winter, a few small stone tools, bow and arrows, *xampu·* [throwing stick for hunting

177

rabbits], and what little clothing we had. We would pack everything on the back of a small burro that my father had and go. My father was a good man. He was never a drinker then. He worked hard and so did my mother.

I can remember when I was pretty young, we used to go and look for *xa·l'ak* (abalone). They used to show me how to find them and get them off the rocks. We used to hunt for fish, shellfish, and other stuff in the ocean and along the edge of the ocean around Ocean Beach. There are so many houses here now I can't find my way any more. [The shore line at Ocean Beach has been filled in part.] Everything looks so bad now; the hills are cut up even. I can remember coming to *mat kun'it'* (Point Loma). There were not many houses then. I was little and don't remember all, but there was a lot of food here then. We had to hunt for plant food all day to find enough to eat. We ate a lot of cactus plants. [*Dudleya* sp. and *Opuntia* sp.]. We ate a lot of shellfish. There were lots of rabbits there too. My grandfather used to tell the boys to eat rabbit eyes especially, because it would make them good hunters. We hunted those things until we couldn't hunt on Point Loma anymore.

DELFINA CUERO, KUMEYAAY

The Ground Cries Out

Not only did strangers come in vast and catastrophic numbers, but their destruction of nature was immense. Grand oak trees that had provided food for centuries were cut for firewood or uprooted merely to create pastures for cattle. Mudflats that once provided a wealth of clams and oysters were filled or dredged. Marshlands that had harbored great flocks of geese and ducks were drained, while at the very same time dry land once rich in rabbits and prong-horn antelope was being irrigated. Mining and logging debris degraded streams and rivers once teeming with salmon. Hunters drove to virtual extinction the great herds of tule elk, the grizzly bear, the condors, and the eagle, while the deer and other game animals were terrorized into hiding. European grasses, thistles, and other weeds replaced many of the native plants upon which Indians had thrived. Pigs were allowed to fatten themselves on acorns, while Indians were excluded from "private" land. Without Indians to burn and tend the land, prairies reverted to brush, open meadows and oak savannahs to dense forests of Douglas fir.

Horrified at the destruction and helpless to stop it, native people mourned the loss of their land, sometimes cursing those who caused such damage, sometimes finding bitter solace in prophecies that recognized a profound religious and ecological truth: those who destroy their land will ultimately be destroyed as well.

The white people never cared for land or deer or bear. When we Indians kill meat, we eat it all up. When we dig roots, we make little holes. When we build houses, we make little holes. When we burn grass for grasshoppers, we don't ruin things. We shake down acorns and pine nuts. We don't chop down the trees. We only use dead wood. But the white people plow up the ground, pull up the trees, kill everything. The tree says, "Don't.

178

I am sore. Don't hurt me." But they chop it down and cut it up. The spirit of the land hates them....

The Indians never hurt anything, but the white people destroy all. They blast rocks and scatter them on the earth. The rocks say, "Don't. You are hurting me." But the white people pay no attention. When the Indians use rocks, they take little round ones for their cooking. The white people dig deep long tunnels. They make roads. They dig as much as they wish. They don't care how much the ground cries out. How can the spirit of the earth like the white man? That is why God will upset the world—because it is sore all over. Everywhere the white man has touched it, it is sore. It looks sick. So it gets even by killing him when he blasts. But eventually the water will come.

KATE LUCKIE, WINTU

I No Longer Believe

Vastly outnumbered, overwhelmed by the lawlessness and cruelty of the strangers, and dwarfed by their technological superiority—especially in weaponry—people often surrendered, not just politically but in some cases spiritually as well.

In 1864 the Modoc were pushed off their land and moved northward to a reservation in Oregon, where they were forced to live side-by-side with their ancestral enemies, the Klamath. Tensions were high and the Modoc wretched, when in 1870 a subchief named Kintpuash—known to whites as Captain Jack—murdered a Klamath shaman and fled, taking with him fifty-three warriors and many women, children, and old people. The band traveled south and hid itself among the caves and jagged outcroppings of the lava bed region near Tule Lake, where for six months they fended off a force of over 1,000 soldiers. The tragic, dramatic, sordid conflict, marked by barbarities and betrayals, became known as the "Modoc War." In the end Captain Jack was captured and hanged, and the Modoc people were dispersed, some remaining on the Klamath Reservation, others being exiled to Oklahoma.

The following narrative touches upon the Modoc War and suggests its cultural aftermath. As everywhere in California, native values were crumbling beneath the onslaught of whites. Overnight elaborate interlocking systems of belief, technology, and social organization were rendered invalid. A massive death rate shattered the familial, tribal, and ceremonial affinities that bound people together and gave them their very identity. Property and territorial rights—developed and sustained for hundreds of years—were instantly swept aside in arbitrary land grabs and treaties. The sinew-backed bow—strong, flexible, polished, and painted—seemed a pitiful toy compared with the rifle; a basket labored over for weeks was less durable than a cheap tin pail; the harpoon, fishing weir, and even the ancient salmon chants were useless in streams choked with mining and logging debris. New diseases and agents of death made the shamans look like doddering, helpless old men and women. Traditional wisdom that stressed co-operation, moderation, and fitting in seemed outmoded in a frontier society which demanded individual initiative and encouraged competition. Although many people hung onto traditional values and beliefs—and indeed there are many who still do—for others the white invasion brought about a cultural as well as a physical collapse. Sadly and achingly, even people of good family and traditional upbringing turned their backs on the beliefs of their people.

In ancient times described in myths the doctors really cured people, but now they just fool them. When I was old enough to remember, my father and another chief wanted a doctor to kill a man forty miles away. The doctor agreed. But I know for sure that he didn't even kill that man. Even when a doctor tries to kill a man living nearby he always fails. But when someone does die the doctor wants all the credit and claims that he killed the man.

During the Modoc War the strongest doctor was supposed to be Curly-headed Doctor. He took a long cord and painted it red and put it around the whole camp. He said that the federal soldiers would fall down and die if they touched the string; they would never be able to cross it. The people believed him and danced with him all night, singing all the while.

A few days later we saw soldiers coming toward our camp. As they came closer we saw that one of the leaders had a sabre. Behind him two other leaders were followed by the troops. As they came close to the string the leaders shouted, "Mark;" the soldiers dropped to their knees. They shouted, "Fire," and the soldiers shot all around. They then ran over the string. The string did not kill the soldiers; Indian bullets did that. I saw it with my own eyes. After that I didn't believe any more.

The doctor claims he can make rain. He can make the strongest wind, too. He can make heavy snow. He can stop wind, rain, or snow. My father once asked a doctor to stop a bad storm. The doctor agreed. But with all his singing and dancing for two nights the storm didn't cease. Sometimes a doctor will sing and dance for five nights and still the bad weather continues. The people are disappointed that the doctor can't change the weather. But they try to believe him, and they try again sometime. Even though they know the doctor can't make it rain or snow they still believe in him. If the rain comes in two or three days, the doctor says that he brought it. If the storm stops, the doctor says that he did it, and everyone believes him. As far as I can remember a doctor never stopped rain or wind.

My father, John Sconchin, was an intelligent man. The last time my father believed in doctors was when the soldiers crossed the string. He said, "This is the last time that we will believe in doctors. We'll ask them no more." Then my father and the others discussed the many times they had asked doctors to kill other people and it never happened; how many times they called doctors to cure and they didn't cure; and how many times they asked for rain and didn't get it. They spoke of how the doctors always claimed they were responsible when these things did happen. My father and the others were badly disappointed in the doctors.

But most people still believe.

PETER SCONCHIN, MODOC

Boarding School

In the last half of the nineteenth century and into the present century, zealous and well-intentioned reform groups rose up throughout the country. There were abolitionists who fought for an end to legal slavery, temperance societies, suffrage groups, labor organizations, and still others who struggled to end child labor, to create settlement houses and hospitals for the urban poor, and to otherwise bring the ugly realities of America into line with what came to be called "the American dream."

The plight of America's indigenous people did not escape the sympathy and attention of the reformers, and various associations were formed, often headquartered in Boston or other eastern cities, to raise money and lobby for the betterment of Indians. The situation was indeed horrendous. Throughout the country Indian people were defeated, dislocated, dispirited, and in many cases quite literally starving to death. Reform was clearly needed, and these groups did much good. Unfortunately, most of these reformers held to the belief that to improve their lot the Indians had no choice but to assimilate into the dominant culture.

The actions of the reformers were many. Among the most far-reaching was the passage of the Dawes Severalty Act of 1887, the so-called General Allotment Act. This act divided up much communally held tribal land into individual allotments, the idea being that private ownership of land would, by its very nature, empower the Indians and endow them with "civilized" virtues. Instead, the act wreaked havoc with tribal sovereignty and traditional systems of land management and tenure. Also, those now owning their land outright often found themselves unable to meet tax payments, and their land was seized. Others often found themselves desperate for money and were unable to resist selling their land to outsiders. The net result of the Dawes Act was that much Indian land was lost to lawyers and speculators.

Reformers also attempted to end the corruption of Indian agents and contractors by turning over the administration of reservations to religious organizations, it being assumed that not only would the clergy be more honest than others, but their building of churches and their missionary activities would help "elevate" the poor Indians. The political and economic power that the religious organizations held was often used to help missionaries spread new beliefs and uproot the older traditions.

Yet another far-reaching reform was the creation of the boarding school system, which removed Indian children from the influence of their families and communities and sent them to distant schools. Here, forbidden to speak their languages and practice their customs, it was expected that they would eventually be cleansed of their "Indianness" and that they would be rendered fit for jobs and life in the dominant society.

Every year the agent of the government school came around in the fall of the year and gathered the children to take them to the school. My mother signed a paper for me to go up there. In the morning (after a two-day trip to Covelo by wagon, flat-bed railroad car, stage coach, and gravel wagon with six other children from the Hopland/Ukiah area), I just kind of stood around and watched the other girls, what they were doing and where

The schoolhouse at Hoopa. *Photo by A.L. Kroeber, 1907. Courtesy of Phoebe Apperson Hearst Museum of Anthropology.*

to go. I didn't know what to say. I think I only knew two words of English, yes and no. I never got to ask my mother why she sent me like that when I didn't know the English language....

There were three girls there from Hopland. I already knew some of their language, it's a different dialect from mine. I couldn't talk the English language in the school at Covelo so I hollered at them when we lined up. Then one of the girls that was in my line reported me. They took me and strapped the heck out of me with a big leather strap. I didn't know what I got strapped for. Three days later those girls told me it was for talking the Indian language on the grounds which I'm not supposed to do.

I was eleven years old [when I went to Covelo], and every night I cried and then I'd lay awake and think and think and think. I'd think to myself, "If I ever get married and have children I'll *never* teach my children the language or all the Indian things that I know. I'll *never* teach them that, I don't want my children to be treated like they treated me." That's the way I raised my children....

I was scared, I had no one to talk to [no one spoke my dialect]. That was sure hard. I felt that if I said something or fought against how we were treated, they might kill me. I cried every night. I couldn't talk to anybody or ask anybody anything because I didn't know how to. I was so dumb, that's the way I felt. They knew that I couldn't understand so nobody talked to me. I was the only one that had my language.

ELSIE ALLEN, POMO

Elsie Allen did have children, and true to her resolve she, like so many of her generation, did not teach them her Pomo language. She did, however, become a masterful weaver of baskets, and until her death in 1990 she was tremendously important in passing along traditional skills and knowledge to her children and to many others.

I Am the Last

Death and cultural destruction continued throughout the nineteenth century at a horrendous rate. The fate of the Chunut, Wowol, and Tachi—three Yokuts groups who lived around the shores of Tulare Lake in the San Joaquin Valley —is typical. They once numbered about 6,500 people, but even by 1850 disease and conquest reduced them to about 1,100. Then came the steady flow of white settlers into the Central Valley. Tribal groups were uprooted and forced onto barren reservations without adequate food or shelter. Eventually economic necessity—more bluntly, desperation—drove people from the reservations into nearby farms, ranches, and cities to seek whatever work they could find. As the older people died, the younger people scattered and inter-married with strangers. In 1933 an eighty-five year old Chunut woman named Yoimut lamented the extinction of her people.

I am the last full-blood Chunut left. My children are part Spanish. I am the only one who knows the whole Chunut or Wowol language. When I am gone no one will have it. I have to be the last one. All my life I want back our good old home on Tulare Lake. But I guess I can never have it. I am a very old Chunut now and I guess I can never see the old days again.

Now my daughter and her Mexican husband work in the cotton fields around Tulare and Waukena. Cotton, cotton, cotton, that is all that is left. Chunuts cannot live on cotton. They cannot sing their old songs and tell their old stories where there is nothing but cotton. My children feel foolish when I sing my songs. But I sing anyway:

Toke-uh lih-nuh Wa-tin-hin nah yo
Hiyo-umne ahe oonook miuh-wah.
That is all.

YOIMUT, YOKUTS

A Fishing Experience

The Kashaya, one of the seven linguistic divisions of the Pomo, lived along the coast of Sonoma County. Their first major white contact was with Fort Ross, the Russian outpost founded in 1812. Unlike the Spaniards who forced the Indians into missions, or the Anglos who stole the land and treated the native residents as trespassers, the Russians came merely to hunt sea otter and grow grain for their Alaskan colony. Their behavior toward the Indians was rela-tively indifferent, even benign. By the time the Russians deserted Fort Ross in 1842 the Kashaya, who had often traded and worked there for wages, had become gradually acclimated to white ways. Thus their subsequent clash with Mexican and Anglo settlers—while harsh—was not totally devastating. Also, since the Sonoma coast offered few harbors, no gold, and poor agriculture, it was settled more sparsely than much of the rest of California.

By the 1870s a white rancher, Charlie Haupt, had married a Kashaya woman, and it was on his sprawling property that many Kashaya people found refuge. Here two villages grew, one of them the Abaloneville mentioned in the following narrative.

From the late nineteenth century to recent times the Kashaya have remained relatively secluded and even aloof, greatly influenced by the isolationist policies of certain spiritual leaders who rose up among them. Perhaps the most influential of these leaders was Annie Jarvis, whose presence dominated the

Roundhouse (left) and dwellings (below) at Haupt Ranch. *Photo courtesy of Phoebe Apperson Hearst Museum of Anthropology.*

Kashaya from 1912 to 1943. She forbade gambling and drinking, banned marriage with the whites, kept the children out of boarding schools, and encouraged the use of the Kashaya language and the retention of many traditional customs. After Annie Jarvis, Essie Parrish, a shaman, held sway until her death in 1979.

Because of their unusual history the Kashaya have survived far better—in terms of both culture and population—than other Central California people. Originally one of the smallest of the Pomo divisions, numbering no more than 600 to 800 people, today (while greatly diminished) they are the largest. Over 150 people identify themselves as Kashaya, the language is still actively spoken by several dozen, and the social and ceremonial life retains many traditional elements.

In recent times the isolation of the past has come pretty much to an end, and people from Kashaya have begun to mix with other Indian groups throughout the state. Wherever they go, they often introduce Kashaya religious and traditional practices into other communities who have lost their own dances, songs, and beliefs. A large part of the religious and cultural revival of the 1980s can be attributed to the activities of this remarkable group.

While the Kashaya escaped annihilation in the last half of the nineteenth century, the immense decline in population indicates that they too underwent great suffering. As ranching and logging cut people off from their hunting and gathering grounds, the Kashaya became more and more dependent upon farm work and day labor. Living on the fringes of white society they often found themselves starving in what had once been a land of plenty. Yet even as they struggled to exist, the old patterns of belief and cooperation among people persisted.

I am going to tell about something we did while living in Abaloneville—going fishing and hunting for food to eat. At the time white food wasn't plentiful—in my youth. We made harpoons. I too knew how to do that. We fastened three nails together and sharpened the one in the middle on the point. Where the two side nails were fastened we called "ears." The harpoon head was then wrapped with cord, smeared with pitch, and smoothed off with a hot rock. A cord was attached to the head and tied onto a pole. That's how we carried it around to spear fish with. We Indians called the harpoon *napa*.

Now I am going to tell how we used to go fishing. We walked a long way to the fish. One time, when we had arisen early in the morning, we set out without much food—without any food except what we had already eaten that morning. Then we went a long way. We went a long way downhill; going downhill was good because we didn't get tired. When we reached the water, we walked upstream. "Upstream is the only way to search for fish," the old time people had said when teaching us. We do the same thing too; if we went downstream the fish would get our scent as we waded across the water. That is why the people of long ago said to go only upstream to fish. We, too, did it that way. We walked along and walked along towards what we call *ahsahq-a* [fish holes], where the fish lie together.

When we had got close to that pool, we looked into the water. One person counted and said, "Sixty fish are gathered." Then we got our poles ready, fastened on the harpoon points, and stabbed. We speared for a long time. All day we worked the fish there. I suppose a few fish were left, but we speared almost all. There must have been sixty fish lying there.

Then we all quit. We were completely soaked; even our bodies, our entire bodies, were soaked. We came up out of the water. We divided the fish up according to how many each could carry. I suppose there were six or seven given to each person, for there were ten of us carrying. Filling our sacks we slung them over our backs and went upwards along the trail that we had come down.

A few people grew tired and weak from hunger. Then they got so that they couldn't move their feet, they had grown so weary. I felt the same way too. Whenever I sat down I just keeled over to sleep and felt completely unable to get up. We walked along that way. That happened to many men—they were sleeping, unable to get up. I was just barely moving along myself—getting up, starting off, walking along. Only a few of us reached the summit. The rest were still being weak from hunger. I felt the same way too, getting terribly weak. Whenever we sat down we went to sleep and didn't feel like getting up. And packing those heavy fish, too, made it even worse. Only a few of us reached home. When we arrived home we were worn out. All the strength that we had felt in us earlier was gone—only a little, just enough to move our legs was left.

When we had arrived home, we explained. "The other men are still resting along the trail, unable to walk, weak from hunger," we said. The other men packed some food and clothes and departed, looking for them. When they had eaten the food and put on the dry clothes, they began to feel better. Before the searchers had left and found them, we had told them where, on which trail, we had gone to the river, so that the men would be found easily. They also found the fish they had been carrying. When they had been fed they became much stronger, and, picking up their fish, they returned.

That is how we used to do things—help one another. If someone should fail somewhere in the wilderness, we would go after him. When he had been strengthened, he would be led home. Even if that happened at night, we would still go.

This that I have told is a true story about what I saw myself. This is the end.

HERMAN JAMES, POMO

Two Gambling Stories

It is almost impossible to overstate the massiveness of the assault upon Indian culture and Indian life. The death rate was horrifying, the suffering and degradation worked into the marrow of those who lived through these cruel and miserable times. Yet, amazingly—and perhaps this is the glory of the human race—life went on, poignant, vital, at times even zany. There were those who still fell in love, had children, sang songs, played traditional games, laughed at the foibles of their neighbors, struggled, somehow survived, and in later years sat back in their rocking chairs to tell wonderfully entertaining stories about it all.

My mother told of this woman from the Ukiah Valley, who was always bragging about herself and her family. She was also a basketmaker and said she was the champion basketmaker among all the Indians. She said this to the white people who were basket buyers so they wouldn't buy from the other women. There was a lot of bad feeling about this woman. I'm not going to say her name because her relatives are still around and it wouldn't be good to start this whole thing up again. Well, it wasn't just her baskets she bragged about; she said she was the best dancer, gambler, singer, the best in everything according to her.

Well, one time, we were all together in the summer picking hops, and she and her family were there too. I remember, it was pay day and there was a lot of talk in the camp about what to do. Some of the ladies got up a stick game. This one lady I'm talking about said she would take on any of the women; she would stand by herself against them all. I watched the ladies play; there were six on one side and just her on the other. Well, they played a long time, and you know, that lady beat those other women. I thought about that a long time and was troubled that she had won the game. Seemed to me she should have lost, the way all the people were talking about her.

I asked my mother about this and why I was troubled. Maybe that lady did something to me to make me feel bad or something. My mother said that for some people their bragging was their luck. They bragged so much that the other people sometimes began to doubt themselves, and doubt their luck too. When they did this, they would lose their luck and make it so that the bragging person would win. Mother said that you want to be careful who you gamble with; you'll lose if the bragging person makes you doubt your luck; and you'll lose too if the other person is better than you. You can win if you know who is who. You know, that's true about most things I've come to find out in my living this long.

When I was a little girl, maybe about ten, the Cloverdale people and the Dry Creek people got together for a doings. There was a hand game and a stick game going on. I don't know just how many games they played, but it seemed like they played all the time; they went all night too. There was this woman married to a Dry Creek man who was playing too. They had lots of money because she came in a two-horse buggy, had an umbrella, lots of good blankets on the seat, and a suitcase [most had flour sacks for our clothes when we traveled], and she had on clothes like the white ladies would wear, and a purse that sounded like she had bells in it.

This lady, sometimes she would get almost all the sticks [counters], and then she would just about lose them all. Before the people had something to eat in the morning, she'd lost just about everything: her money, the horses,

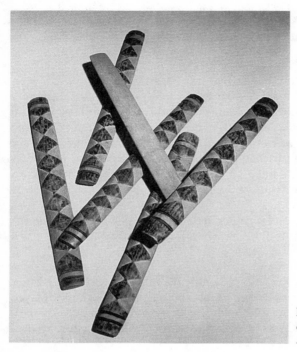

Pomo "stick dice." *Photo courtesy of the Oakland Museum.*

the buggy, her shoes, hat, underskirts, even her blouse. She said she wanted to play one more game and give her luck a chance to win. The other side wanted to know if she was going to bet her skirt since she didn't have anything else. She said no, she wasn't going to bet that. She said, "How much will you give me for my husband; I'll bet my husband. He's worth something. How much will somebody give me?" All the ladies and the young women laughed at this; they thought to themselves that he must not be very good if this lady wants to bet him. Everybody laughed about her bet; but, you know, they were probably right; he probably wasn't much good.

ELSIE ALLEN, POMO

The Judge's Visit

Throughout the sordid history of white/Indian relations in California, Indians resisted as best they could. The resistance at first expressed itself in mission uprisings and revolts, raids upon the cattle, horses, and crops of the intruders; and more organized actions such as the military uprising of Estanislau, the guerrilla activities of the Plains Miwok people near Mount Diablo, and the Modoc War. Even into the 1960s and 1970s, the occupation of Alcatraz Island, the takeover of government land at D-Q University and Ya-Ka-Ama, and the so-called Pit River Rebellion carried on the tradition of resistance. Less

188

well known, however, was the tremendous courage of many individuals throughout the state, who—despite the greatest intimidation—stood up, faced their oppressors, and demanded justice for themselves and their people.

I must have been about eight years old. We already were living in this house [in Requa at the mouth of the Klamath River] and we used to have a gate above, by the road there, and there were two men coming down. We told Granpa, "The dog's barking: there's two men coming." And he says, "Stop the dog." So we stopped the dog from barking and they came down and they knocked at the door and came in and he told us children to sit down over there and be quiet. He said, "Don't make any noise with these people." And that was a Justice of the Peace; his name was Bowie. A well-dressed man, I remember, because this man had a suit on, all dressed up, and he had a small satchel he was carrying with him.

So they came in and Granpa told them to sit down and they sat down. "Hello Billy," the judge says—they called Granpa "Billy." His name was William Brooks. And he shook hands with them. The judge says, "This man is here to see you today," he says, "he come to talk to you." Granpa worked a lot with non-Indians and he could understand English good and he could talk English good. He never had English schooling but he knew how to talk. So he said, "Go ahead and tell me what you're here for and I'll listen."

So he told my grandfather he had sold his timber. That was in 1912 he sold his timber, and that was about at that time. And he says, "William Brooks, known as Billy, I came to tell you that you can't set your net over there in the corner anymore on this property here, where you always set your little net," he says. "You can't set your net there any more, because you're a white man now," he says. "You sold your timber." And I could see Granpa's cheeks right here moving back and forth. He just listened to him, never said a word. So this man got through talking to him and says, "That's what I came for— to tell you that."

And he sat down. We could see that Granpa's face was moving when this man told him that he could no longer set his net over there, you know—but he waited for the man to finish. Then he got up to talk. "All right, Mr. White Man," he says, "you came to tell me what you wanted to tell me. Now you let *me* talk to *you* now." And Granpa says, "From the time I was in the sweat- house—a little boy just so big—when I was getting to be a teenager, I knew how to cross the river to go fishing on that side; I knew how to stand with the men and fish." See, they train them how to stand on the fishing ground to fish on the shore. You don't quarrel, you don't fish and hook in front of another man; every man has his place. If he sees fish in front of him, if he spears it or if he hooks it, it's his, but not the man standing over there's fish. "I was taught like that," Granpa said. "I was taught to fish and learned what to get so that I could survive if something happened to my folks or learn to provide for my family when I grew up. Every kind of a fish I was taught how to fish and to hunt and what to kill and what not to kill." When we went hunting for our costumes, we couldn't kill too many things at once. We just killed so much every year for the Indian costumes, like the woodpecker heads and canary birds, things like that. You just kill so many—not kill them all, you know—so they can come back and nest next year. "That's the way I was taught—to help provide for the home, as soon as I got big enough," he says. "And *you* come here and tell *me* that I can't fish any more for my family. I have children to raise," he said, "that we have to have fish for," he says. "I've got four children; my son died and I have to raise them. That's been my life all my life."

I could see Granpa was getting mad, you know. He was standing up and he said to him, "Now you see that gate up there?" and he moved his foot like this. "Now you get the hell right out of my house," he says, "and don't you ever come back here and tell me how to live and that I cannot fish anymore," he says, "I'll fish as long as I live and as long as I can take care of my net or stand on the beach and fish," he says. "No white man's gonna tell me how to live. Now get out of here as fast as you can and don't you ever come back on this ground again! And Judge Bowie, don't you ever bring another white man here."

And you know we never saw another—never ever saw a game warden here all these years until all this trouble came on here, the trouble with the gillnets right here when the Feds were here. They came here and drove all over, all on this road. *Never*, never saw a game warden here all those years from when I was a girl either eight or nine years old. Here I am—look how old I am—and I think it should be just the way Granpa said: when you're trained how to live and how to fish and how to treat other men on the fishing ground—no quarreling, no swearing at nobody or anything.

Granpa learned to swear because he worked with white people, non-Indians. He used the white man's words; that's why he swore. He didn't talk that way to the Indians, you know. Granpa was mad, so that's what he said. I don't know if he said anything any meaner than that but I know that's what he said. I could remember us kids just curled up right there. And this man got up quick and they walked out fast—out and out—they went up on the road.

GENEVA MATTZ, YUROK

Four Dream Cult Songs

Ever since their first contact with Europeans, California Indians have undergone great cultural changes. These changes have not simply involved giving up traditional ways for western ways. Sometimes it has meant blending the two in original and often surprising combinations—as when in the middle of an old Pomo song one hears the words "Santa Maria;" or when red cloth replaces hard-to-find woodpecker scalps on dance regalia; or when a woman uses a blender instead of a mortar and pestle to pulverize acorns; or when before going to work in a modern office building a person drops a bit of tobacco in front of the doorway as an offering. Sometimes it has meant adopting the customs of Indian people from other parts of the country which may eventually take root and grow to become part of the ongoing cultural life of California Indians.

Beginning in 1870 a series of native messianic movements swept through California. These movements transformed beliefs, gave hope—or at least escape—to a defeated people, and reshaped and revitalized a deeply shaken religious faith. The so-called Ghost Dance cult originated among the Paviotso of Walker Lake, Nevada, and spread westward with unbelievable rapidity. Native "prophets" carried the word from village to village: Indian people must gather together and dance for days on end, after which the ghosts of Indian dead would march back into the world, drive out the whites, and usher in a new age.

As the cult was transmitted from one tribal group to another variations developed. The Earth Lodge cult preached that the end of the world was imminent and that only native people who secluded themselves in traditional earth lodges and performed proper rituals would survive the impending Armageddon.

The Bole-Maru cult, which developed out of the Earth Lodge cult, abandoned doctrines of world destruction and the return of the dead, stressing instead ideas of the afterlife, a Supreme Being, and the importance of dreaming. The Bole-Maru was especially important among the Patwin and Pomo. It helped refocus and invigorate native shamanism (its effects are still felt among shamans practicing today), and it served as a link between traditional belief systems and the Pentecostal Christianity which would provide a backdoor entry for many Indians into the white world and the white way of thinking.

Among the Wintu a local Dream Dance cult emerged in 1872, an apparent outgrowth of the Bole-Maru, and lasted some forty years. A cult dreamer would meet a dead friend or relative in a dream and receive a song. The next day the dreamer sang the song publicly and danced to it, often with elaborate costume and ritual. Afterwards the song became the common property of all who heard it, and anyone might sing it at future Dream Dance rituals.

The songs that individual dreamers received from dead friends and relatives were often hauntingly beautiful.

I.

Down west, down west we dance,
    We spirits dance.
Down west, down west we dance,
    We spirits dance.
Down west, down west we dance,
    We spirits weeping dance,
    We spirits dance.

SADIE MARSH, WINTU

II.

There above, there above,
    At the mystical earthlodge of the south,
    Spirits are wafted along the roof and fall.
There above, there above,
    At the mystical earthlodge of the south,
    Spirits are wafted along the roof and fall.
There above, there above,
    Spirits are wafted along the roof and fall,
    Flowers bend heavily on their stems.

                         WINTU

III.

It is above that you and I shall go;
    Along the Milky Way you and I shall go;
It is above that you and I shall go;
    Along the Milky Way you and I shall go;
It is above that you and I shall go;
Along the flower trail you and I shall go;
    Picking flowers on our way you and I shall go.

                HARRY MARSH, WINTU

IV.

Above where the minnow maiden sleeps at rest
    The flowers droop,
    The flowers rise again.
Above where the minnow maiden sleeps at rest
    The flowers droop,
    The flowers rise again.
Above where the minnow maiden sleeps at rest
    The flowers droop,
    The flowers rise again.

                         WINTU

XI: The Present

"It's hard to be an Indian."

Julian Lang, Karuk

The Truth Will Set You Free

The dreadful events of the recent past have left deep scars. Every person of
Indian descent has been forced to deal not only with ongoing prejudice, but an
inheritance of injury and humiliation that goes back many generations. It
hasn't been easy. Do native people have any choice but to go through life
absorbed in bitterness, feeling in their very bones the anger and shame of being
a defeated and despised people? Is denial the only alternative to hatred of
others and hatred of oneself—denial of the past, denial even of one's own
Indian ancestry? Even in the bleakest of times there have always been other
voices within the Indian community—wise voices, sad and truthful and
proud—that counsel another way of coming to terms with the past.

All kids should know who they are and be proud of who they are....
Before it was so bad to be an Indian that you were ashamed, or you
had to be somebody else. Many of the people would say I'm Filipino, or I'm
from Canada. I'm from the dark French or whatever. They'd be anything
except Indian. At one time, being Indian was so bad, if you got an education,
it didn't do any good anyway. They wouldn't hire you.... You think anybody
would go to a doctor? The banks wouldn't hire you. Nobody would hire you
because you were an Indian. And so in our minds being Indian was so bad,
and we didn't really know why. Why was it so bad to be an Indian? But it's
because of what *they* did to us, and *they* portrayed us that we were the
savages. We were this and we were that. And we thought maybe we were....

The truth will set you free. We can talk about the Holocaust. We can talk
about all the things that happened other places, but you can't talk about
what happened to the Indians. Our kids know it. We tell our kids. We all
know it. And the hurt is still here. So how do you get rid of that hurt? The
way to get rid of the hurt is to put it out. Let everybody know, and after
awhile it will become history.... The truth will set you free. And our kids
won't be so angry.

VIVIEN HAILSTONE, YUROK/HUPA/KARUK

Grandpa Ramsey

The 1970s, 1980s, and 1990s have seen an increased respect for California
Indian people and culture, among natives as well as non-natives. Yet,
poignantly, it has also seen the loss of a generation of elders who spoke the
native languages, knew the customs, embodied the old ways. Languages which
in the 1970s were spoken only by hundreds are today spoken only by a
handful of the most frail and elderly.

For many Native Californians now in their thirties, forties, and fifties, these
are especially significant times. Behind them, in a slowly receding past, are
memories of the older generation, of a time when traditional culture seemed
richer and more secure than it is today. Before them, in a rapidly approaching
future, are their children, prone (as are children everywhere) to the seductions

of mainstream America. This generation, now in its prime of life, finds itself to be an essential link in the chain of tradition, and many are keenly aware that if they do not preserve, embody, and pass on the traditions of their people, these ways will soon cease to be.

In the selection that follows, Darryl Wilson, a writer, storyteller, and tribal scholar, describes his early contacts with elder Ramsey Bone Blake, and his visit years later with his own children.

I t was a summer before I kept track of time. In our decrepit automobile, we rattled into the driveway, a cloud of exhaust fumes, dust, and screaming excited children. A half-dozen ragged kids and an old black dog poured from the ancient vehicle. Confusion reigned supreme. Uncle Ramsey (after we became parents, his official title changed to "Grampa") was standing in the door of the comfortable, little pine-board home just east of McArthur. Aunt Lorena was in her immaculate kitchen making coffee.

Just as quickly as we poured from the vehicle, we disappeared. There was a pervading silence. Always the crystal bowl rested on Aunt Lorena's kitchen table. Usually it held exotic, distant, tasty objects: oranges, bananas, store-bought candy! There seemed to be three hundred black, shiny eyes staring at the contents of that bowl, but we knew that we must wait for Aunt Lorena to say "when" before we could have the contents—which we instantly devoured.

I cannot remember if we had any cares. It was before I began the first grade. I didn't care if I had shoes or clothes. I didn't care about anything—except to not allow my brothers and sisters to have something that I couldn't. And when I did not know that they got something more than me, it didn't matter, really.

It seems that my "thoughts" were already focused upon some other objective. I listened to the old people. I remembered what they said, the tone of their voice, the waving of the hands. My mind registered the long silences between their choppy sentences and between their quiet words.

They spoke in our language, *A-Juma-wi* and *Opore-gee*, and they used a very crude and stumbling English. The English words were strange. I preferred the "old language." As our lives moved into the world of the English-speakers, and our "old" language became less and less important and less and less used, something within the old people hesitated.

Although I hesitated (and possibly shuddered), I did not surrender. Somehow I simply had to capture the "old" ways. Unknown to me, that was my objective long ago. Often the old people would look at me as I huddled around my father's legs and they were talking while my sisters and brothers were screaming and racing through the land, "...that child is different. He is not the same as all the others." It is not true that I was different, it is that *my people are unique* and different from the waves of Europeans that flooded our land. At an early age I was attracted to this phenomenon. At 5-years-old I could not know it, but it simply was a part of my destiny to record as much of the "old way" as possible.

Many years later, 1985:

In order for my twin boys (at that time they were 4-years-old) to be a part of our "real" history, I took them to "Grampa" Ramsey's home in Fall River Mills on a summer Sunday, 1985. We did not know that Grampa Ramsey was nearing his "time." I knew that he was always around long before I was born, and somehow I figured that he would be around long after I departed—like the mountains or the seasons, he was always there. What I failed to acknowledge is that he was human.

Our natural place upon earth is east of Redding, California. Mt. Shasta and Mt. Lassen are what we identify as the western cornerstones of our land. The Warner Range is the eastern boundary. Glass Mountain, Medicine Lake and Goose Lake, in a direction east from Mt. Shasta make the northern line, and an imaginary line from Eagle Lake to Mt. Lassen completes the circuit. This beautiful land holds the dreams and conflicts of my people. It also is the origin of many stories. How the world was created has many variations. How the earth and nature were made is different from tribe to tribe.

There is a deep canyon just south and laying dead west of where Fall River and Pit River merge. It is several miles long and thousands of feet deep. Grampa Ramsey told us how that canyon was made, because if it was not made the valleys clear back up the Pit River and into Dixie would be flooded.

Born one score and four moments after the assassination of Abraham Lincoln, white-haired and balding, built like a little bull with a twinkle in his clouding eyes and a gruff giggle riding on his mischievous sentences, Grampa Ramsey was our private connection to the ethereal.

His employment as a "cowboy" came to an end when a shying horse threw him and he landed on his neck, nearly breaking it. After his days in the saddle faded he worked on various ranches in the Fall River Valley until his retirement.

He spoke to us in *Opore-gee* (Dixie Valley Language), giggling when the twins would say the words correctly after he explained them. We would have to go visit him many times before he would tell us a "real, not fake" story of our people and our history. During these times I took notes because a tape recorder "spooked" him and it mattered little what he was trying to say, the "ghost" inside the tape recorder affected him—he was occupied with the "ghost" instead of with the lesson.

Close to the time of his "departure," he spoke of being "so old that I no longer think about the end, but think about the beginning, again."

As a silent, powerful, unseen ship passing into an endless sea in the darkness, he moved into the spirit world to join his wife and others of our shattered, little nation. He departed during the full moon of October, 1986. Aunt Lorena preceded him by sixteen years.

DARRYL WILSON, ACHUMAWI/ATSUGEWI

Transition and Adaptation

As they learned the western techniques of crocheting, Yurok women nevertheless kept to the old basketry patterns, sometimes using the new medium to
embed the old patterns in modern memories. *Photo courtesy of Phoebe
Apperson Hearst Museum of Anthropology.*

Essie Parrish, renowned healer and spiritual leader of the Kashaya Pomo, in a dress ornamented with dreamed patterns of cloth and shell. *Photo courtesy of Phoebe Apperson Hearst Museum of Anthropology.*

A Kumeyaay house, built of traditional materials but with a western-style pitched roof and rectangular walls. *Photo courtesy of San Diego Museum of Man.*

A traditional brush house converted into a church, Santa Ysabel. *Photo courtesy of the Smithsonian Institution.*

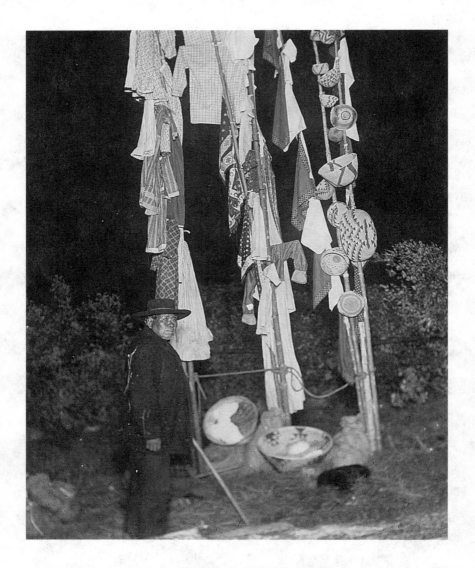

ABOVE: At a Maidu funeral, the goods of the deceased are ceremonially burned, both baskets and modern garments. *Photo by Samuel Barrett, 1908. Courtesy of the American Museum of Natural History, New York.*

OPPOSITE ABOVE: Images of the deceased, in western dress, created for a Luiseño annual mourning ceremony. *Photo by Edward H. Davis, 1904. Courtesy of National Museum of the American Indian.*

OPPOSITE BELOW: A Yurok dugout, outfitted with a sail, crossing the Klamath River. Lillian Ames Salazar is at the bow. *Photo courtesy of Del Norte Historical Museum.*

Annie Burke, respected Pomo basketweaver, passes on the skill to the next generation. *Photo courtesy of California State Library.*

Now I'll Show You How to Do It.

A continual agony that modern Indians have to face is the possibility that their culture may die—that in another twenty years, fifty years, or a hundred years their language will no longer be spoken, their beliefs will exist only in written texts, the complex knowledge and skills acquired over thousands of years will have disappeared from the earth. For those who grew up experiencing the richness of traditional culture, the threat of its demise is horrifying, painful, almost unendurable. In recent years the specter of cultural extinction has inspired many with a sense of urgency and personal responsibility to learn the old ways and to pass them on.

As I grew older, we went to different conferences, and people were saying that the art of basketry was dying. And I couldn't believe that, because I had lived in a home that had all kinds of baskets. And my grandmother made baskets. My mother. And then finally it dawned on me that that would be possible if someone else didn't take over.

And one day I thought to myself—I said, "Well I think I could do that. I think what Grandma is doing I could do." So I went home—asked my mother for materials. My materials she gave me. I whipped out a newborn carrier real fast. I mean, it was like a day. The next day I took it to my grandmother. I said, "Grandma, look." And she looked at that. And I could see that she was really impressed… that I had taken the time to go and make one of these, but she said that it looks like it was made in Japan because I stitched different. And then she said, "Now I'll show you how to do it."

BARBARA BILL, MONO/YOKUTS

Continuing the Song

That so much traditional culture has been lost in the last 150 years is easily understandable. What is amazing, though, is how much has been retained. Throughout the bleakest of times, and despite the mockery and despair of others, there were those who had always kept the old ways alive. Wallace Burrows was one such man. Born in 1886, he learned what he knew from people who had reached adulthood before the coming of whites to the Sacramento Valley. He was a renowned singer and teacher at Grindstone Rancheria in Glenn County, and perhaps the last fluent speaker of the old, conservative Nomlaki language. For year after year he kept the ceremonial life of the roundhouse intact, training new singers and dancers, inspiring others not only with hope but with the necessity of continuing their traditions. He lived remarkably long. The Wintu artist, dancer, and singer, Frank LaPena, recalls a visit with him in 1987, a year before he died at the age of 102.

Knowing and having a teacher such as Wallace Burrows gives us access to the earlier generations and to a time of stability. Wallace, now 101 years old, is a big part of the tradition of the Nomlaki-Wintun people. He's been a dancer and singer all his life.

203

I recently took my son, Craig, to visit Wallace in the hospital in Willows, California. When we came into his hospital room, he was lying there with plastic tubes attached to his body for oxygen, saline solution, and one to help drain and clear his lungs. I felt kind of sad, but when he finally awoke and "warmed up," he was ready to leave for the reservation.

"I will continue to sing and dance," my son said to him.

The old man kind of lit up and said, "So sing." So we both ended up singing to him. We did nine songs, and the way they work, you do them four times. We were in there singing when the nurse came in and told us to hold it down. So we dropped back a bit, but we sang him right to sleep. And there was a real beauty in that. Wallace calls us the "Sacramento Boys." We go up to Willows a lot to help with tribal things, the need to continue the old ways. At that moment in the hospital room I could really feel the bigness of the thing. I could see what the song itself was doing, the spirit of it. He's our teacher. That's why we were there: out of respect for our teacher and to see to it that by the continuation of his songs his music will be the connection for all generations.

FRANK LAPENA, WINTU

Peethivthaaneen

The 1980s and 1990s have seen a remarkable revitalization of Native California culture. Dances are once again well attended, and ceremonies that have been dormant for decades have been revived.

Among the leaders of this revitalization are a number of independent tribal scholars. Many of them grew up in traditional communities and reservations, spent years away going to college or working within the dominant society, and have now returned to take positions of cultural advocacy and leadership. One such scholar is Julian Lang, a member of the Karuk tribe. In love with Karuk culture, Julian has spent countless hours among his elders, assisting them and learning from them. He has also spent thousands more hours in libraries and archives, listening to songs recorded generations ago on wax cylinders, reviewing grammars and texts collected by linguists, poring over the notes of historians and anthropologists.

Like his counterparts throughout the state, Julian is much more than just a scholar. He is a participant in his culture as well, a singer, an artist, a teacher, and a traditionalist. In the selection that follows, he describes the preparations for the World Renewal Dance held at Ka'tim'iin, the Karuk center of the world. The year is 1990, but the tone and content of his account are clearly of another age—an age still very much alive.

We are fixing the Earth. Tonight is the dark of the moon, the beginning of our new year. The Medicine Prayer Man will stand up before all the people, a symbol of strength and good thoughts. For days now he has been fasting and sweating himself in the Best Sweathouse known in our world. Each day he walks along the ancient trails to the fireplaces, where he

204

sweeps the Earth clean of all sickness and prays for abundant food, water-food, and walks-in-the-mountain food. For days we have been shooting our arrows, piercing the Earth, waking it up so the Medicine Man's prayers will be heard. So, our prayers will be heard likewise.

One of our oldest women said to me last night, "You folks must dance and have a good time so the Earth will feel good." Tonight we will have three dances, and a feast. It is Indian New Year at the Center of the World tonight! We will all shake hands and say to each other, "We have fixed the Earth. We have reset the pole that makes the Earth hold fast."

When the Earth was created it was not known how Human was going to do, how Human was going to live. Finally the Spirit People knew Human must eat salmon, acorns, deermeat, and all kinds of plant and water food. The Ikxareeyavs, the Spirit Beings, said, "This is going to be your medicine. This will help you in the hunt. These are your tools. This is your Way." When the First People began to die in multitudes, the Ikxareeyavs were shocked at such imbalance. They sat and talked. "Human must fix the Earth each year," they concluded. So, now we have our Ikxariya'áraar, our Spirit-Man (Medicine Man) who sweeps the world clean just as the Ikxareeyav did the first time. "Human must War Dance, and White Deerskin Dance. That's how to keep away sickness and keep the Earth stable and in balance," the Ikxareeyav said. Tonight we will have finished doing as they once did so many generations ago. "That's the best way there is," our oldest woman said. "Do like they did and you can't go wrong."

JULIAN LANG, KARUK

Half Indian/Half Mexican

At the time of the first contact, there was a sharp distinction between people of European ancestry and Native Californians: language, dress, beliefs, appearance, values—the differences couldn't have been greater. As generation succeeded generation, however, people intermarried, and Indians have adopted more and more of the white world's ways. Today Indians are generally of mixed blood and mixed manners. Coming to terms with the fact that they are part Indian, part something else, and working through the conflicts this raises, is an important part of contemporary Indian life.

I'm half Indian and half Mexican.
I'm half many things.
I'm half compassionate/I'm half unfeeling.
I'm half happy/I'm half angry.
I'm half educated/I'm half ignorant.
I'm half drunk/I'm half sober.
I'm half giving/I'm half selfish.

205

A self made up of many things,
I do not have to be anything for anybody but myself.
I have survived long enough to find this out.
I am 41 years old and am happy with my whole—self.
Don't let your children wait as long…

JAMES LUNA, LUISEÑO

Baskets in Museum Collections

One of the major concerns of contemporary California Indians is the issue of
sovereignty. Politically, this manifests itself as a demand that California natives
be recognized as sovereign (if defeated) nations, capable of having a govern-
ment-to-government relationship with the United States, deserving of freedom
from certain state laws, heirs to certain unsurrendered rights more readily
granted to native people outside California than within.

The issue of sovereignty also goes beyond politics. Also being questioned is
the extent to which development on Indian sacred land interferes with religious
freedom; the right of universities to dig up Indian burial sites and keep the
bones of people's ancestors for study; and the moral, if not legal, authority of
museums to possess Indian goods, such as baskets or dance regalia, and keep
these out of Indian hands.

Museums keep our baskets
        they say
safe and out of harm's way—
preserving them for all time.
Well, that may sound fine
        at first listening
but something is majorly
        missing.
For while offers of access
        to our baskets
        may seem generous
we wonder why it is
        that we
must seek permission
        and prove
        our worth
to visit the baskets
        of our birth?
And if we do manage
        a visit within
the walls of the institution
we find there's a "white glove"
        policy

206

to make sure that
    we
don't damage the baskets
through contact with
    our skin.
Oh, don't you see that both
    symbolically
    and literally
here is one more "white"
    barrier
between Indian people
    and their
    culture?
Hey, I know it's nothing new—
    but isn't it also true that
sometimes it is so intrinsically
    built into our reality
that we don't readily recognize
    the gross inequity?
We've got this problem of
    conflicting
    cultural perspective—
one that feels protective measures
preserve these basket treasures.
The other believes that separation
    from the people has been
    too long
and like a song no longer sung
    a basket un-touched
    and un-used
    will die—
    its spirit will be gone.
Science took bones
    of our ancestry
away from the places
    they should be—
measured and examined them
    and reduced them
    to objects of
    scientific curiosity.
In some ways our baskets
have met the same fate
but it's not too late
to address with sensitivity
    this issue of
    cultural sovereignty.

Maybe museums can be seen as
        friends—
as temporary guardians—
and now that the times are
        ready for change
        we can arrange
to bring our baskets home again.
But museums will first have to
        learn to forget
to view our baskets as
        financial assets—
money in the bank so to speak.
This will be a hard one
        I know—
and some may never want
        to let go.
For losing power and control
        is seldom met
        with favor—
in fact more often what you'll get
        is resistant
        behavior.
But just as apartheid is dying slow
        the movement toward
                justice
        for native peoples
                lives
        and continues to grow.
The time is ripe and we'll prepare
        to care
for our baskets in our own way—
        we'll give them life
        and keep them strong
        at home
        with us
        where they
        belong.

LINDA YAMANE, RUMSEN OHLONE

For the White Poets

At the same time Indians continue to suffer from prejudice and exploitation in certain areas of life, they are paradoxically held up as objects of worship by other segments of society. The last two decades in particular have seen an interest—even a fascination—by whites in Indian ways. Whites flock to Indian reservations, museums, trading posts, and to acorn dances and "big-times;" Indian basketweavers often have a following of whites learning the ancient craft; shamans are pursued by would-be apprentices; sweatlodge ceremonies are being conducted by non-Indians; non-Indian people read (and write) ever-increasing numbers of books on Indians. Is this just another form of exploitation? After having robbed people of their land, language, culture, and life have we whites now returned to pluck from them bits of wisdom, philosophy, and poetry with which to ornament our lives? Can our culture integrate ancient wisdom and values in any meaningful way? Can Indian culture, so fragile and overpowered by the culture of the dominant society, maintain its authenticity in the face of so many newfound "friends?" Poet Wendy Rose issues an uncomfortable yet necessary challenge.

For the white poets who would be Indian
just once. Just long enough
to snap up the words
fishhooked from our tongues;
you think of us now
when you kneel on the earth,
when you turn holy
in a temporary tourism
of our souls.

With words
you paint your faces,
chew your doeskin, touch breast
and tree as if
sharing a mother were
all it takes, could bring
instant and primal knowledge.

You think of us only when
your voice wants for roots,
when you have sat back on
your heels and become
primitive.

You finish your poems
and go back.

WENDY ROSE, MIWOK/HOPI

Prayer of Welcome

After decades of brutal assault, much of Native California culture has been lost. Yet despite the savagery of the dominant society, Indian life is far from extinguished. Even today, dances are still performed, new roundhouses are being built, shamans still practice healing, baskets are being made, and teachings are being passed on. It is not unusual to find in the freezers of even the most acculturated—along with the frozen peas and ice cream, a bag of acorn meal, saved for special occasions. In a bureau drawer, among the socks and handkerchiefs, is a flicker-shaft bandeau, awaiting the next dance.

What has kept Indian culture alive? Perhaps it was in part resiliency, secrecy, isolation, and humor—survival traits of conquered and persistent people everywhere. Also significant was religious practice and a spiritual cast of mind that could look beyond suffering. Be thankful for what you have, the old teachings insist. Don't complain, don't ask for more. Thank the people, the plants, the animals, all things and all beings, for they provide for you. Gratitude, not complaint, is close to the heart of Indian religion.

In June, 1991, native basketweavers gathered from all over California at the Ya-Ka-Ama Indian cultural center in rural Sonoma County. Gladys Gonzales, a Kashaya Pomo elder then living in Fresno, was present and was asked to give a blessing over the first meal. She did, praying in her native language. Afterwards she explained in English what the prayer was about.

I first addressed my Father in heaven and thanked Him for this beautiful land that He had created for us to come and meet together as native people of this land. I said that we're grateful for this land, beautiful land, and to have the opportunity to come and gather once in a while. And lots of Indian people come here [to Ya-Ka-Ama], and they dance or they sing songs for the land, and they bless the land. And this day we're having this food that was prepared for us today by the women, and we're grateful for them. And we ask our Heavenly Father to bless the food that we are going to partake so that we could enjoy good health and strength throughout our lives here upon the earth. And we're grateful to be together and to put arms around— to greet each other and welcome each other and put arms around each other and show our love to each other. And let us continue to be like this. Loving and showing our love. Extending our love that we have within our hearts. And we thank thee Heavenly Father for all that thou has blessed us with..... I was honored to be here with you good people today.

GLADYS GONZALES, POMO

A Good Life to Look Forward To

Because of the efforts of tribal scholars and the persistence and teaching of elders, many among the younger generation of Indians are dedicating themselves to relearning and practicing the old ways. Rochelle Marie O'Rourke, a young mother of three children, talks of her love of basketry and her vision of herself in the future. While other Americans may dream of a future in the suburbs, with two cars and modern conveniences, Rochelle sees something different for herself. The past is her future, and she accepts it with a warm embrace.

I love [basketweaving]. You create something that is alive. You put your heart and spirit into it, and it's alive. Whatever's in you, you put into the basket.

It's part of my life, and I want it to be part of my kids' life too. I want them to live it, not just know it. I, too, need to live it, so that my children will live it. It can't go away. If it goes away, we go away. We die. There's no other way to explain it.

I want to weave baskets and live the responsibility of it. I want it to be part of my cooking, of my eating, of my raising children. These baskets are utensils. I want to be using them every day. I like to see myself cooking acorns with baskets and rocks, with kids all around me, somewhere along the river. And someday when I'm an elder I want to put my grandchildren in baby baskets made by me. That's pretty neat. It's a good life to look forward to.

ROCHELLE MARIE O'ROURKE,
TOLOWA/YUROK/ACHUMAWI

José Albañas, Luiseño, holding turtle shell rattle. (See page 75.) *Photo courtesy of Southwest Museum.*

Elsie Allen, Pomo basketweaver, at home with her family collection. (See pages 64-65, 181-183, 186-188.) *Photo by Scott Patterson, 1981. Courtesy of Mendocino County Museum.*

RIGHT: Sally Bell, Sinkyone, at the Needle Rock Crossroads. (See pages 165-166.) *Photo courtesy of Bancroft Library.*

BELOW: William Ralganal Benson, Pomo, with feathered basket. (See pages 87, 126-129, 166-173.) *Photo by Jaime de Angulo, 1931. Courtesy of Phoebe Hearst Museum of Anthropology.*

Wallace Burrows (Nomlaki) in 1970. (See pages 203-204.) *Photo courtesy of Dorothy Hill Collection, California State University at Chico.*

Delfina Cuero, Kumeyaay. (See pages 176-178.) *Photo courtesy of San Diego Museum of Man.*

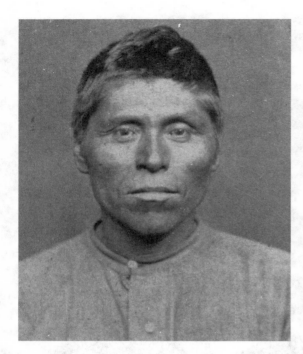

LEFT: Curly-headed Doctor, Modoc, in official prison photo taken at the close of the Modoc War. (See pages 179-180.) *Courtesy of California Department of Parks and Recreation.*

BELOW: Old Dominic, Nomlaki, in front of his house at Paskenta. (See page 51.) *Photo by F.E. Clements, 1928. Courtesy of Phoebe Apperson Hearst Museum of Anthropology.*

Fanny Flounder, Yurok shaman. Note chin tattoos. (See page 104-106.)
Photo courtesy of Special Collections, Humboldt State University.

ABOVE: Gladys Gonzales, Kashaya Pomo, after having delivered the prayer at the First Annual Basketweavers Gathering, 1991. (See page 210.) *Photo by Malcolm Margolin.*

LEFT: Samson Grant, Atsugewi. (See pages 20-22.) *Photo by E.W. Gifford, 1922. Courtesy of Phoebe Apperson Hearst Museum of Anthropology.*

RIGHT: Jerry James, Wiyot, 1910. (See page 88.) *Photo courtesy of Bancroft Library.*

BELOW: Vivien Hailstone, Yurok/ Hupa/Karuk, 1989. (See page 194.) *Photo by Heather Hafleigh. Courtesy of California Indian Project, Phoebe Apperson Hearst Museum of Anthropology.*

ABOVE: Billy Joe (William Joseph), Nisenan, standing in front of the old Auburn Roundhouse. (See pages 38, 63.) *Photo 1932 by Hans Uldall. Courtesy of Elizabeth Uldall.*

LEFT: Julian Lang, Karuk. (See page 193.) *Photo by Heather Hafleigh.*

RIGHT: Frank LaPena, Wintu, with one of his sculptures, Wuk'Wuk, 1991. (See pages 203-204.) *Photo courtesy of Carla Hills.*

BELOW: Emma Lewis, Hupa. (See pages 130-135.) *Photo courtesy of Phoebe Apperson Hearst Museum of Anthropology.*

223

ABOVE: Phoebe Maddux, Karuk, in traditional attire. (See pages 30-33, 103-104.) *Photo by John P. Harrington, 1929. Courtesy of Smithsonian Institution.*

OPPOSITE ABOVE: Geneva Mattz, Yurok, in front of an old-style house. (See pages 188-190.) *Photo by Michelle Vignes.*

OPPOSITE BELOW: McCann, Hupa, measuring dentalia against calibration marks tattooed on his arm. (See page 89.) *Photo by Pliny Goddard, 1901. Courtesy of Phoebe Apperson Hearst Museum of Anthropology.*

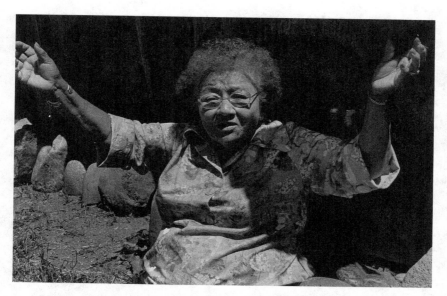

225

Rochelle Marie O'Rourke, Tolowa/Yurok/Achumawi, holding baby, Mech, 1991. (See page 211.) *Photo by Malcolm Margolin.*

ABOVE: Old Sconchin and Captain Jack, Modocs, in official prison photo after the Modoc War, 1873. (See pages 179-180.) *Photo courtesy of Bancroft Library.*

LEFT: Lucy Smith, Dry Creek Pomo, on her 80th birthday, 1986. (See page 95.) *Photo courtesy of Lucy Smith.*

Robert Spott, Yurok, in ceremonial regalia. (See pages 48-50.) *Photo courtesy of California Department of Parks and Recreation.*

LEFT: Tom Williams, Sierra Miwok. (See pages 45, 108-109, 114-115.) *Photo courtesy of Phoebe Apperson Hearst Museum of Anthropology.*

BELOW: Amanda Wilson, Maidu, and granddaughter. (See pages 11, 29.) *Photo by B.P. Cody, 1940. Courtesy of Southwest Museum.*

Darryl Wilson, Achumawi/Atsugewi, with twin sons, Ch-har-te-see and Ro-nee-we (Hoss and Boss). (See pages 198-200.) *Photo courtesy of Darryl Wilson.*

RIGHT: Yoimut, Chunut Yokuts. (See page 183.) *Photo courtesy of Yosemite National Park Research Library.*

BELOW: Lucy Young, Lassik/ Wintun, in 1936. (See page 159.) *Photo courtesy of Mendocino County Historical Society, Robert J. Lee Collection.*

Notes

Page 11. LIVELY, LIVELY. From Frances Densmore, *Music of the Maidu Indians of California* (Los Angeles: Southwest Museum, 1958), p. 20. This song, a "duck dance song," was collected in Chico in 1937 from a Maidu woman named Mrs. Amanda Wilson, then in her seventies.

Page 12. THE CRADLE. From Walter Goldschmidt, "Nomlaki Ethnography," *University of California Publications in American Archaeology and Ethnology*, 42, No. 4 (1951), p. 371. Narrated by Jeff Jones, a Nomlaki, in 1936. Jones was then about seventy years old. A photograph taken at the time shows him to have been a strikingly handsome and intelligent-looking man, with great drooping moustachios and laughing eyes.

Page 14. WHEN I WAS A CHILD. From Verne F. Ray, *Primitive Pragmatists: The Modoc Indians of Northern California* (Seattle: University of Washington Press, 1963), pp. 107-109. As reprinted in *News From Native California*, 4, No. 3 (1990), p. 12.

Page 15. CHILDHOOD GAMES. From Marie Potts, *The Northern Maidu* (Happy Camp, Calif.: Naturegraph Publishers, Inc., 1977) pp. 22, 23, 45.

Page 16. MY GRANDFATHER. From Elizabeth Colson, *Autobiographies of Three Pomo Women* (Berkeley: Archaeological Research Facility, Department of Anthropology, University of California at Berkeley, 1974), p. 129. The narrator, whose name is not revealed, was born in 1882 and dictated her reminiscences in 1941.

Page 17. LEARNING TO HUNT. From Leslie Spier, "South Diegueño Customs," *University of California Publications in American Archaeology and Ethnology*, 20 (1923), p. 336. The reminiscence was dictated in 1920 near present-day Campo in San Diego County by a man named Jim McCarthy, then over eighty years old.

Page 18. A MAN WITHOUT FAMILY. From Burt and Ethel Aginsky, *Deep Valley* (New York: Stein and Day, 1967), p. 18. The statement was narrated in 1935 by a man who was reputed to have been 112 years old.

Page 20. BECOMING A MAN. From Susan Parks, *Samson Grant, Atsuge Shaman* (Redding, Calif.: Redding Museum and Art Center). As reprinted in *News From Native California*, 1, No. 2 (1987), p. 4.

Page 22. PUBERTY DANCE SONG. From Stephen Powers, *Tribes of California* (Washington: U.S. Government Printing Office, 1877), p. 236. The song was recorded by Powers in 1871 or 1872.

Page 22. ROLLING HEAD. From Cora Du Bois and Dorothy Demetracopoulou, "Wintu Myths," *University of California Publications in American Archaeology and Ethnology*, 28 (1931), p. 362. Told by Syke Mitchell of the McCloud branch of the Wintu in 1929.

Page 24. SAND PAINTING SERMON. From Alfred Kroeber, *Handbook of the Indians of California* (Washington: U.S. Government Printing Office, 1925), p. 684.

Page 26. INITIATION INTO THE GHOST SOCIETY. From Alfred Kroeber, *Handbook of the Indians of California* (Washington: U.S. Government Printing Office, 1925), p. 188.

Page 29. I AM A FINE-LOOKING WOMAN. From Frances Densmore, *Music of the Maidu Indians of California* (Los Angeles: Southwest Museum, 1958), p. 50. The song was recorded in 1937. (See endnote for p. 11, "Lively, Lively.")

Page 30. HOW THE WOMAN GOT EVEN. From John Harrington, "Karuk Indian Myths," *Bureau of American Ethnology Bulletin*, 107 (1932), p. 12. Narrated by a sixty-five year old Karuk woman, Phoebe Maddux, whose Indian name, Imkanvan, meant "Wild-sunflower-greens-gatherer."

Page 34. THREE LOVE SONGS. From Dorothy Demetracopoulou, "Wintu Songs," *Anthropos*, 30 (1935), p. 492.

Page 35. THE HANDSOME MAN. From Cora Du Bois and Dorothy Demetracopoulou, "Wintu Myths," *University of California Publications in American Archaeology and Ethnology*, 28 (1931), p. 326. Told by Jenny Curl of the McCloud branch of the Wintu in 1929.

Page 38. FOOTBALL FREE-FOR-ALL. From Hans Uldall and William Shipley, "Nisenan Texts and Dictionary," *University of California Publications in Linguistics*, 46 (1966), p. 91. A reminiscence collected in 1930 or 1931, most likely from a Nisenan man named William Joseph of Auburn, who at the time was about seventy-five years old.

Page 38. THE TOLOWIM-WOMAN AND BUTTERFLY MAN. From Roland Dixon, "Maidu Myths," *Bulletin of the American Museum of Natural History*, 17 (1902) p. 95.

Page 40. WOMEN ARE TROUBLEMAKERS. From Walter Goldschmidt, "Nomlaki Ethnography," *University of California Publications in American Archaeology and Ethnology*, 42, No. 4 (1951), p. 370. (See endnote for p. 11, "The Cradle.")

Page 45. THE YOUNG CHIEF. From Edward W. Gifford, "Central Miwok Ceremonies," *University of California Anthropological Records*, 14, No. 4 (1955), p. 262. This speech was transcribed and translated from a phonograph recording made by a man named Molestu (Tom Williams), chief of the Central Miwok village of Chakachino in Tuolumne Couty. Williams was over eighty years old when the recording was made, some time in the second or third decade of the the present century.

Page 46. TARANTULA. From Edward W. Gifford, "Coast Yuki Myths," *Journal of American Folklore*, 50 (1937), p. 170.

Page 48. THE OSEGEN SLAVE AT ESPEU. From Robert Spott and Alfred Kroeber, "Yurok Narratives," *University of California Publications in American Archaeology and Ethnology*, 35 (1942), p. 152. Robert Spott, born in 1888, dictated this and other narratives between the years 1933 and 1940 to Alfred Kroeber. Kroeber was struck with Spott's excellent memory, his intellectual inclinations, and his "extraordinary sensitivity to the value of native culture."

Page 51. PROPERTY. From Walter Goldschmidt, "Nomlaki Ethnography," *University of California Publications in American Archaeology and Ethnology*, 42, No. 4 (1951), p. 333. (See endnote for p. 11, "The Cradle.")

Page 51. VERY STRICT LAWS. From Lucy Thompson, *To the American Indian: Reminiscences of a Yurok Woman*. (Berkeley: Heyday Books, 1991), pp. 177-178. Lucy Thompson was born in Pecwan in 1853, a woman (as she described herself) "of highest birth." Although English was not her first language, she wrote and self-published her remarkable book in 1916 to tell the truth about her people.

Page 53. TREE CARE. From Lucy Thompson, *To the American Indian: Reminiscences of a Yurok Woman*. (Berkeley: Heyday Books, 1991), pp. 28-33. (See endnote for p. 51, "Very Strict Laws.")

Page 56. CHOOSING A CHIEF. From C. Darryl Forde, "Ethnography of the Yuma Indians," *University of California Publications in American Archaeology and Ethnology*, 28 (1931), p. 135. The account was given by a Quechan man named Patrick Miguel in 1929, who was in his early fifties at the time.

Page 57. BUILDING A DANCE HOUSE. From Walter Goldschmidt, "Nomlaki Ethnography," *University of California Publications in American Archaeology and Ethnology*, 42, No. 4 (1951), p. 422. Narrated by Jeff Jones. (See endnote for p. 11, "The Cradle.")

Page 59. MESSENGERS. From Walter Goldschmidt, "Nomlaki Ethnography," *University of California Publications in American Archaeology and Ethnol-

ogy, 42, No. 4 (1951), p. 342. (See endnote for p. 11, "The Cradle.")

Page 60. FEAST ORATION. From Samuel Barrett, "Wintun Hesi Ceremony," *University of California Publications in American Archaeology and Ethnology*, 14 (1919), p. 461. The speech was originally recorded in 1906.

Page 63. FOOTBALL BIG-TIME. From Hans Uldall and William Shipley, "Nisenan Texts and Dictionary," *University of California Publications in Linguistics*, 46 (1966), p. 91. A reminiscence most likely of William Joseph. (See endnote for p. 38, "Football Free-For-All.")

Page 64. HOW A DISPUTE WAS SETTLED. From David W. Peri, "The Game of Staves, "*News From Native California*, 1, No. 3 (1987), p. 5.

Page 65. WARFARE. From Walter Goldschmidt, "Nomlaki Ethnography," *University of California Publications in American Archaeology and Ethnology*, 42, No. 4 (1951), p. 341. Narrated by Jeff Jones. (See endnote for p. 11, "The Cradle.")

Page 67. THE SWEATHOUSE. From Lucy Thompson, *To the American Indian: Reminiscences of a Yurok Woman*. (Berkeley: Heyday Books, 1991), pp. 39-40. (See endnote for p. 51, "Very Strict Laws.")

Page 69. THE GREAT HORNED OWLS. From Robert Oswalt, "Kashaya Texts," *University of California Publications in Linguistics*, 36 (1964) p. 163. The story was collected in 1958 from Herman James, then nearly eighty years old. An accomplished storyteller, James learned this and other tales from his maternal grandmother who was born some eight years before the Russians settled at Fort Ross in 1812.

Page 75. AT THE TIME OF DEATH. From Constance Du Bois, "The Religion of the Luiseño and Diegueño Indians of Southern California," *University of California Publications in American Archaeology and Ethnology*, 8, No. 3 (1908), p. 110. Recorded soon after the turn of the century from an elderly man named José Albañas.

Page 76. THE MEN I KNEW. From William Wallace, "Personality Variation in Primitive Society," *Journal of Personality*, 15 (1947), p. 321.

Page 79. OLD GAMBLER'S SONG. From Stephen Powers, *Tribes of California*. (Washington: U.S. Government Printing Office, 1877) p. 308. Collected in the early 1870s.

Page 79. GRANDFATHER'S PRAYER. From Dorothy Demetracopoulou Lee, "Some Indian Texts Dealing With The Supernatural," *Review of Religion*, 5 (1941), p. 407. The prayer was recalled by a granddaughter, Sadie Marsh.

Page 80. CRYING. From Elizabeth Colson, *Autobiographics of Three Pomo Women*. (Berkeley: Archaeological Research Facility, Department of Anthropology, University of California at Berkeley, 1974), p. 116. The anonymous narrator was born in 1882 and dictated her reminiscences in 1941.

Page 81. DEATH SONG. From Jane Hill and Rosinda Nolasquez, *Mulu'wetam: The First People; Cupeño Oral History and Language*. (Banning, Calif.: Malki Museum Press, 1973), p. 78a.

Page 81. BURIAL ORATION. From Cora Du Bois, "Wintu Ethnography," *University of California Publications in American Archaeology and Ethnology*, 36, No. 1 (1935), p. 79.

Page 82. THE LAND OF THE DEAD. From Ruth Benedict, "Serrano Tales," *Journal of American Folklore*, 39 (1926), p. 8.

Page 84. SUMMONS TO A MOURNING CEREMONY. From Edward W. Gifford, "Central Miwok Ceremonies," *University of California Anthropological Records*, 14, No. 4 (1955), p. 263. This speech was collected at Bald Rock in 1913 from a man know as Chief Yanapayak.

Page 87. PLANTS ARE THOUGHT TO BE ALIVE. From Edwin Loeb, "Pomo Folkways," *University of California Publications in American Archaeology and*

Ethnology, 19, No. 2 (1926), p. 149. The narrator, William Ralganal Benson, was hereditary chief of the "Stone people" and the "Water-lily people," two Pomo subtribes who lived on the shores of Clear Lake.

Page 88. THE PLEIADES AND THEIR PURSUER. From Edward Curtis, *The North American Indian*. (Norwood, Mass.: Plimpton Press, 1924), p. 196. The story, collected by the photographer Edward Curtis, was narrated by a man named Jerry James, born in 1859.

Page 89. THE LUNAR ECLIPSE. From Pliny Goddard, "Hupa Texts," *University of California Publications in American Archaeology and Ethnology*, 1, No. 2 (1904), p. 196. The story was told at the turn of the century by a man known as McCann. He was described as being white-haired, perhaps seventy or seventy-five years old. (Like other Native Californians born before the coming of whites, he did not know his exact age.)

Page 89. SUN AND MOON. From Roland Dixon, "Maidu Myths," *Bulletin of the American Museum of Natural History*, 17 (1902), p. 78.

Page 90. THE GREEDY FATHER. From William Bright, "The Karok Language," *University of California Publications in Linguistics*, 13 (1957), p. 215. The narrator was Lottie Beck of modern-day Orleans, who told the story in the early 1950s.

Page 91. THE STICK HUSBAND. From Edward W. Gifford, "Coast Yuki Myths," *Journal of American Folklore*, 50 (1937), p. 168.

Page 93. THE GIRL WHO MARRIED A RATTLESNAKE. From Samuel Barrett, "Pomo Myths," *Bulletin of the Public Museum of the City of Milwaukee*, 15 (1933), p. 373. The story was told soon after the turn of the century by a man named Charley Brown, who spoke the northern Pomo language, which before the coming of whites was used from present-day Ukiah and Willits west to the coast.

Page 94. THE MAN AND THE OWLS. From Alfred Kroeber, "Myths of South Central California," *University of California Publications in American Archaeology and Ethnology*, 4, No. 4 (1907), p. 228. The story was collected from an anonymous storyteller of the Yawdanchi Yokuts tribal group which inhabited the Tule River drainage in the foothills northeast of present-day Bakersfield.

Page 95. MANY RELATIVES. From David W. Peri and Scott M. Patterson, *Ethnobotanical Resources of the Warm Springs Dam-Lake Sonoma Project Area, Sonoma County, California* (San Francisco: U.S. Army Corps of Engineers, 1979). As reprinted in *News From Native California*, 6, No. 2 (1992), p. 29.

Page 98. PRAYER FOR GOOD FORTUNE. From Alfred Kroeber, *Handbook of the Indians of California* (Washington: U.S. Government Printing Office, 1925), p. 511. Recorded from the Yawelmani Yokuts group of the Kern River area.

Page 98. INITIATION SONG. From Alfred Kroeber, *Handbook of the Indians of California* (Washington: U.S. Government Printing Office, 1925), p. 194.

Page 99. TO THE EDGE OF THE EARTH. From Dorothy Demetracopoulou, "Wintu Songs," *Anthropos*, 30 (1935), p. 488. The song was recorded in 1929.

Page 100. MY MOUNTAIN. From Julian Steward, "Two Paiute Autobiographies," *University of California Publications in American Archaeology and Ethnology*, 33 (1934), p. 423. This selection was excerpted from a longer work narrated by a Paiute man named Jack Stewart in 1927 or 1928. Stewart, whose Indian name was Hoavadunaki, was nearly a hundred years old at the time and had already reached maturity when the whites first settled in Owens Valley in 1861.

Page 103. THE LONG SNAKE. From John Harrington, "Karuk Indian Myths," *Bureau of American Ethnology Bulletin* 107 (1932), p. 9. Narrated by a sixty-five year old woman, Phoebe Maddux. (See endnote for p. 30, "How the Woman Got Even.")

Page 104. A DOCTOR ACQUIRES POWER. From Robert Spott and Alfred

Kroeber, "Yurok Narratives," *University of California Publications in American Archaeology and Ethnology*, 35 (1942), p. 158. (For more information on the narrator, Robert Spott, see endnote for p. 41, "The Osegen Slave at Espeu.")

Page 106. HOW I GOT MY POWERS. From Alfred Kroeber, *Handbook of the Indians of California* (Washington: U.S. Government Printing Office, 1925), p. 65.

Page 108. PORTRAIT OF A POISONER. From Lucy Freeland and Sylvia Broadbent, "Central Sierra Miwok Dictionary with Texts," *University of California Publications in Linguistics*, 23 (1960), p. 64. The account was given by Tom Williams betweeen 1921 and 1923. Williams, who spoke the western dialect of the Central Sierra Miwok language, was living in the foothill town of Jamestown at the time.

Page 109. A FEARFUL ENCOUNTER. From Pliny Goddard, "Kato Texts," *University of California Publications in American Archaeology and Ethnology*, 5 (1907), p. 237. The account was narrated in 1906 by Bill Ray, a man between sixty and sixty-five years old at the time.

Page 110. SEARCHING AFTER A SOUL. From C. Darryl Forde, "Ethnography of the Yuma Indians," *University of California Publications in American Archaeology and Ethnology*, 28 (1931), p. 193. Told by Patrick Miguel in 1929 when Miguel was in his early fifties.

Page 110. THE RAINMAKER. From C. Darryl Forde, "Ethnography of the Yuma Indians," *University of California Publications in American Archaeology and Ethnology*, 28 (1931), p. 197. Told by a man named Joe Homer, aged sixty, in 1929.

Page 111. THE RATTLESNAKE SHAMAN. From Leslie Spier, "South Diegueño Customs," *University of California Publications in American Archaeology and Ethnology*, 20 (1923), p. 313. The narrator was Jim McCarthy, a man over eighty years old in 1920 when he gave this account.

Page 113. RATTLESNAKE CEREMONY SONG. From Alfred Kroeber, *Handbook of the Indians of California* (Washington: U.S. Government Printing Office, 1925), p. 506.

Page 114. THE SHAMAN AND THE CLOWN. From Lucy Freeland and Sylvia Broadbent, "Central Sierra Miwok Dictionary with Texts," *University of California Publications in Linguistics*, 23 (1960), p. 66. (See endnote for p. 108, "Portrait of a Poisoner.")

Page 116. A GREAT AND WISE SHAMAN. From Verne Ray, *Primitive Pragmatists*. (Seattle: University of Washington Press, 1963), p. 68. The narrator, Jenny Clinton, was born about 1858 on the shores of Tule Lake. When she was very young, she and her family were moved to Oklahoma as punishment for their participation in the Modoc War. She returned to Klamath Reservation in 1903, and gave this account in the mid-1930s.

Page 117. I DREAM OF YOU. From Alfred Kroeber, *Handbook of the Indians of California* (Washington: U.S. Government Printing Office, 1925), p. 471.

Page 118. DANCE OF THE SPIRITS. From Constance Du Bois, "The Religion of the Luiseño and Diegueño Indians of Southern California," *University of California Publications in American Archaeology and Ethnology*, 8, No. 3 (1908), p. 154. The story was collected at the turn of the century from an aged man, probably Salvador Cuevas, who was then a major ceremonial leader of the Luiseño.

Page 118. HOUSE OF SILVER-FOX. From Jeremiah Curtin, "Achomawi Myths," *Journal of American Folklore*, 22 (1909), p. 286.

Page 119. A SHAMAN'S DREAMS. From Edward Curtis, *The North American Indian*, Vol. 2. (Norwood, Mass.: Plimpton Press, 1908), p. 55. Related by a shaman named Ahweyama.

Page 120. VISIT TO KUMASTAMHO. From Alfred Kroeber, *Handbook of* the *Indians of California* (Washington: U.S. Government Printing Office, 1925), p. 783.

Page 123. COTTONTAIL AND THE SUN. From Julian Steward, "Myths of the Owens Valley Paiute," *University of California Publications in American Archaeology and Ethnology*, 34, No. 5 (1936), p. 371. This myth was narrated by a man named Tom Stone of Bishop.

Page 124. BIRTH OF THE WORLD-MAKERS. From Lucile Hooper, "The Cahuilla Indians," *University of California Publications in American Archaeology and Ethnology*, 16 (1920), p. 317.

Page 125. THE CREATION. From Roland Dixon, "Maidu Myths," *Bulletin of the American Museum of Natural History*, 17 (1902) p. 39.

Page 126. MARUMDA AND KUKSU MAKE THE WORLD. From Jaime de Angulo and William Ralganal Benson, "Creation Myths of the Pomo Indian," *Anthropos*, 27 (1932) p. 264. Benson was more than seventy years old when he narrated this myth in about 1930. (For information about William Ralganal Benson, see the endnote for p. 87, "Plants Are Thought to Be Alive.") The translator was Jaime de Angulo, linguist and later the author of *Indian Tales*, who had a fine ear for native speech and the literary talent to render it into English.

Page 129. REMAKING THE WORLD. From Cora Du Bois and Dorothy Demetracopoulou, "Wintu Myths," *University of California Publications in American Archaeology and Ethnology*, 28 (1931), p. 286. Told by Jenny Curl.

Page 130. WOMAN'S LOVE MEDICINE. From Pliny Goddard, "Hupa Texts," *University of California Publications in American Archaeology and Ethnology*, 1, No. 2 (1904), p. 308. The story was told by Emma Lewis in 1901. She was in her mid-fifties at the time, and had lived all her life in Hoopa Valley.

Page 133. HE-LIVES-IN-THE-SOUTH. From Pliny Goddard, "Hupa Texts," *University of California Publications in American Archaeology and Ethnology*, 1, No. 2 (1904), p. 160. Like the previous tale, told by Emma Lewis. The title is a literal translation of the foundling boy's name, Yinukatsisdai.

Page 136. THE TAR WOMAN. From J. Alden Mason, "The Language of the Salinan Indians," *University of California Publications in American Archaeology and Ethnology*, 14 (1918), p. 109. This myth was told by Maria Ocarpia in 1916. She was a member of the Migueleño division of the Salinan.

Page 139. A LONG TIME AGO. From William Shipley, "Maidu Texts and Dictionary," *University of California Publications in Linguistics*, 33 (1963), p. 61. Narrated by a woman named Maym Gallagher who lived in Payner Creek, California.

Page 140. COYOTE AND SPIDER. From Gladys Nomland, "Bear River Ethnography," *University of California Anthropological Records*, 2, No. 2 (1938), p. 119. The story was collected in 1928.

Page 141. COYOTE AND THE ACORNS. From Jean Sapir, "Yurok Tales," *Journal of American Folklore*, 41 (1928), p. 254. The story was narrated by a Yurok woman named Mrs. Haydom in the summer of 1927.

Page 142. COYOTE'S JOURNEY. From William Bright, *American Indian Cultural and Research Journal*, 4 (1980), p. 23.

Page 147. COYOTE AND HIS GRANDMOTHER. From Gladys Nomland, "Bear River Ethnography," *University of California Anthropological Records*, 2, No. 2 (1938), p. 121. The story was collected in 1928.

Page 148. TWO COYOTE ADVENTURES. From William Shipley, ed. and trans., *The Maidu Indian Myths and Stories of Hánc'ibyjim* (Berkeley: Heyday Books, 1991), pp. 104-116 passim. Narrated originally in 1902 or 1903.

Page 154. COYOTE AND BULLFISH. From Cora Du Bois and Dorothy Demetracopoulou, "Wintu Myths," *University of California Publications in American Archaeology and Ethnology*, 28 (1931), p. 383. Narrated by a person named Jo Bender of the Upper Sacramento River.

Page 155. COYOTE AND TRAP. From Julian Steward, "Myths of the Owens Valley Paiute," *University of California Publications in American Archaeology and Ethnology*, 34, No. 5 (1936), p. 378. Tom Stone, who lived in Bishop, was described as an "exceptionally good storyteller who immensely enjoyed his own talent."

Page 156. COYOTE STEALS FIRE. From Alfred Kroeber, "Myths of South Central California," *University of California Publications in American Archaeology and Ethnology*, 4, No. 4 (1907), p. 202.

Page 157. COYOTE AND FALCON CREATE PEOPLE. From Samuel Barrett, "Myths of the South Sierra Miwok," *University of California Publications in American Archaeology and Ethnology*, 16, No. 4 (1919), p. 8.

Page 159. MY GRANDPA, BEFORE WHITE PEOPLE CAME. From Edith V. A. Murphey, "Out of the Past: A True Indian Story," *California Historical Society Quarterly*, 20, No. 4 (December 1941), pp. 349-350.

Page 160. THE DEATH OF FATHER QUINTANA. From Edward D. Castillo, ed. and trans., "The Assassination of Padre Andrés Quintana by the Indians of Mission Santa Cruz 1812: The Narrative of Lorenzo Asisara," *California History*, 68, No. 3 (Fall 1989), pp. 116-125.

Page 163. THE ARRIVAL OF WHITES. From Walter Goldschmidt, "Nomlaki Ethnography," *University of California Publications in American Archaeology and Ethnology*, 42, No. 4. (1951), p. 311. The account was narrated by Andrew Freeman in 1936. Freeman, who was sixty-five at the time, must have heard of these incidents from people of his parents' and grandparents' generation.

Page 165. THE MASSACRE AT NEEDLE ROCK. From Gladys Nomland, "Sinkyone Notes," *University of California Publications in American Archaeology and Ethnology*, 36, No. 2. (1935), p. 166. The narrator, Sally Bell, was over ninety years old when she gave this account in 1928 or 1929. She was one of the last of the Sinkyone.

Page 166. THE STONE AND KELSEY MASSACRE. From William Ralganal Benson, *California Historical Society Quarterly*, 11 (1932), p. 268. Benson, who was born in 1862, heard of these events directly from those who took part. (For more information on Benson, see endnote for p. 87, "Plants Are Thought to Be Alive.")

Page 173. REFUGE. From Evelene Mota, "A Story," *News From Native California*, 1, No. 2 (1987), p. 18.

Page 176. WE HAD TO MOVE AGAIN. From Florence Connolly Shipek, *Delfina Cuero: Her Autobiography, An Account of Her Last Years and Her Ethnobotanic Contributions*. (Menlo Park, Calif.: Ballena Press, 1991), p. 23-27.

Page 178. THE GROUND CRIES OUT. From Cora Du Bois, "Wintu Ethnography," *University of California Publications in American Archaeology and Ethnology*, 36, No. 1 (1935). As reprinted in *News From Native California*, 6, No. 2 (1992), p. 36.

Page 179. I NO LONGER BELIEVE. From Verne F. Ray, *Primitive Pragmatists: The Modoc Indians of Northern California*. (Seattle: University of Washington Press, 1963), p. 67. The narrator, Peter Sconchin, was born in 1850 and served as one of Captain Jack's warriors. His father, John Sconchin, was second in command to Captain Jack and was hanged with him; his uncle, known generally as Old Sconchin, had been head chief of the Modoc until 1864.

Page 181. BOARDING SCHOOL. From "School Days in Northern California: The Accounts of Six Pomo Women," *News From Native California*, 4, No. 1 (1989), p. 40-41. Recorded by Vic Bedoian and Roberta Llewellyn.

Page 183. I AM THE LAST. From Frank Latta, *Handbook of the Yokuts Indians*. (Bakersfield, Calif.: Kern County Museum, 1949), p. 276. The narrator, a woman named Yoimut, died in 1933.

Page 183. A FISHING EXPERIENCE. From Robert Oswalt, "Kashaya Texts," *University of California Publications in Linguistics*, 36 (1964) p. 287. (See endnote for p. 69, "Great Horned Owls.")

Page 186. TWO GAMBLING STORIES. From David W. Peri, "The Game of Staves," *News From Native California*, 1, No. 3 (1987), p. 6.

Page 188. THE JUDGE'S VISIT. From Helene H. Oppenheimer, *Salmon War on the Klamath, 1978—Remembered by a Yurok Family*. (Berkeley: The Bancroft Library's Donated Oral History Collection), pp. 54-57.

Page 190. FOUR DREAM CULT SONGS. The first three songs are from Dorothy Demetracopoulou, "Wintu Songs," *Anthropos*, 30 (1935), p. 485-487. The fourth song is from Cora Du Bois, "The 1870 Ghost Dance," *Anthropological Records*, 3, No. 1 (1939), p. 57. Songs 2 and 4 were anonymous.

Page 193. IT'S HARD TO BE AN INDIAN. From Julian Lang, "It's Hard to Be an Indian," *News From Native California*, 3, No. 1 (1989), p. 3.

Page 194. THE TRUTH WILL SET YOU FREE. From Bev Ortiz, "Beyond the Stereotypes," *News From Native California*, 5, No. 1 (1990/91), p. 33. Vivien Hailstone is a basketweaver who has been active and tremendously effective in California Indian arts, education, and political action.

Page 194. GRANDPA RAMSEY. From Darryl Babe Wilson, "How the Great Canyon Was Made," *News From Native California*, 5, No. 3 (1991), pp. 4-5. After many years as a poet, activist, and father, Darryl Wilson has returned to school and is working toward an advanced degree in literature.

Page 203. NOW I'LL SHOW YOU HOW TO DO IT. From Barbara Bill, *News From Native California*, 6, No. 1 (1991/92) p. 27. Recorded by Bev Ortiz. Barbara Bill weaves and demonstrates weaving, and has been active in a newly formed association of California Indian basketweavers.

Page 203. CONTINUING THE SONG. From Frank LaPena, "The Art of Living," *News From Native California*, 2, No. 1 (1988) p. 19. Frank LaPena, a well-known artist, teaches at California State University at Sacramento and is a member of the Maidu Traditional Dancers.

Page 204. PEETHIVTHAANEEN. From Julian Lang, "Peethivthaaneen," *News From Native California*, 6, No. 2 (1992) p. 17.

Page 205. HALF INDIAN/HALF MEXICAN. From "James Luna: Half Indian/Half Mexican," *News From Native California*, 5, No. 4 (1991) p. 11. James Luna is an artist as well as a poet.

Page 206. BASKETS IN MUSEUM COLLECTIONS. From Linda Yamane, "Baskets in Museum Collections," *News From Native California*, 5, No. 4 (1991) p. 7. Linda Yamane is an artist, scholar and mother who now lives in the Monterey Bay area.

Page 209. FOR THE WHITE POETS. From Wendy Rose, *Academic Squaw*. (Marvin, South Dakota: Blue Cloud Quarterly, 1977). Wendy Rose, part Miwok and part Hopi, was born in Oakland, in 1948. A graduate of the University of California at Berkeley, she is an artist and an anthropologist, in addition to being a poet.

Page 210. PRAYER OF WELCOME. From Gladys Gonzales, *News From Native California*, 6, No. 1 (1991/92) p. 16. Recorded by Bev Ortiz.

Page 211. A GOOD LIFE TO LOOK FORWARD TO. From Rochelle Marie O'Rourke, *News From Native California*, 6, No. 1 (1991/92) p. 35. Recorded by Malcolm Margolin.

Index

I

Ikxareeyavs. *See supernatural beings: creator beings*
illness and disease 6, 19, 26, 54, 78, 100-101, 108, 109, 110, 163, 164, 165, 205. *See also medicines; menstrual practices; shamans*
initiation. *See ceremony: initiation and puberty; songs*
Ipai. *See Kumeyaay*

J

Jakalunus 115-116
James, Herman 69-71, 185-186
James, Jerry 88, **221**
Jarvis, Annie 184
Joe, Billy. *See Joseph, William*
Jones, Jeff 12, 40, 51, 57-58, 59-60, 67
Joseph, William 38, 63, **222**

K

Karok. *See Karuk*
Karuk 5, **19**, 30-32, **32**, 51, 90-91, 103-104, 135, 142-147, 193, 194, 204-205, **221**, **222**, **224**
Kashaya. *See Pomo*
Ka'tim'iin 204
Kato 109
Kelsey, Andy. *See Stone and Kelsey Massacre*
Kintpuash. *See Captain Jack*
Kixunai. *See supernatural beings: creator beings*
Klamath [tribe] 115, 116, 179
Klamath Reservation 179
Klamath River 2, **32-33**, 48, 51, 131, 133, **134**, 135, 189, **201**
Konkow 79, 174-176. *See also Maidu*
Kuksu. *See supernatural beings: creator beings*
Kumastamho. *See supernatural beings: creator beings*
Kumeyaay 17-18, **97**, 111-112, 176-178, **199**, **217**

L

land. *See environment; property*
Lang, Julian 193, 204-205, **222**
language 1-2, 6, 7, 24, 80, 94, 142, 165, 177, 181, 182, 183, 185, 194, 204. *See also specific tribal groups and languages*
LaPena, Craig 204
LaPena, Frank 203-204, **223**
Lassen, Mount 196
Lassik 159, **231**
leadership. *See political organization*
legal systems 19, 48-50, 52-53, 64-65, 76-78. *See also fishing; political organization*
Lewis, Emma 131, 133-134, **223**
love [romantic] 29-40, 131, 133
Luckie, Kate 178-179
Luiseño 24-26, 75, 118, **201**, 206, **213**
Luna, James 206

M

Maddux, Phoebe 30-31, 103-104, **224**
magic. *See shamans*
Maidu 3, 7, 11, 16, 29, 39, 82, 89, 114, 125-126, 139, 148-154, 174-176, **200**, **229**. *See also Konkow; Nisenan*
Major, Mary 174-176
Marongo, Rosa 82-83
marriage 19, 34, 40, 46, 59, 92-93, 93-94. *See also family*
bride price 30-32, 38, 49
Marsh, Harry 34, 35, 192
Marsh, Sadie 191
Marumda. *See supernatural beings: creator beings*
Mastamho. *See supernatural beings: creator beings*
Mattz, Geneva 189-190, **225**
Mayan 2
McCann 89, **225**
McCarthy, Jim 17-18, 111-112
Medicine Lake 196
medicine men. *See shamans*
medicines 53-54, 101, 131, 133, 205. *See also illness and disease*

245

trickster figures 140. *See also supernatural beings: animal people: Coyote*
Trinity River 51, 52, **52,** 53
Tsimshian 2
Tubatulabal 3
Tulare Lake 183
Tule Lake 2, 14, 179

V

vegetation. *See environment*
villages 48, 51, 57, 67, **68,** 72
visions 25, 107
   dreams 6, 22, 23, 56, 100, 101,
     103, 104, 110, 112, 113,
     117-121, 129-130, 136-137,
     191-192, **198**

W

warfare **66**
   intergroup 65-67, 119, 120, 179
   with whites 163-165, 179-180.
     See also resistance to Europeans
Washo **13**
watercraft
   boats 2-3, **4-5,** 9, 133, **201**
   rafts 3, **5,** 125-126
wealth 19, 30, 31, 49-50, 76. *See also money; property*
weirs. *See fishing*
Whilkut 78
whistle **97**
White Deerskin Dance. *See ceremony*
Williams, Tom 45, 108, 114-115,
   229
Wilson, Amanda 11, 29, **229**
Wilson, Boss (Ro-nee-we) **230**
Wilson, Darryl 195-196, **230**
Wilson, Hoss (Ch-har-te-see) **230**
Wintu 22, 23-24, 34-35, 35-38,
   51, 60-63, **62,** 79-80, 81-82, 94,
   99, 130, 154-155, 178-179,
   191-192, 203-204, **223**
Wintun 159, 203, **231.** *See also Nomlaki; Patwin; Wintu*
Wiyot 88, **221**
woodpecker feathers 31, 107, 115,
   190. *See also wealth*
World-Maker. *See supernatural beings: creator beings*

world renewal. *See ceremony*
Wowol. *See Yokuts*

Y

Ya-Ka-Ama 188, 210, **220**
Yamane, Linda 206-208
Yanapayak [Chief] 84-85
Yoimut 183, **231**
Yokuts 3, 94, 98, **113,** 113-114,
   156, 203
   Choinumni 3
   Chunut 183, **231**
   Tachi 183
   Wowol 183
Young, Lucy 159, **231**
Young, Tom. *See Hanc'ibyjim*
Yuki 2, 26-27, 46-47, 91-92, 98
Yuma. *See Quechan*
Yuman 2
Yurok 2, 9, **32-33, 42, 43,** 48-50,
   50, 52-53, 53-54, **68,** 67-69,
   76, 104-106, 106-108, 135,
   141-142, 189-190, 194, **197,**
   201, 211, **219, 221,** 225, **226,**
   228

MALCOLM MARGOLIN grew up in Boston and has been living in the San Francisco Bay Area since 1970. His first published book, *The Ohlone Way: Indian Life in the San Francisco–Monterey Bay Area,* was named by the *San Francisco Chronicle* as one of the hundred most important nonfiction books written by a Western writer in the twentieth century. Margolin is the former publisher of Heyday, which he founded in 1974. He is also the former publisher of *News from Native California,* a quarterly magazine devoted to California Indian history and ongoing culture, which he launched in 1987. He is the recipient of many prestigious awards, including awards from Lannan Foundation, the San Francisco Foundation, the Book Club of California, UC Berkeley's Bancroft Library, the Wallace Alexander Gerbode Foundation, the American Association of State and Local History, the Society for California Archaeology, the Before Columbus Foundation, the Society of Professional Journalists, California Indian Health Services, and the California Council for the Promotion of History. From the Bay Area Book Reviewers Association he received the Fred Cody Award for Lifetime Achievement.

CALIFORNIA
HISTORICAL
SOCIETY since 1871

About the California Historical Society
Founded in 1871, the California Historical Society (CHS) is a nonprofit organization with a mission to inspire and empower people to make California's richly diverse past a meaningful part of their contemporary lives.

Public Engagement
Through high-quality public history exhibitions, public programs, research, preservation, advocacy, and digital storytelling, CHS keeps history alive through extensive public engagement. In opening the very heart of the organization—our vast and diverse collection—to ever wider audiences, we invite meaning, encourage exchange, and enrich understanding.

CHS Collections
CHS holds one of the state's top historical collections, revealing California's social, cultural, economic, and political history and development—including some of the most cherished and valuable documents and images of California's past. From our headquarters in San Francisco to the University of Southern California and the Autry National Center in Los Angeles, we hold millions of items in trust for the people of California.

Library and Research
Open to the public and free of charge, our North Baker Research Library is a place where researchers literally hold history in their hands. Whether you're a scholar or are simply interested in learning about the history of your neighborhood, city, or community, you have hands-on access to the rich history of our state.

Publications
From our first book publication in 1874, to our ninety-year history as publisher of the *California History* journal, to the establishment of the annual California Historical Society Book Award in 2013, CHS publications examine the ongoing dialogue between the past and the present. Our print and digital publications reach beyond purely historical narrative to connect Californians to their state, region, nation, and the world in innovative and thought-provoking ways.

Support

Over the years, the generosity and commitment of foundations, corporations, cultural and educational institutions, and private donors and members have supported CHS's work throughout the state.

Learn More

www.californiahistoricalsociety.com